STANDARD & POOR'S

GUIDE TO MONEY & INVESTING

VIRGINIA B. MORRIS

KENNETH M. MORRIS

LIGHTBULB

PRESS

LIGHTBULB PRESS
Project Team

Design Director Dave Wilder
Design Mercedes Feliciano, Kara W. Hatch
Editors Sophie Forrester, Mavis Morris, Michael Mraz, Tania Sanchez, Tina Satter, Kristin Szostek
Production and Illustration Krista K. Glasser, Tina Sbrigato, Rachel Schneidmill, Matt Spiegler, Thomas F. Trojan

PICTURE CREDITS
American Bank Note Company, American Stock Exchange, Bureau of Engraving and Printing, Chase Manhattan Archives, Chicago Board of Trade, CUC International, Museum of the City of New York, NASD, New York Stock Exchange, The Nasdaq Stock Market, Pax World, The Options Industry Council, T. Rowe Price Investment Services, United States Mint

SPECIAL THANKS
Standard & Poor's: David Blitzer, Managing Director & Chairman of the Standard & Poor's Index Committee; David Brezovec, Managing Editor, Credit Market Services; Zoe Brunson, Associate Director, Portfolio Advisor Services; Phil Edwards, Managing Director, Portfolio Advisor Services; George Gulla, Vice President, Equity Research Services; James Holloway, Vice President of Editorial for Equity Research Services; Joseph Lisanti, Editor-in-Chief, The Outlook; Rosanne Pane, Director & Mutual Fund Strategist, Portfolio Advisor Services; Peter Roffman, Managing Director, Portfolio Advisor Services; Kenneth Shea, Managing Director, Global Equity Research Services; and Sam Stovall, Chief Investment Strategist

The Options Clearing Corporation: Dan Busby and Bill Ryan

Cynthia Cain, Bess Newman, Mina B. Samuels

Almost 15 years ago, the first Lightbulb guide on money and investing made its debut. Unlike other financial guides available to consumers at that time, the guide offered clear explanations of financial concepts and topics—from understanding stocks and bonds to trading derivatives—combined with highly colorful, informative, and often witty design—that have since become the hallmark of all Lightbulb guides.

Since that initial publication, we have experienced one of the longest bull markets in history, several market corrections, a crash, and a bubble burst that sent the markets reeling and had a devastating impact on many individual portfolios. We have also seen the introduction or popularization of a whole new range of financial products, including exchange traded funds (ETFs), index fund investing, hedge funds, managed accounts, and real estate investment trusts (REITs), as well as the emergence of online trading. Even futures and options, once thought to be too esoteric for all but the wealthiest and most sophisticated investors, have started to figure in the investment strategies and portfolios of many more people.

Given these changes in the investment world, the guide was due for a dramatic overhaul. In this effort, we were fortunate to be able to draw upon the resources of Standard & Poor's, whose experts worked closely with us to ensure that the guide was timely, complete, and comprehensive. We want to acknowledge and thank them for their immeasurable contribution to the guide.

For those of you already familiar with Lightbulb guides, or for those of you picking one up for the first time, you'll find that the *Guide to Money & Investing* holds to our founding principle—namely, to provide clear, objective, and practical financial information that everyone can understand and act upon. As with our other guides, we are not offering financial advice in these pages so much as helping investors know what to look for, and what to look out for.

We hope that all of our readers find this guide a worthy successor to our earlier work, and derive both enjoyment and knowledge in learning about and participating in the fascinating world of money and investing.

Virginia B. Morris
Kenneth M. Morris

CONTENTS

STANDARD & POOR'S
GUIDE TO MONEY & INVESTING

MONEY & MARKETS

STOCKS

BONDS

CONTENTS

INDEXES & INDEX INVESTING

MUTUAL FUNDS

OPTIONS

FUTURES

ALTERNATIVE INVESTMENTS

Understanding Capital Markets

Buyers and sellers interacting in a common space use wealth to create more wealth.

Essentially, capital is wealth, usually in the form of money or property. Capital markets exist when two groups interact: those who are seeking capital and those who have capital to provide. The capital seekers are the businesses and governments who want to finance their projects and enterprises by borrowing or selling equity stakes. The capital providers are the people and institutions who are willing to lend or buy, expecting to realize a profit.

A CAPITAL IDEA

Investment capital is wealth that you put to work. You might invest your capital in business enterprises of your own. But there's another way to achieve the same goal: Let someone else do the investing for you.

By participating in the stock and bond markets, which are the pillars of the capital markets, you commit your capital by investing in the equity or debt of issuers that you believe have a viable plan for using that capital. Because so many investors participate in the capital markets, they make it possible for enterprises to raise substantial sums—enough to carry out much larger projects than might be possible otherwise.

The amounts they raise allow businesses to innovate and expand, create new products, reach new customers, improve processes, and explore new ideas. They allow governments to carry out projects that serve the public—building roads and firehouses, training armies, or feeding the poor, for example.

All of these things could be more difficult—perhaps even impossible—to achieve without the financing provided by the capital marketplace.

A DIFFERENT PERSPECTIVE

There are times when individual investors play a different role in the capital markets and become seekers, rather than suppliers, of capital. The best example is a mortgage.

HOUSE FOR SALE

Those providing capital

GOING TO MARKET

Sometimes investors buy and sell stocks and bonds in literal marketplaces—such as traditional exchange trading floors where trading deals are struck. But many capital market transactions are handled through telephone orders or electronic trading systems that have no central location. As more and more of the business of the capital markets is conducted this way, the concept of a market as face-to-face meeting place has faded, replaced by the idea of the capital markets as a general economic system.

PRIMARY AND SECONDARY

There are actually two levels of the capital markets in which investors participate: the **primary markets** and the **secondary markets**.

Businesses and governments raise capital in primary markets, selling stocks and bonds to investors and collecting the cash. In secondary markets, investors buy and sell the stocks and bonds among themselves—or more precisely, through intermediaries. While the money raised in secondary sales doesn't go to the stock or bond issuers, it does create an incentive for investors to commit capital to investments in the first place.

OTHER PRODUCTS, OTHER MARKETS

The capital markets aren't the only markets around. To have a market, all you need are buyers and sellers—sometimes interacting in a physical space, such as a farmer's market or a shopping mall, and sometimes in an electronic environment.

There are a variety of financial markets in the economy, trading a range of financial instruments. For example, currency markets set the values of world currencies relative to each other. In this case, market participants exchange one currency for another either to meet their financial obligations or to speculate on how the values will change. Similarly, the commodity futures market and the money market, among others, bring together buyers and sellers who have specific financial interests.

Those seeking capital

Many investors put money into securities hoping that prices will rise, allowing them to sell at a profit. But they also want to know they'll be able to liquidate their investments, or sell them for cash at any time, in case they need the money immediately. Without robust secondary markets, there would be less participation in the primary markets—and therefore less capital could be raised. (Of course, there are also other reasons why investors may stay away from primary markets.)

THE PRICE IS RIGHT

One of the most notable features of both the primary and secondary financial markets is that prices are set according to the forces of supply and demand through the trading decisions of buyers and sellers. When buyers dominate the markets, prices rise. When sellers dominate, prices drop.

You've undoubtedly experienced the dynamics of market pricing if you've ever haggled with a vendor. If the two of you settle on a price at which you're willing to buy and the vendor is willing to sell, you've set a market price for the item. But if someone comes along who is willing to

Investors trading among themselves

pay more than you are, then the vendor may sell at the higher price.

If there are a limited number of items and many buyers are interested, the price goes up as the buyers outbid each other. But if more sellers arrive, offering the same item and increasing the supply, the price goes down. So the monetary value of a market item is what someone is willing to pay for it.

In fact, price often serves as an economic thermometer, measuring supply and demand. One of the problems in **command economies**, in which prices are set by a central government authority instead of the marketplace, is that, without changing prices to clue them in, producers don't know when to adjust supplies to meet demands, resulting in chronic overstocks and shortages.

Raising Capital

Capital is the lifeblood of businesses, large and small.

Companies typically need capital infusions at several stages in their lives: at birth, as they grow, and if they're facing financial problems. Fortunately, they can seek capital from several sources, though availability may vary depending on the age and size of the company. And each source has some advantages as well as potential drawbacks.

THREE KINDS OF CAPITAL INFUSION

Investing public capital

Venture capital

Seed capital

CAPITALIZING A START-UP

Imagine for a moment that you want to start a company. You'll need capital to buy equipment, set up an office, hire employees, and attract clients, among other things. Most of the **start-up capital**—also known as **seed capital**—may be your own money. You may liquidate your investments, tap your bank accounts, or maybe even mortgage your home to get the capital you need.

The good thing about using your own capital to finance your enterprise is that you don't incur any obligations to others, and you maintain control because you're the only one with a stake. The risk, of course, is that if your business fails, all the money you lose is your own. And unless you're unusually wealthy, there's probably a limited amount of money you can—or are willing to—invest.

A second major source for raising seed capital is friends and family or other early stage investors who are willing and able to commit money, either buying an equity interest or providing favorable-rate loans. As a group, they're known as **angel investors**, though they may not all be saints.

VENTURING OUT

Private companies may seek funding from **venture capital** firms—often referred to as VCs—that specialize in investing large sums at a particular stage of a company's development. While some venture firms may assume the risk of backing start-ups, the majority invest in companies that seem poised for significant growth or that operate in a particular industry in which the VC firm specializes.

Venture capitalists are willing to take bigger risks than most other suppliers of capital because they have enough resources to make substantial investments in several companies at the same time. While each business by itself may pose a significant risk, if even a few succeed, the venture capital firm may realize large profits.

LIMITED LIABILITY

Most equity investors enjoy limited liability status. That means the most they can lose is the capital they put up. The distinction of being the first limited liability company goes to the British East India Company, which was formed in 1662.

A LITTLE PRIVACY

Investment banks can also arrange for companies to get financing through **private placement**. In that case, a smaller, limited group of wealthy investors is offered the opportunity to invest. Private placements don't have the same registration and reporting requirements as public offerings.

COMPANIES IN NEED OF CAPITAL

Venture capitalists may consider hundreds of businesses before they find the handful that show the right potential. They then provide an infusion of capital in exchange for part ownership, or **equity**, including the right to share in the company's profits. Ownership rights also give venture capitalists a say in how the companies they invest in are run, and, in some cases, there may be provisions for additional controls or increased equity if certain financial targets are not met.

Venture capital involvement isn't necessarily a bad deal for a company, however, since VCs generally have experience in a particular market and can provide valuable insights, business contacts, and financial management. But in accepting capital from outside investors, businesses do concede a degree of control to their new partners.

Venture capitalists also play a major role in determining what happens to the companies they invest in. Typical resolutions include a merger with or acquisition by a larger firm or an initial public offering (IPO).

SHOPPING THE CAPITAL MARKETS

Not even the wealthiest venture capital firms can provide as much capital as the **capital markets**, where anonymous investors buy stocks and bonds. A company can often raise significant amounts of money by selling stock through an initial public offering (IPO). And a company with a solid financial record can often borrow more cheaply by selling bonds than it can by taking a bank loan.

The decision to turn to the capital markets for financing opens up a massive source of cash—but it also affects how the business operates. Companies that issue stock must grant shareholders certain rights. And companies that issue **debt securities**, such as bonds, enter into legally binding contracts to repay.

TAKING IT TO THE BANK

Some of the biggest players in the capital markets are large, multinational firms known as **investment banks**, which specialize in corporate financing. That means providing services and advice to companies that want to raise capital or are involved in mergers and acquisitions.

Investment banks help companies determine the best way to secure financing: through debt or equity, using private placement or public offering. Then they help companies navigate the requirements and paperwork involved in registering and offering securities for sale, including **underwriting** the offering—finding buyers and setting prices. Investment banks can also create new investment vehicles out of existing securities, cutting them up or combining them to offer specialized products for certain investors.

GOING TO THE BANK

Businesses may also be able to raise a limited amount of capital by applying for bank loans, though borrowing may have certain drawbacks. First, since repayment begins as soon as the loan is secured, monthly cash flow is affected. Second, the bank is likely to demand **collateral**, or security, for the loan.

But a major advantage of raising capital with a loan is that once it's paid off, the company hasn't given away any equity. If the company succeeds, the original owners derive all the benefit of the increased value.

Market Regulation

Rules and referees help keep the investment markets fair.

In a perfect world, every player in the capital markets would always deal honestly and fairly with every other player. The field would be perfectly level, giving everyone the same access to information and opportunities.

But in the absence of perfection, there is regulation. The system that has developed in the United States to regulate the capital markets is designed to keep them fair and efficient by setting and enforcing standards and rules, settling disputes among market participants, mandating changes, and initiating improvements.

The ultimate goal of regulation is often described as maintaining investor confidence. But why is that so important? The reason is that investor dollars are the fuel on which the economy runs. If the public distrusts the markets, investors keep their money out of investments—and out of US businesses. But when people trust the markets, they're willing to put money into investments like stocks and bonds, giving companies money to innovate and expand.

In fact, one common explanation for the wealth of the US capital markets is that the US regulatory system is the strictest in the world, thereby earning investor confidence.

SEC

State Regulators

Government Regulators

MEET THE REFEREES

Given the scope and complexity of the job, no single regulator can supervise all aspects of the capital markets or the securities industry. Instead, regulation is carried out by a number of organizations with different and sometimes overlapping jurisdictions.

There are two major groups of market regulators: **government regulators**, at both the federal and state levels, and **self-regulatory organizations (SROs)**, through which industry players govern themselves.

At the federal level, the **Securities and Exchange Commission (SEC)** oversees all aspects of the nation's securities industry, enforcing laws passed by Congress as well as its own rules. The SEC also supervises the SROs and has the right to demand changes in their rules. Each state also has its own securities

regulator to supervise business within its borders and regulate activities that fall outside the SEC's scope.

The largest industry self-regulator is **NASD**, formerly known as the National Association of Securities Dealers. It oversees roughly 5,200 brokerage firms and over 660,000 brokers—which is nearly all of them. The other major SROs are the markets and exchanges where trading occurs. For example, the **New York Stock Exchange (NYSE)** regulatory arm supervises trading and sets and enforces standards for its listed companies.

Similarly, the exchanges where options and futures contracts are traded have federal regulators—the SEC in the case of options and the Commodities Futures Trading Commission (CFTC) for futures—and act as self-regulating bodies.

TOO MUCH OR NOT ENOUGH?

Regulation is a dynamic, evolving system of guidelines and controls, adapting to changes in the market environment and to events—such as scandals and failures—that reveal vulnerabilities in the current setup.

When things go wrong, however, not everyone believes that more regulation is necessarily the best solution. Although few people argue for zero government oversight, what's often debated is exactly how much oversight is the right amount.

Opponents of regulation argue that the markets work best when government lets them alone—what is sometimes referred to as *laissez faire*. From this perspective, government interference increases the cost or difficulty of doing business, stifles innovation, and prevents ordinary market forces of supply and demand from determining prices and products. Regulation opponents also point out that industries already regulate themselves, and suggest that government dollars can be better spent elsewhere.

But proponents of government regulation point to the industry's failure to prevent past problems as the reason to appoint and strengthen a third-party watchdog, especially since the securities markets are so central to the health of the US economy. They argue that outside policing is necessary to protect investors, whose interests may conflict with industry interests. When investor confidence is shaken, they maintain, government intervention is needed to calm public concerns, especially in cases where the public doesn't believe the industry can resolve its own problems.

The Sarbanes-Oxley Act of 2002 mandated reforms to enhance corporate responsibility and financial disclosures and to combat corporate and accounting fraud. It also created the Public Company Accounting Oversight Board (PCAOB) to oversee the auditing profession.

NASD NYSE AMEX Nasdaq

SROs
Self-Regulatory Organizations

UNTYING THE KNOTS

Deregulation occurs when strict regulation of an industry is ended or relaxed. Lawmakers who support deregulation believe that fewer government controls will mean greater benefits for the public—such as lower costs and more choices—when new companies are allowed to enter a previously limited market or are given greater freedom to set prices and offer new products and services.

In the securities industry, deregulation in the 1970s allowed brokerage firms to set their own commissions, rather than charging the government-set rate. The result was lower fees, and the birth of discount brokers. More recently, in 1999, the Gramm-Leach-Bliley Act repealed the Glass-Steagall Act of 1933 and dissolved the legal barriers that existed between banks, insurance companies, and investment firms. Now a single company can be all three.

HOW IT BEGAN

Regulation was once solely self-regulation, as markets like the NYSE encouraged honest and efficient practices among their members.

But as investing worked its way west, away from the established financial centers of eastern cities, inexperienced investors often fell victim to aggressive and fraudulent sales tactics. In response, states began passing their own securities laws, beginning with Kansas in 1911.

After the 1929 stock market crash revealed weaknesses in even the most respected securities markets, Congress passed several laws that became the foundation of today's market regulation system. Among other things, it established the SEC, required fair disclosure for investments, and mandated registration of investment advisers.

The Role of the SEC

The nation's top securities industry watchdog barks and bites.

Despite the complexities of the US securities industry, there's a notable level of public confidence in the marketplace. One of the major reasons that an investor in Kansas feels comfortable putting money into a California-based company through a trading system based in New York is that most of what happens in the nation's securities markets falls under the jurisdiction of a single federal watchdog: the **Securities and Exchange Commission**, or **SEC**.

The SEC was established in 1934, when the public's confidence in investment markets had been undermined. In response, Congress passed, and President Roosevelt signed, the first comprehensive federal securities laws in the United States and established the SEC to interpret and enforce them.

INSIDE THE SEC
Commissioners

The SEC is led by five commissioners, who are appointed by the US president to five-year terms. One commissioner, designated by the president and confirmed by Congress, serves as chairman. To keep the Commission nonpartisan, no more than three commissioners can belong to the same political party. However, there are periods when seats remain vacant, which can shift the balance of power.

Divisions

- The **Division of Corporate Finance** handles and oversees the various filings that companies are required to make.
- The **Division of Market Regulation** oversees the players in the securities markets, including exchanges and broker-dealers.
- The **Division of Investment Management** oversees the investment management industry, including mutual funds and investment advisers.
- The **Division of Enforcement** investigates wrongdoing and recommends action when appropriate.

TAKING ACTION

If the SEC discovers potential wrongdoing, it has several options, depending on the nature of the alleged violation and the solution it believes will benefit investors most. There are two types of actions the SEC can take: **civil actions**, which are decided in US District Courts, and **administrative actions**, which are decided by administrative law judges.

CAVEAT EMPTOR

Caveat emptor, Latin for "buyer beware," is the principle that underlies US securities laws.

Rather than evaluating the investments that companies offer in seeking to raise capital, federal law focuses on **disclosure**—requiring that investors have access to the facts they need to make informed investment decisions. This includes both positive and negative information about the issuer, covering its business activities and strategies, the composition of its management, its financial health, and any foreseeable risks.

To make this information readily available, any company that wants to sell securities to the public must file specific, comprehensive documentation with the SEC. New securities must be registered and potential investors provided with a prospectus. In addition, companies must report periodically on their business and financial standing in an annual, audited report known as the **10-K**, and in a quarterly, unaudited report known as the **10-Q**.

The SEC reviews these documents to make sure they meet the requirements for public disclosure and makes the information available for free through its EDGAR database (www.sec.gov/edgar/searchedgar/webusers.htm).

MAKING THE RULES

While the nation's securities laws establish broad requirements, a big part of the SEC's job is to turn the language of the laws into rules that the industry can follow. For instance, since the law makes insider trading illegal, the SEC defines what corporate officers must do to ensure that their trades are legal.

SEC rules are regularly revised to keep pace with changes in the industry. New or amended rules are of great concern to all market participants, so the rulemaking process allows all interested parties to comment before a rule is finalized.

The process usually begins with a **proposed rule**, written by staff and presented to the Commission for review. If the SEC wants public feedback before drafting a proposal, it sometimes describes the issue in a **concept release** and asks for comments.

If the Commission likes a proposed rule, it presents the rule to the public, and everyone with an interest in the outcome has a month or two to register a point of view. After reviewing the comments, the staff generally revises the rule and presents it again to the Commission for final approval. If a rule touches on a highly sensitive, far-reaching issue or represents a major change, it may be the subject of litigation and may ultimately be approved—or rejected—by Congress.

LOOKING OUT FOR INVESTORS

Along with full disclosure, the other major principle on which federal securities laws are built is that investment advisers have a fiduciary responsibility and are obligated to put investors' interests first. So, for example, if an adviser recommends that an investor buy or sell a certain stock or bond, it should be because that action is in the investor's interest—not just because the trade, and any associated fees and commissions, are good for the adviser or the adviser's firm.

To enforce these protections, the SEC registers and regulates investment companies and investment advisers, who are paid for providing advice. It also oversees NASD, which regulates broker-dealers, who buy and sell securities for their clients.

WHAT'S AN NRSRO?

The term nationally recognized statistical rating organization (NRSRO) is used by the SEC to designate entities that issue publicly available credit ratings and that also meet certain conditions. These conditions are elaborated on at the SEC website (www.sec.gov).

The NRSRO designation was initiated by the SEC to provide investors with the ability to differentiate among different rating entities. There are currently five firms that have the NRSRO designation.

Self-Regulation

There's a lot to the adage that honest business is good for business.

The first securities industry regulator in the United States was the industry itself. By 1817, the US securities markets had grown large, complex, and unruly. So the brokers who had been trading securities on Wall Street decided to form what would become the **New York Stock Exchange (NYSE)**.

As their first regulatory act, they drew up a formal constitution, establishing rules for members to follow. Today, such self-regulation is considered central to the integrity of the US financial markets, and the bodies that police themselves are known as **self-regulatory organizations (SROs)**.

While regulation may have been born of self-interest, today the law requires markets and exchanges to regulate themselves. And the broker-dealers who make a business of trading securities are regulated through the nation's largest SRO, **NASD**—originally the National Association of Securities Dealers.

While SROs have changed and expanded over the years, their purpose remains much the same: setting and enforcing standards and rules to govern themselves. They work in tandem with the states and the SEC, cooperating in investigations and helping support the government's regulatory goals of protecting investor rights and keeping the markets efficient, fair, and honest.

TOO CLOSE FOR COMFORT?

One of the major advantages SROs have as regulators is that, as insiders, they understand the practical workings of the securities industry and can monitor activity where and when it actually happens. SROs have access to the trading floor, to the offices of the member firms, and to the trading data as it comes in. They're also close to people and firms within the industry, so they're positioned to hear about problems early on. But the very closeness to the activity that gives SROs their insights and perspective may also represent a big weakness.

The Logic of Self-Regulation

Besides the most obvious reason—that the law requires it—the securities industry has its own reasons for regulating itself.

For one thing, when a firm acts dishonestly, it may cast a shadow on honest firms as well. So it's in the interest of honest firms to keep a close eye on unfair practices. Furthermore, self-regulatory bodies have the power to enforce standards that can make business more efficient—such as establishing a centralized reporting system for trades, or developing a single, standard licensing examination for brokers.

Practically speaking, self-regulation may be less expensive and more efficient than government regulation. But ultimately the strongest reason for self-regulation is that it makes the public more confident about the securities markets. That means more money flowing into investments—and more profits for the securities industry.

That's because as self-regulators, SROs may tend to see issues from the point of view of the brokerage and investment banking firms that make up their membership. This isn't always bad news, since firms usually have an interest in keeping costs down and processes efficient—all of which are good for investors. But occasionally, the industry may seem reluctant to institute reforms that will benefit investors but appear to work against their own self-interest.

As a result, effective self-regulation is typically a matter of balance: making sure regulators are close enough to the business they regulate to do their job, without being so close that it creates a conflict of interest.

For example, NASD once owned and operated the Nasdaq Stock Market, the first electronic securities market. Serious criticism was leveled at NASD when it became apparent that its business interest in Nasdaq was in conflict with its role as a regulator. To fix the problem, NASD turned Nasdaq into a separate, publicly owned corporation, and redefined NASD as a nonprofit private organization solely focused on regulation.

Similar concerns at the NYSE led to huge corporate governance reforms in 2003 to make the NYSE's regulatory arm more independent of its business interests. Still more changes are likely to come as regulators continue to seek the right balance.

SRO Responsibilities

NASD

Oversight
- Brokerage firms
- Branch offices
- Registered representatives (stockbrokers)

Main regulatory activities
- Supervision of market trading on Nasdaq and certain other markets
- Licensing and continuing education of registered representatives
- Mediation and arbitration of 90% of industry disputes, including those between investors and firms
- Review of advertising materials to protect investors from misleading or false information
- Increased market efficiency through centralized information systems
- Investigations and disciplinary actions, including censure, fines, suspensions, or barring from practice

MARKETS & EXCHANGES

Oversight
- Members
- Member firms
- Listed companies

Main regulatory activities
- Market surveillance—monitoring trading activity in person and electronically
- Audits and reviews of member firms' finances and business practices
- Administering qualifying exams and providing continuing education
- Setting and monitoring the listing requirements for companies, including financial and corporate governance requirements
- Investigations and disciplinary actions

INSIDE THE COMPANY

Firms in the securities industry also have internal self-regulation: their compliance departments. Among the tasks of a corporate compliance department are to review sales material and other documents that the company generates, investigate customer complaints, and take disciplinary action against company employees if necessary. By using in-house enforcement, companies hope to stay on the right side of the law—and to avoid the cost, inconvenience, and damage to their reputations that a full outside regulatory investigation may sometimes bring.

Global Capital Markets

The quest for capital—and for places to invest it—extends beyond national borders.

When companies open business operations abroad, or form joint partnerships with companies based in other countries, they become players in an international capital marketplace. The same is true when individual or institutional investors put their capital to work outside their national borders.

UPS AND DOWNS

One benefit of cross-border investing is that strong economic growth in one part of the world can stimulate growth in other regions. That can be good for the investors and good for the economies where the markets operate. One potentially negative consequence of globalization, however, is that problems in the economy of one nation or region may have a ripple effect on the economies of many others—even though the major factor in any nation's financial health is what's happening at home.

DEVELOPED AND EMERGING

Broadly speaking, world markets fall into two categories: developed and emerging.

Developed markets, including those in Europe, North America, Australia, New Zealand, and Japan tend to be highly regulated and have an efficient system for matching seekers with providers of capital and foster an active secondary market.

Emerging markets are usually significantly smaller and newer than developed markets and have fewer active participants, resulting in less liquidity and greater volatility. The trading mechanisms are often less efficient as well. These markets may also be more vulnerable to political instability, particularly if the country has a short history of democracy or if ethnic and religious controversies threaten to disrupt economic development.

Being labeled as developed or emerging is not always a clear indication of how a market operates. For example, some emerging markets are more mature and stable than others, and tend to attract more investor attention because they offer opportunities for long-term gain. This is especially true where large populations are becoming more affluent and the economies have shown sustained growth.

At the same time, some developed markets may suffer through long periods of stagnation or other economic problems that deter international investors.

MARKET EVOLUTIONS

Some markets are open to all investors, while others limit the participation of nonresidents. That's because some nations face a dilemma in seeking international capital: On the one hand, this capital can provide welcome growth. But at the same time, it has the potential to undermine domestic control and stability.

When they do seek to attract international investment, though, securities markets in emerging economies have strengthened their regulatory practices, improved transparency, and streamlined their clearance and settlement systems for handling the exchange of securities and cash payments.

WHAT'S GOOD FOR THE GOOSE

US investors seeking greater diversification may look abroad when they have capital to invest. At the same time, companies based abroad may want to tap the wealth of the US markets. If they do, they may offer shares of their stock on the US market through a US bank, which is known as a depositary.

In this arrangement, the depositary bank holds the issuing company's shares, known as **American depositary shares (ADSs)**. The bank offers investors the chance to buy a certificate known as an **American depositary receipt (ADR)**, which represents ownership of a bundle of the depositary shares.

To have their ADRs listed on an exchange, companies must provide English-language versions of their annual reports, adhere to accepted US accounting practices, and grant certain shareholder rights. In addition, they must meet listing requirements imposed by the exchange or market where they wish to be traded.

In reality, many ADRs aren't listed on an exchange, often because they are too small to meet listing requirements. Instead, they're traded over the counter (OTC). Some of the issuing companies register with the SEC and submit the required filings. Others do not, which means you may not be able to get the same level of information about the company as you can with a registered ADR. The OTC markets are also generally less liquid than the major exchanges, which can make OTC ADRs more difficult to sell at the time and price you want.

GOING GLOBAL

When a company makes depositary arrangements to sell its stock in two or more countries, the shares are called global depositary shares and they are sold as global depositary receipts (GDRs). In all other ways, they work the same way as ADRs.

THE WORLD BANK

The World Bank, or more formally, the International Bank for Reconstruction and Development (IBRD), is an investment bank that raises money by issuing bonds to individuals, institutions, and governments in more than 100 countries. The bonds are guaranteed by the governments of the 178 countries who own the bank.

The World Bank lends the money from its investors to the governments of developing countries at affordable interest rates to help finance internal projects and economic policy reforms. In fact, long-term loans to the poorest nations through the bank's International Development Association (IDA) are interest free.

The Bank's International Finance Corporation (IFC) provides funds for private enterprise in emerging nations and helps stimulate additional financing from other investors. Its affiliate, the Multilateral Investment Guarantee Agency, promotes private investment by providing guarantees that protect investors from political risks, such as the possibility of nationalization. Without this safety net, investors might otherwise be reluctant to participate.

BROADER HORIZONS

When US companies invest in non-US businesses, there may be increased value for their shareholders. In fact, by one calculation, 35% of the returns on the **Standard & Poor's 500 Index**—which includes only US companies—are attributable to business outside the country.

The World of Money

Currencies are floated against each other to measure their worth in the global marketplace.

A currency's value in the world marketplace reflects whether individuals and governments are interested in using it to make purchases or investments, or in holding it as a source of long-term security. If demand is high, its value increases in relation to the value of other currencies. If it's low, the reverse occurs.

Some currencies are relatively stable, reflecting an underlying financial and political stability. Other currencies experience wild or rapid changes in value, the sign of economies in turmoil as the result of runaway inflation, deflation, defaults on loan agreements, serious balance-of-trade deficits, or economic policies that seem unlikely to resolve the problems.

Similarly, certain currencies are used widely in international trade while others are not. That's the result of the relative stability of the currencies and the volume of goods and services a country or economic union produces.

HOW TRADING WORKS

Most bank transactions are conducted over the telephone and registered in a computerized dealing system.

Make a market

If a bank wants to buy a particular currency, a trader calls for a quote from a bank that is a market maker for that currency. That means the bank specializes in handling it.

Get a bid

The bank responds with the price that it would bid to buy and the price at which it would sell since it doesn't know if the caller wants to buy or sell.

NOTHING IS FIXED

Currency values of even the most stable economies change over time as traders are willing to pay more—or less—for dollars or pounds or euros or yen. For example, great demand for a nation's products means great demand for the currency needed to pay for those products.

If there's a big demand for the stocks or bonds of a particular country, its currency's value is likely to rise as overseas investors buy it to make investments. Similarly, a low inflation rate can boost a currency's value, since investors believe that the value of long-term purchases in that country won't erode over time.

HOW CURRENCY VALUES ARE SET

Between 1944 and 1971, major trading nations had a fixed, official rate of exchange tied to the US dollar, which could be redeemed for gold at $35 an ounce. Since 1971, when the gold standard was abandoned, currencies have floated against each other, influenced by supply and demand and by various governments' efforts to manage their currency. Some countries, for example, have sought stability by pegging, or linking, their currency to the value of the US dollar. In Europe, the European Union established the euro as a common currency for participating member nations. By 2002, euro bank notes and coins had replaced many individual currencies for all transactions.

EURO-DOLLARS

are US dollars on deposit in non-US banks. They can earn interest, be loaned, or used to make investments in US or international companies. For example, US banks borrow Eurodollars regularly.

Agree to terms

If the caller wants the deal, he or she says so. The bank that quoted a price confirms the details—what's being bought or sold and the price—and the caller verifies the terms.

Confirm deal

The caller who initiated the transaction enters the information in the dealing system and gets a confirmation.

The trade details are also entered in the bank's in-house system, and confirmed with the responding bank at the end of the day, either by phone, fax, or messenger.

Transfer payment

Payment is sent by wire transfer to a corresponding currency bank. For example, a New York bank would send payment in yen to its Tokyo branch, or to a designated Japanese bank if it didn't have a branch there.

SEEKING STABILITY

Governments generally try to keep their currencies **stable**, maintaining constant relative worth with the currencies of their major trading partners. One way to control the value of currency is by adjusting the **money supply** according to demand, depending on how much business is being transacted in that currency.

Another way to control currency values is by adjusting **interest rates**. When rates are high, international investors are more likely to buy investments in that currency. When rates are low, demand for the investments in that currency falls, along with its exchange value.

Sometimes governments deliberately **devalue** their currency, bringing the exchange rate lower relative to other countries. One reason is that this makes the country's exports relatively cheap, giving it a trade advantage.

BIG DEALS

Large-scale currency trading in the global foreign exchange market, or **forex**, is handled on telecommunications networks controlled by banks or other financial institutions.

In **spot trading**, the deal is **settled**, or finalized, within two days at current rates. **Forward transactions** involve setting an exchange rate that will apply when the currency is traded on a set date in the future. **Currency swaps** involve exchanging one cash flow for another, such as a stream of income in one currency in exchange for a stream of income in another currency at a preset exchange rate.

International Investing

In the new economy, investors looking for ways to diversify their portfolios have a world of opportunity.

If you want to balance some of the risks of investing in only US securities, you can diversify your portfolio by also investing in equities and debt available on overseas markets. Although the economic situation in one country or region may have an impact on securities markets around the world, domestic factors tend to play the most important role in determining investment return in any particular market. This means by investing globally, you're in a position to benefit from strong performances in multiple markets. And if returns in other markets are strong in a period when US markets are flat or falling, those gains may offset potential losses.

THERE ARE REWARDS

Investing abroad can produce rich returns. In the best of all possible worlds, investors win three ways, in what investment pros call the **triple whammy**:

- The investment rises in price, providing **capital gains**
- The investment pays **dividends**
- The country's **currency rises against the dollar**, so that when investors sell they get more dollars

BUT ALSO RISKS

Investing abroad is no less risky than buying at home. Prices do fall and dividends get cut. Plus, there may be hidden traps that can catch unwary investors. Here are some of the common ones:

- Tax treatments of gains or losses differ from one country to another
- Accounting and trading rules may be different
- Converting dividends into dollars may add extra expense to the transaction
- Some markets are only loosely regulated
- It can be hard to find information
- Giving buy and sell orders can be complicated by distance and language barriers
- Unexpected changes in overseas interest rates or currency values can cause major upheavals
- Political instability in a country or region can affect the value of investments there

ANOTHER PERSPECTIVE

Overseas investors make money in US stocks when the dollar is strong against their currency and stock prices are climbing. If the dollar weakens, though, the value of their investment drops as well.

The Currency Risk—and Its Reward

The greatest variable in calculating the risks and rewards of international investing hinges on changes in currency values. If the dollar shrinks in value, US investors make more when they sell at a profit. But just the opposite happens if the dollar gets stronger.

STOCK PRICE IN EUROS

BUY
- Dollar is stronger than euro

One Share
EUR **50**

SELL
- Stock rises
- Dollar weaker

One Share
EUR **60**

SELL
- Stock rises
- Dollar unchanged

One Share
EUR **60**

SELL
- Stock drops
- Dollar weaker

One Share
EUR **45**

SELL
- Stock rises
- Dollar stronger

One Share
EUR **60**

SELL
- Stock drops
- Dollar stronger

One Share
EUR **45**

WAYS TO INVEST

There are several ways for a US investor to invest internationally:

- Big US brokerage firms with branch offices abroad can invest directly
- Some international and multinational companies list stocks directly on US exchanges
- Multiple mutual fund firms offer international funds that invest overseas
- The stock of some of the largest companies is sold as **American depositary shares (ADSs)**

CROSS-BORDER BONDS

Investors are often more comfortable investing in bonds issued in their own currency by an overseas entity than buying bonds in another currency. International bonds, known generically as Eurobonds, are usually issued by a borrower in a country other than its own, in a currency other than its own—often in the currency of the intended purchasers. There are also dual-currency bonds, where interest is paid in one currency but the bonds are redeemed in another.

In this example, a US investor buys a German stock for 50 euros per share. A year later, the investor sells for 60 euros per share. Clearly that's a profit, but how much?

Since the price has gone up 10 euros per share, from 50 to 60, there's a gain of 20%. That's also what a German investor would have made on the deal. But the revaluation of the currency also affects the return. If the dollar were worth less—say 90 cents per euro instead of $1.10—a US investor would have a greater gain.

But if the dollar had gained ground against the euro and was worth $1.20 per euro, the US investor would have a net loss despite selling the stock for a profit in euros.

To figure the stock price, divide the price per share by the exchange rate.

$$\frac{\text{Price per share}}{\text{Exchange rate}} = \text{Stock price}$$

To figure the gain or loss, divide the difference between the sale price and the initial cost by the initial cost.

$$\frac{\text{Sale price} - \text{initial cost}}{\text{Initial cost}} = \text{Gain or loss}$$

EXCHANGE RATE	STOCK VALUE IN DOLLARS
Dollar = EUR **1.10**	**$45.45**
Dollar = EUR **.90**	**$66.67**
Dollar = EUR **1.10**	**$54.55**
Dollar = EUR **.90**	**$50.00**
Dollar = EUR **1.20**	**$50.00**
Dollar = EUR **1.20**	**$37.50**

GAIN OR LOSS

47% GAIN
The double advantage of a higher stock price and a lower dollar produced a $66.67 sale price, for a $21.22—or 47%—per-share profit.

20% GAIN
Because the stock price increased and there was no change in the exchange rate, the $54.55 sale price was $9.10 more than the purchase price, a 20% gain.

10% GAIN
Investors can make money on a dropping share price if the value of the dollar also drops. In this example the price drops to 45 but there's a $4.55, or 10%, profit.

10% GAIN
US investors often lose money when the dollar increases in value if they bought when it was worth less. Here the 20% gain in euro price means only a 10% gain in dollars.

17.5% LOSS
The biggest losses occur when the value of the dollar increases and the share price drops. Here a loss of 5 euros a share represents a $7.95 loss in dollars.

Trading Around the Clock

Stock trading goes on around the world, around the clock, in an electronic global marketplace.

Stock trading goes on nearly 24 hours a day, on dozens of different exchanges on different continents in different time zones.

As the trading ends in one city, activity shifts to a market in another city, sweeping the changes in price around the world. The opening prices in Tokyo or Sydney are influenced by the closing prices in the United States—just as Asia's closing prices affect what happens in European trading, and what happens in Europe influences Wall Street. Just after the New York markets close, for example, trading begins in Wellington. Two and a half hours after Tokyo closes, London opens. And with two hours to go in London, trading resumes in New York.

The global market explains why a stock can end trading one day at a specific price and open the next day at a different price.

What's still evolving is the extent to which the markets are interrelated. One reason is the growing number of multinational companies that trade on several exchanges. Another is the increasing tendency for investors to buy in many markets, not just their own.

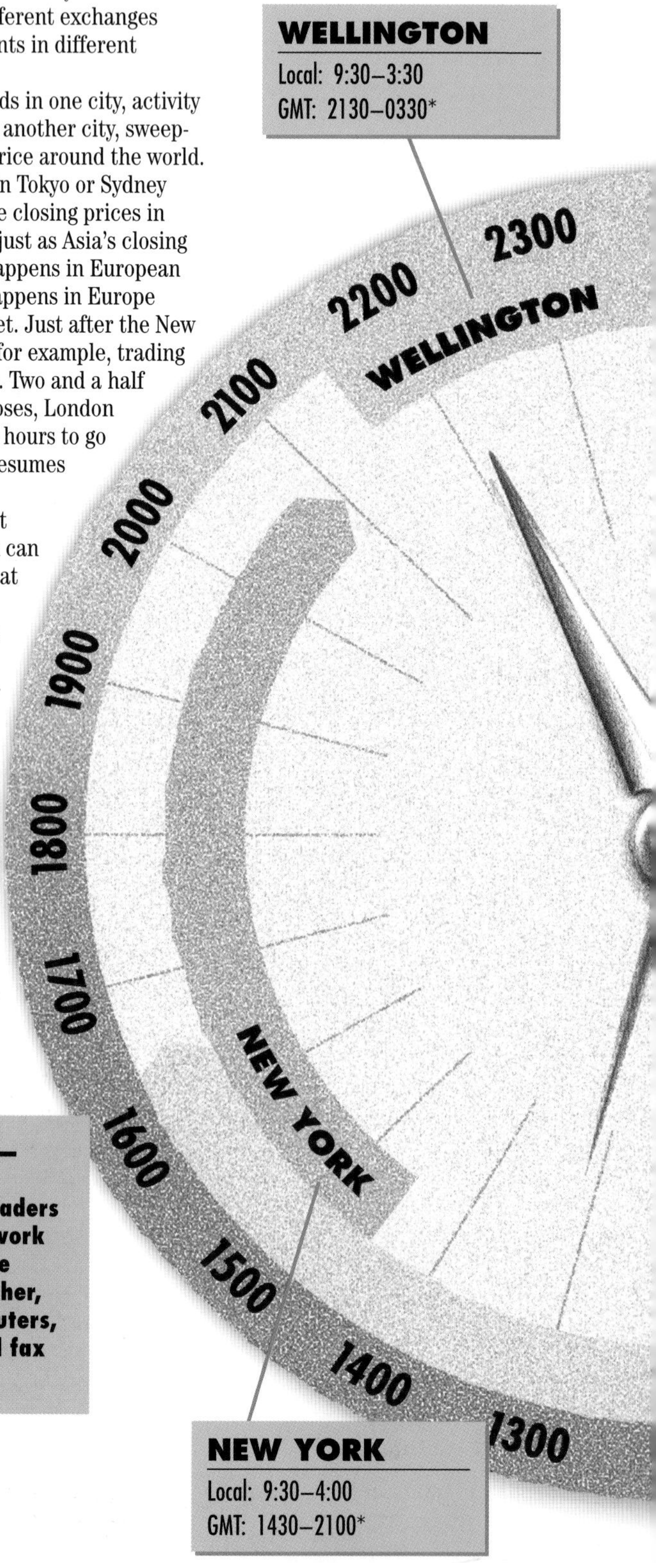

ZONING OUT— OR IN
International traders can—and do—work in one time zone and live in another, thanks to computers, telephones, and fax machines.

WELLINGTON
Local: 9:30–3:30
GMT: 2130–0330*

NEW YORK
Local: 9:30–4:00
GMT: 1430–2100*

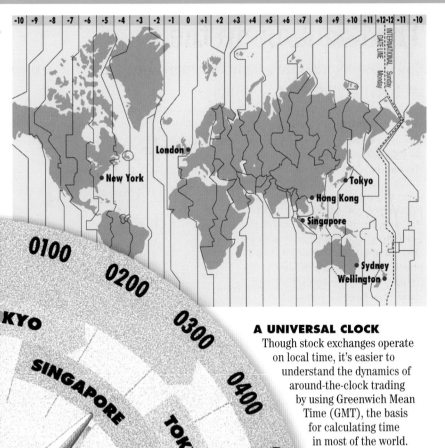

A UNIVERSAL CLOCK

Though stock exchanges operate on local time, it's easier to understand the dynamics of around-the-clock trading by using Greenwich Mean Time (GMT), the basis for calculating time in most of the world. There's a market open somewhere 24 hours a day, Monday through Friday. Taiwan and South Korean markets are open on Saturday morning.

TOKYO
Local: 9:00–11:00/12:30–3:00
GMT: 0000–0200/0330–0600

SINGAPORE
Local: 9:00–12:30/2:00–5:00
GMT: 0100–0430/0600–0900

LONDON
Local: 8:30–4:30
GMT: 0830–1630

*Standard time. Markets operate on daylight saving time part of the year.

The Banking System

Banks are an integral part of the capital markets and keep things fluid.

Investors help keep the capital markets healthy by investing in securities, often for the long term. But what about capital that they may need for more immediate use?

While there are a number of short-term investment alternatives, people may prefer to deposit their extra cash in a bank. It's safer than keeping money in a drawer or carrying it around, and it's easily accessible. The money that people and organizations deposit in bank accounts is the capital that banks put to work.

By lending money to businesses to meet short-term financing needs, banks help keep the economy fluid, or liquid. And by providing long-term mortgages, banks provide individuals with the capital they seek to purchase homes. In fact, banks are such an important source of community funding for both business and individuals that their lending practices have sometimes been credited—or blamed—for the economic health of local areas.

WHAT'S A BANK?

Commercial banks traditionally differed from **investment banks** because their main business was making loans and accepting **transaction deposits** on which you can write checks, **demand deposits**, from which you can withdraw your money at any time, and **time deposits**, on which you receive interest for a fixed term. But banks can also underwrite corporate debt and initial public offerings of common stock, advise clients who are planning a merger or an acquisition, and handle other investment banking functions through the division of their institutions that is described as a **merchant bank**.

Since the passage of the Gramm-Leach-Bliley Act in 1999, which deregulated the financial industry, the differences between a commercial bank, an investment bank, a brokerage firm, and an insurance company have been blurred.

Similarly, savings banks, thrift institutions (also known as savings and loan associations), and credit unions once were restricted to accepting deposits and lending money. Today they offer many of the same services that commercial banks offer.

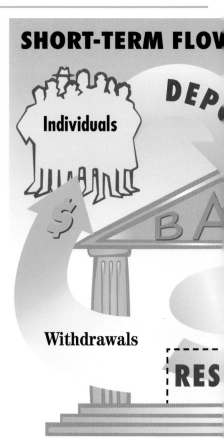

SHORT-TERM FLOW

Individuals

Withdrawals

RES

A DOUBLE SYSTEM

Most developed nations have a centralized banking system and a single authority charters, regulates, and supervises all of the country's banks. The United States is unusual in having a dual system.

Banks may be federally chartered or state chartered. Federal banks are subject to the laws, regulations, standards, and supervision of the national central banking system under the jurisdiction of **The Office of the Comptroller of the Currency (OCC)** and the **Federal Reserve System**, or the **Fed**. In contrast, a state-chartered bank is supervised by regulators in the state where it operates and may be governed by laws that don't apply to federal banks.

In fact, while there are sometimes differences about which regulations take precedence—laws governing lending practices are one example—federal and state laws tend to be compatible. State banks can be members of the Fed system while maintaining their state charters.

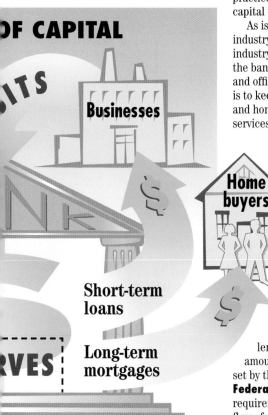

OF CAPITAL

ITS

Businesses

Home buyers

Short-term loans

Long-term mortgages

RVES

CONTROLLING THE CURRENCY

The OCC charters, regulates, and supervises the activities of national banks, their international branches, and US branches of non-US banks. Among its primary tasks are oversight of lending and investment practices—the ways in which a bank puts capital to work.

As is the case with the securities industry, regulation of the banking industry governs both the institutions—the banks themselves—and the directors and officers who work for them. The goal is to keep the banking system secure and honest and to ensure that banking services are widely available.

IN RESERVE

Much of a bank's business comes from lending the money in its deposit accounts. But because customers can draw on demand deposits whenever they like, the bank has to have money on hand to meet those demands. So banks don't actually lend out all the money they take in from deposits.

The money a bank doesn't lend is known as its **reserves**. The amount a bank must hold in reserve is set by the US central banking system, the **Federal Reserve**, which uses reserve requirements as one way to control the flow of money in the economy.

And even if they aren't members, they can use the Fed's check-processing and other services for a fee.

So why maintain two systems? To most bank customers, the differences are imperceptible. But you may benefit more than you know. The dual banking system is credited with adding an element of competition to US banks that promotes innovation. For example, state banks have pioneered many of the industry's best ideas, including the checking account.

IT'S MONEY IN THE BANK

Public confidence in the banking system, and the financial system as a whole, is built, at least in part, on the **Federal Deposit Insurance Corporation (FDIC)**, which insures bank deposits up to $100,000. That adds up to a total of more than $3 trillion across the country.

Remember, though, that securities are not insured even when you purchase them through a bank or they carry the bank's name.

KEEPING AN EYE ON COMMERCIAL BANKS	
Regulator	**Jurisdiction**
Federal Reserve System	All federal banks and state banks that are members of the system
Office of the Comptroller of Currency (OCC)	All federal banks, federal branches of non-US banks, and international branches of federal banks
Federal Deposit Insurance Corporation (FDIC)	State-chartered banks that are not members of the Federal Reserve System
State banking regulators	State-chartered banks in their state

The Federal Reserve System

The Federal Reserve System is the guardian of the nation's money—banker, regulator, controller, and watchdog all rolled into one.

Like other countries, the United States has a national bank to oversee its economic and monetary policies. But the Federal Reserve System, known informally as the Fed, isn't one bank. It's 12 separate district banks and 25 regional branches spread across the country, so that no one state, region, or business group can exert too much control.

Each district bank has a president and board of directors, and the system itself is run by a seven-member board of governors. The Fed's Open Market Committee is responsible for guiding day-to-day monetary decisions.

The Federal Reserve's Many Roles

The Fed plays many roles as part of its responsibility to keep the economy healthy.
   The Fed handles the day-to-day banking business of the US government. It gets deposits of corporate taxes for unemployment, withholding, and income, and also of federal excise taxes on liquor, tobacco, gasoline, and regulated services like phone systems. It also authorizes payment of government bills like Social Security and Medicare as well as interest payments on Treasury bills, notes, and bonds.

POLICYMAKER

By authorizing buying and selling of government securities, the Fed tries to balance the flow of money in circulation. When the economy is stable, the demand for goods and services is fairly constant, and so are prices. Achieving that stability supports the Fed's goals of keeping the economy healthy and maintaining the value of the dollar.

BANKER

The Fed maintains bank accounts for the US Treasury and many government and quasi-government agencies. It deposits and withdraws funds the way you do at your own bank, but in bigger volume: Over 80 million Treasury checks are written every year.

LENDER

If a bank needs to borrow money, it can turn to a Federal Reserve bank. The interest the Fed charges banks is called the **discount rate**. Bankers don't like to borrow from the Fed, since it may suggest they have problems. And they can often borrow more cheaply from other banks.

Seattle
Helena
Portland
Salt Lake City
Denver
★ SAN FRANCISCO
Los Angeles
El Paso

Key:
★ **Regional bank**
● **Branch bank**

MONEY & MARKETS

HOW THE FED WORKS

Though it is structured as a corporation owned by banks, the Fed works more like a government agency than a business. Under the direction of its chairman, it sets economic policy, supervises banking operations, and has become a major factor in shaping the economy.

The governors are appointed to 14-year terms by the president and confirmed by Congress. Their long terms are designed to insulate them from political pressure. However, the chairman serves a four-year term and is often chosen by the president to achieve specific economic goals.

MANAGING MONEY

The **Federal Open Market Committee (FOMC)**, under the leadership of the Fed chairman, meets about every six weeks to evaluate the state of the economy and issues what's known as a **risk statement**, indicating if it thinks that either inflation or economic weakness pose a potential threat to the economy. It may also conclude the risks seem balanced.

The risk statement, which tends to have an impact on the stock and bond markets, is generally interpreted as an indication of the action the FOMC is likely to take at its next meeting or the one following to tighten or loosen the money supply.

REGULATOR

CONTROLLER

GUARDIAN

ADMINISTRATOR

The Fed interprets laws that Congress passes into regulation, and monitors the business affairs and audits the records of all of the banks in its system. Its particular concerns are compliance with banking rules and the quality of loans.

When currency wears out or gets damaged, the Fed takes it out of circulation and authorizes its replacement. Then the Treasury has new bills printed and new coins minted.

Gold stored by non-US governments is held in the vault at the New York Federal Reserve Bank—some 10,000 tons of it.

That's more gold in one place than anywhere else in the world, as far as anyone knows. Among its many tasks, the Fed administers the exchange of bullion between countries.

The Fed is also the national check clearing house. It facilitates quick and accurate transfer of more than $39.3 trillion in 42.5 billion check transactions a year.

Controlling the Money Flow

Keeping a modern economy running smoothly requires a pilot who'll keep it from stalling or overaccelerating.

The United States, like most other countries, tries to control the amount of money in circulation. The process of injecting or withdrawing money reflects the monetary policy that the Federal Reserve adopts to regulate the economy.

Monetary policy isn't a fixed ideology. It's a constant juggling act to keep enough money in the economy so that it flourishes without growing too fast.

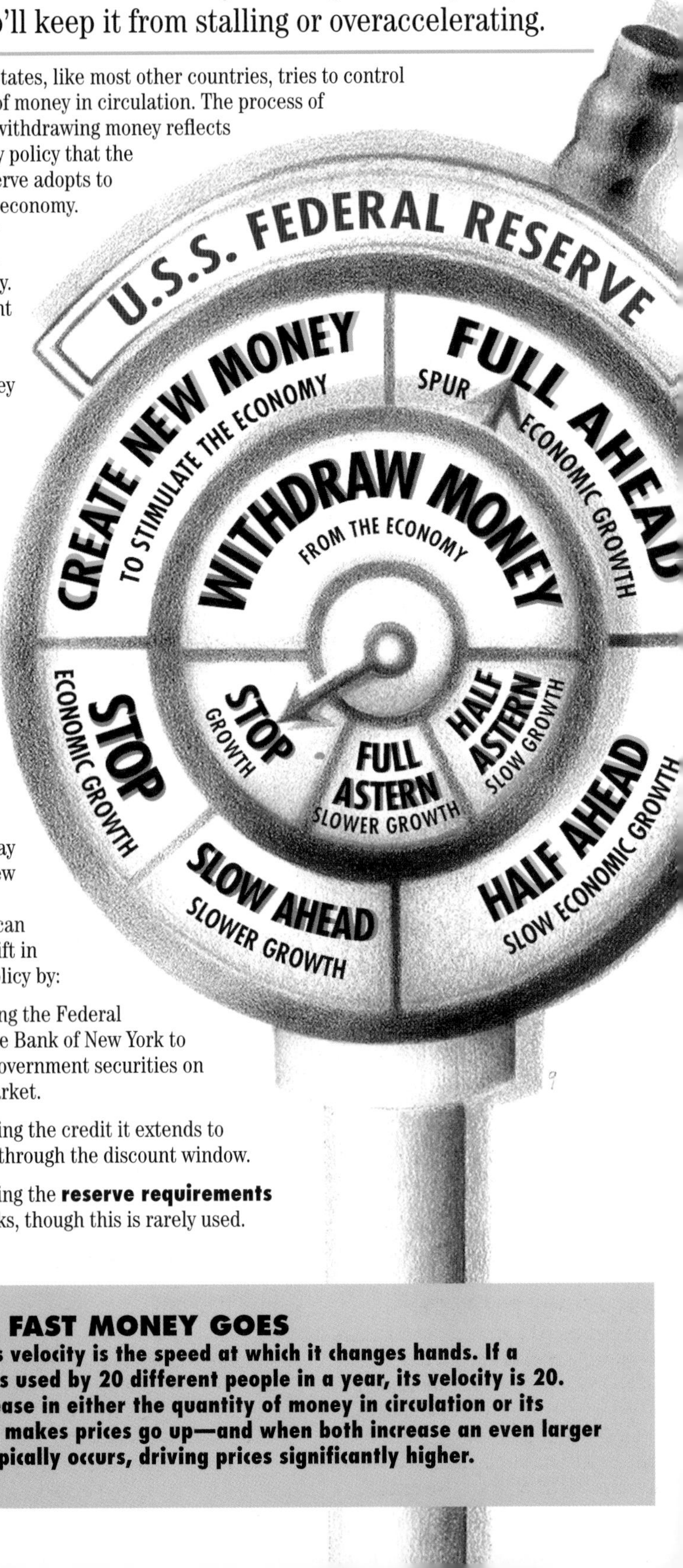

HOW IT WORKS
Changes in monetary policy tend to be gradual, though over a period of months it may move in a new direction.

The Fed can initiate a shift in monetary policy by:

1 Ordering the Federal Reserve Bank of New York to buy or sell government securities on the open market.

2 Adjusting the credit it extends to banks through the discount window.

3 Changing the **reserve requirements** at banks, though this is rarely used.

U.S.S. FEDERAL RESERVE

CREATE NEW MONEY TO STIMULATE THE ECONOMY

FULL AHEAD SPUR ECONOMIC GROWTH

WITHDRAW MONEY FROM THE ECONOMY

STOP GROWTH

STOP ECONOMIC GROWTH

FULL ASTERN SLOWER GROWTH

HALF ASTERN SLOW GROWTH

SLOW AHEAD SLOWER GROWTH

HALF AHEAD SLOW ECONOMIC GROWTH

HOW FAST MONEY GOES
Money's velocity is the speed at which it changes hands. If a $1 bill is used by 20 different people in a year, its velocity is 20. An increase in either the quantity of money in circulation or its velocity makes prices go up—and when both increase an even larger jump typically occurs, driving prices significantly higher.

The Fed's reserve requirement makes banks keep a portion, usually 10%,

RESERVE 10%

of their deposits in a fund to cover any unusual demand from customers for cash.

PUTTING POLICY TO WORK

The Federal Reserve's Federal Open Market Committee (FOMC) implements monetary policy by the control it exerts over the **federal funds rate**, which is the rate that banks charge other banks for overnight access to the balances in their Reserve Bank accounts. Changes in the rate affect other short-term interest rates almost immediately, and also influence long-term rates, the value of the dollar against other currencies, and stock prices.

The dilemma, from the FOMC's perspective, is that it must rely on estimates to make policy decisions and to assess whether or not the policies it adopts are working. For example, it can't be certain what effect a change in the federal funds rate will actually have or how soon the economy will respond.

CHANGING THE SUPPLY

About 11:15 a.m. every day, the New York Fed decides whether to buy or sell government securities to implement the FOMC policy decisions.

To slow down an economy where too much money is in circulation, it sells securities, taking in the cash that would otherwise be available for lending. To give the economy a shot in the arm, it creates money by buying securities.

For all practical purposes, there isn't any limit on the amount of money the Fed can create. In a typical month, it might pump as much as $4 billion or as little as $1 billion into the economy.

ADJUSTING THE RATE

The Fed can also increase or decrease the **discount rate**, the rate it charges banks to borrow money. If the rate is increased, banks tend to borrow less and have less available to lend to their clients. If the rate is decreased, banks tend to borrow more and lend at attractive rates.

CREATING MONEY

To create money, the New York Fed buys government securities from banks and brokerage houses. The money that pays for the securities hasn't existed before, but it has value, or worth, because the securities the Fed has bought with it are valuable.

More new money is created when the banks and brokerages lend the money they receive from selling the securities to clients who spend it on goods and services. These simplified steps illustrate how the process works.

1

The Fed writes a check for $100 million to buy the securities from a brokerage house. The brokerage house deposits the check in its own bank (A), increasing the bank's cash.

2

Bank A can lend its customers $90 million of that deposit after setting aside 10%. The Fed requires all banks to hold 10% of their deposits (in this example, $10 million) in reserve. A young couple borrows $100,000 from Bank A to buy a new house. The sellers deposit the money in their bank (B).

3

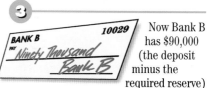

Now Bank B has $90,000 (the deposit minus the required reserve) to lend that it didn't have before. A woman borrows $10,000 from Bank B to buy a car, and the dealer deposits her check in Bank C.

4

Bank C can now loan $9,000.

This one series of transactions has created $190,099,000 in just four steps. Through a repetition of the loan process involving a wide range of banks and their customers, the $100 million that the Fed initially added to the money supply could theoretically become almost $900 million in new money.

The Economic Cycle

Experts work hard to predict and control the ups and downs of the economy.

Economies tend to move through normally recurring cycles of growth and slowdown. But there can be problems if growth results in runaway inflation or if a slowdown ends in recession. The Federal Reserve works to prevent either situation.

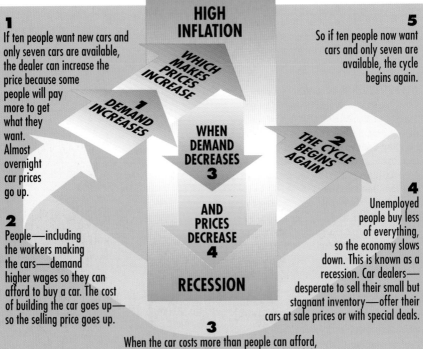

HIGH INFLATION

WHICH MAKES PRICES INCREASE

DEMAND INCREASES

1
If ten people want new cars and only seven cars are available, the dealer can increase the price because some people will pay more to get what they want. Almost overnight car prices go up.

2
People—including the workers making the cars—demand higher wages so they can afford to buy a car. The cost of building the car goes up— so the selling price goes up.

WHEN DEMAND DECREASES 3

AND PRICES DECREASE 4

RECESSION

THE CYCLE BEGINS AGAIN

5
So if ten people now want cars and only seven are available, the cycle begins again.

4
Unemployed people buy less of everything, so the economy slows down. This is known as a recession. Car dealers— desperate to sell their small but stagnant inventory—offer their cars at sale prices or with special deals.

3
When the car costs more than people can afford, they stop buying. Fewer cars are needed, and the factory lays off workers.

THE INFLATION STRUGGLE

Most economists agree that inflation isn't good for the economy because, over time, it destroys value, including the value of money. If inflation is running at a 10% annual rate, for example, a book that cost $10 one year would cost $20 just seven years later. For comparison's sake, if inflation averaged 3% a year, the same book wouldn't cost $20 for 24 years.

Since inflation typically occurs in a growing economy that's creating jobs and reducing unemployment, politicians are willing to risk its consequences. But the Federal Reserve prefers to cool down a potentially inflationary economy before it gets out of hand. Since it also wants to prevent any long-term slowdown, it typically reverses its monetary policy when the economy seems likely to shrink.

WHO GETS HURT?

The people hit the hardest by inflation are those living on fixed incomes. For example, if you're retired and have a pension that was determined by a salary

TIME AS MONEY

In 1800, you could travel from New York to Philadelphia in about 18 hours by stagecoach. The trip cost about $4.

Today the train costs about $53, but takes 75 minutes. While the trip's price has **inflated** about 1,225%, the travel time has **deflated** about 93%. So if time is money, today's traveler comes out ahead.

you earned in less inflationary times, your income will buy less of what you need to live comfortably. Workers whose wages don't keep pace with inflation can also find their lifestyle slipping.

But inflation isn't bad for everyone. Debtors love it because the money they repay each year is worth less than it was when they borrowed it. If their own income keeps pace with inflation, the money they repay is also an increasingly smaller percentage of their budget.

WHEN THERE'S NO INFLATION

When the rate of inflation slows, it's described as **disinflation**. Several years of 1% annual increases in the cost of living are disinflationary after a period of more rapid growth. Employment and output can continue to be strong, and the economy can continue to grow.

Deflation, though, is a widespread decline in the prices of goods and services. But instead of stimulating employment and production, deflation has the potential to undermine them. As the economy contracts and people are out of work, they can't afford to buy even at cheaper prices.

Stagflation, a confounding combination of slow economic growth and high inflation, is yet another example of how components of the standard cycle can be out of step.

CHARTING A RECESSION

Recessions are periods when unemployment rises while sales and industrial production slows. Government officials, the securities industry, investors, and policymakers all try to anticipate when they will occur, but the factors that produce economic prosperity are so complex that no predictor is always reliable.

The Index of Leading Economic Indicators, released every month by the Conference Board, a business research group, provides one way to keep an eye on the economy's overall health. Generally, three consecutive rises in the Index are considered a sign of growth and three

CONTROLLING THE CYCLE

Most developed economies try not to let the economic cycle run unchecked because the consequences could be a major worldwide **depression** like the one that followed the stock market crash of 1929. In a depression, money is so tight that the economy virtually grinds to a halt, unemployment escalates, businesses collapse, and the general mood is grim.

THE RULE OF 72

The rule of 72 can be a reliable guide to the impact of high inflation. You simply divide 72 by the annual inflation rate to find out the number of years it will take prices to double. For example, when inflation is at 10%, prices will double in seven years ($72 \div 10 = 7$). But when it's 3%, they may double in 24 years ($72 \div 3 = 24$).

You can also use the rule of 72 to estimate how long it will take you to double the money you're saving. If you're earning a 5% return on your investment portfolio, you should double your principal in 14.4 years. But if your return is 10%, it should double in half the time.

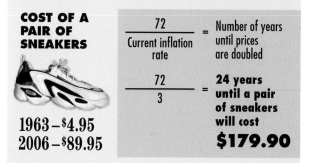

COST OF A PAIR OF SNEAKERS

1963 – $4.95
2006 – $89.95

$$\frac{72}{\text{Current inflation rate}} = \text{Number of years until prices are doubled}$$

$$\frac{72}{3} = \text{24 years until a pair of sneakers will cost}$$

$179.90

drops a sign of decline and potential recession. Its movement may signal economic downturns 18 months in advance, and it correctly forecast the recessions of 1991 and 2001. But it has also pointed to recessions that never materialized.

The National Bureau of Economic Research (NBER), which tracks recessions, describes the low point of a recession as a **trough** between two **peaks**—the points at which the recession began and ended. Of course, peaks and troughs can be identified only in retrospect, though the fact that there's a slump in the economy is evident.

Recessions are typically shorter than the period of economic expansion they follow. But they can be quite severe even if they're brief, and recovery can be slower from some recessions than from others.

For example, the economy may expand while unemployment rates stay high if there's an increase in **productivity**. That means fewer workers are creating more goods and services.

Stock: Sharing a Corporation

When you buy stock, or shares, you
own a slice of the company.

Stock is an **equity** investment. If you buy stock in a
corporation, you own a small part of that corporation
and are described as a **stockholder** or **shareholder**.
You buy stock because you expect it to increase in value,
or because you expect the corporation to pay you dividend
income, or a portion of its profits. In fact, many
stocks provide both growth and income.

When a corporation issues stock, the
company receives the proceeds from that
initial sale. After that, shares of the stock are
traded, or bought and sold among investors,
but the corporation gets no income from those
trades. The price of the stock moves up or
down depending on how much you and other
investors are willing to pay for it at the time.

COMMON STOCK

Most stock issued in the United States is
common stock. Owning it entitles you to
collect dividends if the company pays
them, and you can sell shares at a profit
if the price increases. But stock prices
change all the time, so you have to recognize that your shares could lose value,
especially in the short term. Some common
stocks are **volatile**, which means their
prices may increase or decrease rapidly.

Despite the risk, investors have been
willing to buy common stock because over
time stocks in general—though not each
individual stock—have provided stronger
returns, or price increases plus dividends,
than other investment securities.

PREFERRED STOCK

Some companies issue **preferred stock**
in addition to common stock. These equity
investments, which also trade in the secondary market, are listed separately from
the company's common stock and trade at
a different price.

Preferred stock dividends are paid
before common
stock dividends and are
often guaranteed, unlike those
on common stock. Preferred shareholders
are also more likely to recover some of
their investment if the company fails. And,
in some cases, preferred stock can be converted to common stock at a preset price.

The prices of preferred
stock tend to change little
over time, which means
they pose less risk. But the
dividends typically aren't
increased if the company's
earnings increase, which
limits potential gains.

The combination of these
various characteristics help
explain why preferred shares
are sometimes described as
hybrid investments—a combination of
fixed income and equity.

COMMON STOCK

- Owners share in
  success if stock
  price goes up
- Stock may drop if
  company falters

StrwdHtlRsrt	HOT	1.34e	4.2	5	5796	32
StateSt	STT	.56	.6	34	4087	89
StatnIslBcp	SIB	.36f	2.2	15	841	16
StationCno	STN		...	dd	1111	1
StationCno pf		3.50	7.0	...	82	
Steelcase A	SCS	.44	2.7	11	974	
Steinway	LVB		...	15	.143	
Stepan	SCL	.60	2.6	11	48	
Steris				22	805	

**Classes
of stock**

Preferred stock

BLUE CHIP

is a term borrowed from poker, where the blue chips are the most valuable. Blue chips refer to the stocks of the largest, most consistently profitable corporations. The list isn't official—and it does change.

PREFERRED STOCK

- Dividend payment has priority over common stock dividends

- Dividends don't increase if company prospers

SPLIT STOCK

- More shares created at lower price per share

- Stockholders profit if price goes back up

STOCK SPLITS

When the price of a stock increases significantly, you and other investors may be reluctant to buy, either because you think the price has reached its peak or because it costs so much. Corporations have the option of splitting the stock to lower the price, which they expect to stimulate trading. When a stock is split, there are more shares available, but the total market value is the same.

Say a company's stock is trading at $100 a share. If the company declares a two-for-one split, it gives you two shares for each one you own. At the same time the price drops to $50 a share. If you owned 300 shares selling at $100 you now have 600 selling at $50—but the value is still $30,000.

The initial effect of a stock split is no different from getting coins in exchange for a dollar bill. But the price may move up toward the presplit price, increasing the value of your stock.

Stocks can split three for one, three for two, ten for one, or any other combination.

REVERSE SPLITS

In a **reverse split** the corporation exchanges more shares for fewer—say ten shares for five—and the price increases accordingly. Typically the motive is to boost the price so that it meets a stock market's minimum listing requirement or makes the stock attractive to institutional investors, including mutual funds and pension funds, which may not buy very low-priced stocks.

CLASSES OF STOCK

Companies may issue different classes of stock, label them differently and list them separately on a stock market. Sometimes a class indicates ownership in a specific division or subsidiary of the company. Other times it indicates shares that sell at different market prices, have different dividend policies, or impose voting or sales restrictions on ownership.

Public and Private Companies

There's a range of differences between what's public and what's private.

The terms *public* and *private* have a range of opposite meanings that are relevant to a discussion of stock. Public means open or available to everyone and private means restricted to a particular group. Thus, anyone can buy shares in a **public company** but not in a **private company**. When a private company goes public, it sells shares through an initial public offering (IPO). When a public company goes private, all its shares are purchased by a limited group of investors.

What can be confusing, though, is that both public and private companies are part of the **private sector**. That's the opposite of the **public sector**, which refers to federal, state, and local governments. As companies can move from public to private, or the reverse, they can also move between sectors.

THE PUBLIC SECTOR

The public sector includes the departments, offices, agencies, and corporations run by municipal, state, and federal governments. These public enterprises may be funded by tax dollars, by money raised by selling bonds, or, in some cases, by charging fees for services they provide.

The public sector provides citizens with services, such as education, transportation, law enforcement, and social welfare programs, through their agencies or offices. Privatization occurs when a government sells all or part of a government enterprise to individual and institutional investors or turns over previously public functions to private firms.

WHY PRIVATIZE?

There are many reasons to privatize, most of them economic. Some people believe that private sector enterprises are more efficient than public sector ones, so that privatization provides better service at lower cost. Whether those benefits materialize or not, privatization shifts responsibility for those services from the government.

Selling off attractive assets or making them available for private development can raise substantial amounts of cash to offset public debt or provide cash infusions to bolster the economy and reduce taxes. Another reason to privatize is to dispose of holdings that may be a drain on public resources, such as hospitals or public transportation systems, because they're expensive to operate and are often not profitable. In the same vein, turning over the operation of prisons, schools, and other facilities to private companies may reduce the number of employees.

TAKING SOME RISKS

Investors take risks whether they buy shares in a privately held company that has become public or a former government enterprise that has been privatized—though the risks are somewhat different.

In both, there are the questions of whether the company will be profitable in the marketplace, whether it will provide income in the form of dividends and growth in the form of increased share price, and how much debt it has and whether that debt will hamper its ability to succeed.

PRIVATIZATION

In the case of privatized assets, investors must consider the potential for government interference, especially if it remains a partial owner or regulator.

PROS AND CONS

In the privatization debate, there are strong arguments for and against, often fueled by political philosophy.

Pros:
- Provides infusion of capital
- Introduces stronger management
- Eases or eliminates debt

Cons:
- Potential loss of jobs and employee benefits
- Service quality driven by profit motive
- Redistribution of wealth into few hands

THE PRIVATE SECTOR

WHY GO PUBLIC?

Business owners, who typically sell only a portion of their company when taking it public, may have a number of motives. Sometimes it's primarily a way to raise enough capital to expand the business and outstrip the competition. In other cases, it's a way for the founders to reap substantial financial rewards from their ingenuity and business success.

If the founders continue to run the company successfully while owning a substantial number of shares, they can be richer and more powerful than they might have been at the head of a private firm. In other cases, founders or the descendants of founding families leave the firm once it has become a public company.

Of course, not all private companies go public. For many small firms, it's not a viable alternative even if it seems a potential way to attract capital. And there are a number of large, powerful companies in the United States and around the world that continue to be privately held.

Sometimes the alternative is a private placement, which means that a private company sells some or all of its shares directly to investors rather than offering shares to the public. A private placement doesn't have to be registered with the SEC or meet other disclosure criteria since the shares can't be traded among investors.

The reverse process, called **nationalization**, occurs when a government takes over a private company. It may occur for economic reasons—if companies need public subsidies to survive, as a way to preserve jobs, or in an effort to keep profits within the country—or for a variety of political reasons.

NATIONALIZATION

CAPITAL

Government and shareholder scrutiny

MUTUAL COMPANIES

HYBRID COMPANIES

Some insurance companies aren't really publicly held, but they're not completely private either. Rather, they're mutual companies, which means that they are owned by their policyholders. Any profit the companies make is shared by these owners, as it might be in a publicly held company, in the form of dividends or rebates on future premiums. But the dividends these mutual companies pay are not the same as dividends paid by a public company.

Certain savings banks and federal savings and loan associations are mutual companies as well, with their depositors entitled to a share of the profits. In the case of insurance companies and savings and loans, members have a right to vote for directors, as shareholders of public companies do. That's not the case with savings banks.

Some mutual companies convert to public ownership and sell shares to outside investors, though in some states they may have to use any profits to benefit their customers before they can pay dividends to their shareholders.

Initial Public Offerings

The first time a company issues stock, it's called **going public.**

Going public, or taking a company public, means making it possible for outside investors to buy the company's stock. Selling shares gives the company's owners access to more capital than they can raise elsewhere and, unlike a loan, it never has to be repaid.

HOW YOU INVEST

When an IPO comes to market, shares are available through brokers affiliated with the chief underwriter or a firm that's part of the selling syndicate working with the underwriter. In most cases, though, the shares go to the broker's best clients—those with the biggest accounts, longest history, or some other advantage.

You can buy shares as soon as trading begins, but there may be good reasons to wait at least six months, until the first analysts' reports are available. Despite the buzz they may create, many IPOs trade at lower prices than comparably sized companies for several years after issue.

GOING PUBLIC

The **initial public offering (IPO)** process traditionally begins when a company that wants to be publicly traded contacts an **underwriting firm**, usually an investment bank. The underwriter agrees to buy all the public shares at a set price and resell them to the public. The risk the underwriter assumes is offset by the fee it charges, usually a percentage of each share's price. If the IPO is successful, those fees are the underwriter's profit.

The underwriters and the company prepare a prospectus that is filed with the Securities and Exchange Commission (SEC) and made available to potential investors as a way to assess the potential strengths of the company and the risks that investing in it may pose. The SEC must approve the offering before it can proceed.

ATTRACTING INVESTORS

The proposed stock sale is publicized in the financial press. The ads are commonly known as **tombstones** because of their black border and heavy print.

The underwriters may also organize meetings between the company's management and institutional investors, such as pension managers or mutual funds. The day

> A company gets the money only when its stock is issued. All subsequent trading means a profit or loss for the stockholder, but not for the company that issued it.

before the actual sale, underwriters **price the issue**, or establish the price at which it will be offered to investors. Everyone who buys shares in the IPO pays that price.

When the stock begins trading the next day, the price can rise or fall, depending on whether investors agree or disagree with the underwriters' valuation of the new company.

DIRECT SALES

Some companies prefer to go public by auctioning shares to any investor who wants to submit a competitive bid. The bidding process, sometimes described as a Dutch auction, determines the sale price. Everyone who has bid the sale price or higher while the auction is in progress purchases shares at the sale price.

One reason that a company may prefer a direct sale is that investors typically pay more per share than in a conventional IPO, where the price at issue may be lower than market value. A higher price increases the capital the company raises.

SECONDARY OFFERINGS

If a company has already issued shares, but wants to raise additional **capital**, or money, through the sale of more stock, the process is called a **secondary offering**.

Companies are often wary of issuing more stock, since the larger the supply of stock outstanding, the less valuable each share already issued may be.

For this reason, a company typically issues new shares only if its stock price is high. To raise money, it may decide to issue bonds, or sometimes convertible bonds or preferred shares.

LOVE ME TENDER

Just as it may issue additional shares, a company may choose to **repurchase**, or buy back, shares of its stock, either gradually in the stock market or by **tender offer**, giving shareholders the right to sell at a specific price. The company's motive may be to boost its stock price or to reduce dilution that results from granting stock options. Or it may decide a buyback is a better use for extra cash than investing in a new company, reinvesting in its own business, or paying a dividend.

The Right to Vote

Owning stock gives you the right to vote on important company issues and policies.

As a stockholder, you have the right to vote on major policy decisions, such as whether a company should issue additional stock, sell itself to outside buyers, or change the board of directors. In general, the more stock you own, the greater your voice in company decisions. But even if you own just a small number of shares you may present a proposal to be voted on at the annual meeting, provided it meets the requirements of the Securities and Exchange Commission (SEC) and you've held the shares for more than a year.

ALL STOCKS ARE NOT EQUAL

Usually, each share of stock gives you one vote. Some companies, however, issue different classes of stock with different voting privileges. When stocks carry extra votes, a small group of people can control a company's direction while owning fewer than 50% of the shares.

THE WAY YOU VOTE

You can attend the company's annual meeting and vote in person. Or you can vote online at the designated website, using an electronic ballot, vote by telephone, or cast your vote by mail using a ballot called a **proxy**. A 2005 survey reports that 80% of proxies in the United States and 70% in Canada are returned, mostly online or by phone.

Before the annual meeting you receive a **proxy statement**, a legal document that presents information on planned changes in company management that require shareholder approval. By law, it must also present shareholder proposals, even if they are at odds with company policy. It also takes positions on each question, stating management's recommendation.

SEC rules require proxies to show, in chart form, the total compensation of the company's top five executives. The proxy must also report the company's stock performance in relation to comparable companies in the industry and to the S&P 500 Index.

The proxy asks shareholders to elect a board of directors. The directors oversee the operation of the company and set long-term policy goals. You can support them all, vote against them or vote for some but not others.

The proxy lets shareholders vote yes or no or abstain on shareholder proposals and other issues affecting the corporation. The directors want you to vote yes on the issues they support and no on the others. If you don't return your proxy, your vote isn't counted.

X Please mark your votes as in this example.

Unless otherwise specified, proxies will be voted FOR the election of the nominees for directo FOR proposals 2 and 3, and AGAINST proposals 4, 5 and 6.

The Board of Directors recommends a vote FOR election of directors and proposals 2 and 3.

	FOR	WITHHELD		FOR	AGAINST	ABSTAIN
1.Election of Directors (see reverse)	X		2. Approval of Amendments to the 1987 Stock Option Plan	X		
FOR, except vote withheld from the following nominee(s):			3. Appointment of Independent Auditors		X	

The Board of I stockholder pr

4. Stockholder proposal

5. Stockholder proposal

6. Stockholder proposal

SIGNATURE(S) _John Q. Investor_   DATE _9/19_

NOTE: Please sign exactly as name appears hereon. Joint owners should each sign. When signing as attorney, executor, administrator, trustee or guardian, please give full title as such.

CHANGING ATTITUDES

Institutional investors, such as mutual funds and pension plans, who hold blocks of company stock also vote their proxies. That puts them in a stronger position than individual investors to influence company policy or the make-up of the board of directors. And some of these investors have flexed their muscles in recent years.

For example, some institutional investors have pressed companies to change environmental and employee policies and confront certain ethical issues. Other funds, though, have generally supported management positions.

A ruling by the Securities and Exchange Commission that took effect in 2004 compels mutual funds to file a report disclosing the way they vote. Among other things, this information allows fund investors to evaluate how well a fund's public position on issues corresponds to its voting record. Some funds, including many socially responsible funds, had already adopted the policy.

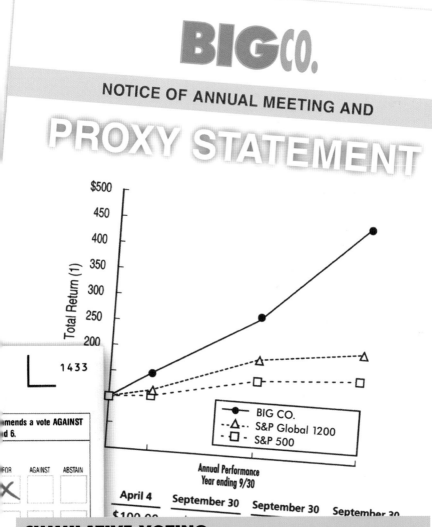

BIGCO.

NOTICE OF ANNUAL MEETING AND

PROXY STATEMENT

1433

mends a vote AGAINST
d 6.

FOR   AGAINST   ABSTAIN

| BIG CO. | S&P Global 1200 | S&P 500 |

Annual Performance
Year ending 9/30

April 4   September 30   September 30   September 30

$100.00

CUMULATIVE VOTING

As a shareholder, you typically get one vote for each share of stock you own. But when you vote for the board of directors in some companies, you may have the opportunity to cast your votes in a nontraditional way. In traditional corporate voting—called statutory voting—you cast the same number of votes for each director running for election. In cumulative voting, on the other hand, you can combine your votes and cast different numbers of votes for different candidates.

For example, if you owned 100 shares and eight directors were running for election, in a statutory vote, you'd cast 100 votes for each of the candidates, for a total of 800 votes. In a cumulative vote, you could still do that, or you could distribute your 800 votes among some of the candidates, assigning no votes to others. You could even cast all 800 votes for a single candidate. The purpose of cumulative voting is to give small shareholders more voice in corporate governance.

The Stock Markets

Stocks change hands every trading day on traditional and electronic markets.

The first stock exchange in America was organized in Philadelphia in 1790. But by the time the traders who met every day under a buttonwood tree on Wall Street adopted the name **New York Stock Exchange (NYSE)** in 1817, New York had become the center of market action.

The rival **New York Curb Exchange** was founded in 1842. The name said it all: Trading actually took place on the street until it moved indoors in 1921. In 1953, the Curb Exchange became the **American Stock Exchange**.

A STREET BY ANY OTHER NAME

Wall Street, which got its name from the stockade built by early settlers to protect New York from attacks from the north, was the scene of New York's organized stock trading. Now it lends its name to the financial markets in general—though lots of traders never set foot on it.

TRADITIONAL TRADING

At the New York Stock Exchange, the American Stock Exchange, and regional exchanges in Boston, Philadelphia, and Chicago, brokers gather on a centralized trading floor to buy and sell shares. In some ways, these auction-style transactions are handled as they have always been, in an energetic, competitive give-and-take to get the best price.

But in other ways, these traditional stock markets have changed dramatically in recent years. Transactions are increasingly routed, executed, and reported electronically. Clearing and settlement is almost totally electronic, which speeds up the process of paying for purchases and delivering securities to their new owners.

In what may be a sign of things to come, computer-based stock trading has replaced face-to-face bargaining in most of the world. Trading in London and Tokyo is exclusively electronic, as are the stock markets of emerging nations.

CHANGES IN THE WIND

Expanded electronic trading isn't the only thing changing in traditional markets. The NYSE, for example, has proposed a sweeping structural reorganization that would mean becoming a publicly traded company rather than a private association.

And the Securities and Exchange Commission (SEC) has instituted Regulation NMS (for National Market Structure). Under this rule, brokers will be required to send orders to the market with the best immediately accessible publicly quoted price rather than to what they consider the fastest market.

New markets, sometimes called trading platforms, may emerge to increase competition and reduce costs.

THE STOCK MARKET

The **Nasdaq Stock Market**, which opened in 1971 as the world's first electronic market, has no central trading location and no exchange floor, though its MarketSite Tower, in New York's

Times Square, serves as a center for financial news broadcasts and provides up-to-the-minute trading information.

Nasdaq is a publicly traded company with two trading divisions: the National Market, which lists a wide range of companies, from emerging firms to corporate giants, including Microsoft and Intel, and the Small-Cap Market. The Small-Cap specializes in smaller firms, including many newly public companies.

MAKING THE LIST

When a stock is listed on an orderly, organized market like the NYSE or the Nasdaq—or on rare occasions listed on both—it gains prestige and also a number of tangible benefits. Because the markets are highly regulated and prices are accurately and continuously reported, investors can be confident that trades are legitimate and prices are fair. That encourages active trading, and the more trading there is, the more liquid the market. That means investors know they can sell when they want, though not always at the price they want.

OVER-THE-COUNTER TRADING

Stocks in many small and new companies aren't listed on either the Nasdaq or a traditional market. Instead, they're bought and sold **over-the-counter (OTC)**. The term originated at a time when US investors actually bought stock over-the-counter at their local broker's office. Today, transactions are handled over the telephone or by computer.

Many OTC stocks are comparatively inexpensive and **thinly**, or infrequently, traded. There are two quotation services for OTC stocks—the Pink Sheets' Electronic Quotation Service (www.pinksheets.com), and the NASD OTC Bulletin Board (www.otcbb.com). Both quotation services provide online real-time quotations for OTC stocks—the Bulletin Board for the approximately 3,800 OTC stocks that are registered with the SEC, and the Pink Sheets LLC for the OTC stocks that are not registered with the SEC.

REQUIREMENTS FOR STOCK MARKET LISTING

The major US stock markets impose specific requirements that companies must meet before their stock can be listed or traded on that market. If they qualify for all three, the companies can choose where they wish to be listed.

Exchange	Requirements*	Average daily volume*	Listing fee*
NYSE New York Stock Exchange	1.1 million publicly held shares minimum; $100 million minimum market capitalization	1.6 billion shares	$250,000 initial fee $500,000 annual fee maximum
NASDAQ® The Nasdaq Stock Market	There are sets of quantitative and qualitative requirements for companies listed on the Nasdaq National Market and the Nasdaq Small-Cap Market	1.7 billion shares	$150,000 initial fee $75,000 annual fee maximum
Amex. American Stock Exchange	500,000 publicly held shares minimum; $3 million minimum market capitalization	65 million shares	$60,000 initial fee $45,000 annual fee maximum

*As of August 2005

Trading on a Traditional Market

A stock exchange is both the activity of buying and selling and the place where those transactions take place.

The New York Stock Exchange, the largest traditional exchange in operation, provides the facilities for stock trading and rules under which the trading takes place. It has no responsibility for setting the price of a stock. That is the result of supply and demand, and the trading process.

Trading on the floor of the NYSE is **auction** or **open outcry style**: In each transaction, stock is sold at the highest bid and bought for the lowest offer. The difference between them is the **spread**.

THE TRADING FLOOR
The NYSE's trading area is known as the **trading floor**.

1 The trading day begins at 9:30 a.m. EST/EDT and ends at 4:00 p.m. when the bell is rung from the **podium**. Usually the honor of ringing the bell goes to the executives of a listed company or some group the exchange wants to recognize.

8 Confirmation is made when the floor broker sends the successful trade details back to the branch office where the order originated. About 20% of all NYSE trades are completed on the floor.

7 After every deal, a reporter uses a digital scanning device to record the stock symbol, the price, and the initiating broker. The scanner transmits the information within seconds to the Exchange's electronic tape. It also begins an **audit trail** in the event that something about the trade is suspicious.

A MATTER OF DEBATE
Advocates of the specialist system insist that face-to-face trading ensures the best prices for buyers and sellers. Critics point out abuses of the system, such as specialist **forerunning**, or trading ahead of orders for their own benefit, as one reason that electronic systems are superior.

6 Post display units show the day's activity at the post. They report the stocks traded, the last sale price, and order size.

AMERICAN DEPOSITARY RECEIPTS

The NYSE lists stocks of domestic companies, companies headquartered in other countries, and a special category of stocks known as American depositary receipts (ADRs). They're certificates representing shares of a non-US company that are held in trust for investors by a US bank. You buy and sell an ADR exactly as you do domestic shares, and the trustee handles dividend payment, tax withholding, and all other paperwork.

2 The Exchange rents **booths** to brokerage firms. Each booth is home base for a firm's floor brokers. When an order is received from one of its brokerage offices, a floor broker takes the order to the appropriate **specialist** post to carry out the transaction.

3 The Exchange rents space to **specialist** firms—the brokers to the brokers. A specialist keeps a list of unfilled orders. As buy and sell orders move in response to price changes, the specialist processes the transactions.

The specialists' other job is to maintain an orderly market in a stock. If the **spread** between the **bid** and **asked**—the gap between the highest price offered by a buyer and the lowest price asked by a seller—becomes too wide, specialists buy and sell stock. This narrows the spread and stimulates trading—a good thing for the vitality of the Exchange and for the specialists as well, since the more they trade, the more they have the potential to earn.

4 Various stocks or groups of stocks are traded at **trading posts** near the specialists' positions. Each company's stock trades at only one post on the floor of the Exchange so the trading can be tracked accurately. However, the stock of several different companies may be traded at the same post. The number of companies assigned depends on the combined volume of business they generate.

5 Floor brokers can use a specialist if they choose. But many trades actually occur among floor brokers who show up at the post at the same time.

On a typical day a floor broker walks—or runs— an average of

12 MILES

in crisscrossing the floor.

Trading on an Electronic Market

Thousands of stocks are traded electronically—using computers and telephones—on the Nasdaq Stock Market.

The most obvious difference between a traditional and an electronic market is where transactions take place. A traditional exchange has a trading floor where everything happens, and an electronic market does not. Instead, trades occur on a complex, sophisticated telecommunications network of phones and computers.

An equally important but less visible difference is the difference between an auction market and a dealer's market. Trading on the Nasdaq Stock Market is through an open market, multiple dealer system, with many market makers competing to handle transactions in each individual stock. That's a contrast to the auction system, where floor brokers who are representatives for buyers and sellers interact directly and transactions in each stock are handled by a single specialist. Since there are a number of market makers at the Nasdaq, more transactions can take place at the same time.

A market maker posts buy and sell prices for a guaranteed number of shares—usually one round lot, or 100 shares. When an order arrives, the market maker fills it at the posted price or finds a buyer or seller to complete the trade. If there's not an instantaneous match, the market maker becomes the buyer for the seller and the seller to the buyer.

MAKING MARKETS

A market maker, in fact, is a firm rather than a person. What's distinctive about this trading system is that the firm commits itself to trade a particular stock by quoting a specific price for 100 shares and is ready to execute an order at that price or better. In fact, when a transaction occurs, the market maker actually owns the stock for the period between the sale and the purchase—a period that may be as brief as a few seconds or as long as overnight, depending on when the purchase is made.

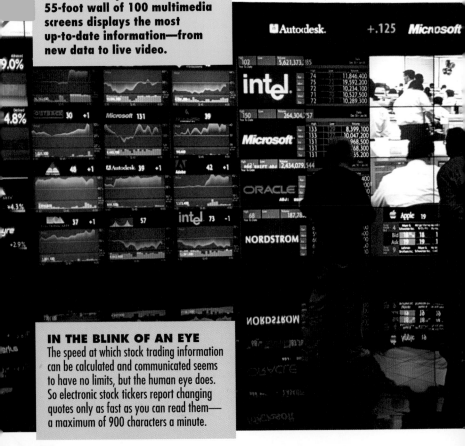

At the Nasdaq MarketSite, a 55-foot wall of 100 multimedia screens displays the most up-to-date information—from new data to live video.

IN THE BLINK OF AN EYE
The speed at which stock trading information can be calculated and communicated seems to have no limits, but the human eye does. So electronic stock tickers report changing quotes only as fast as you can read them— a maximum of 900 characters a minute.

There are typically a number of market makers in the same stock—10 is average, and some stocks have more than 50. So the price competition can be quite intense. In contrast, there may be less competitive bidding in unlisted stocks that are traded over-the-counter (OTC) rather than on the Nasdaq or one of the exchanges. Fewer firms make a market in these stocks, demand is often more erratic, and trading may be thin, or infrequent.

A RANGE OF PRICES

If your order is for 200, 300, or 1,000 shares rather than 100, you may actually pay different prices for every 100 shares if your order goes through a market maker—though your confirmation will give the average price per share. That's because each quotation typically governs 100 shares, and larger orders may be filled with a series of transactions.

Large orders from institutional investors may be quoted and filled in larger lots. For example, an order for 20,000 shares may be filled in 1,000 or 5,000 share lots.

DUAL LISTING

The Nasdaq Stock Market offers US stocks the possibility of dual listing on national markets, similar to dual listing of international companies on a market in their

GETTING CONFIRMATION
Whether your trade is executed on a traditional or electronic market, your broker sends you a written confirmation describing the number of shares you bought or sold, the name of the security, the price you paid or received, fees and commissions, the date the order was executed, and the settlement date. It's important to keep this slip with your investment records, as you'll need it to calculate potential capital gains and losses.

home country and also on a US market. Before this innovation was introduced in 2004—with six stocks—the only dual stock listings occurred when stocks were listed both on the NYSE or the AMEX and a regional exchange.

The primary reason to dual list, according to Nasdaq, is increased liquidity. Because more people are making a market in the stock, active buying and selling increases. However, stocks don't have to be dual listed to trade on multiple markets. Brokers send trades for execution to the market where they get the best price in the fastest time, independent of where the stock is listed.

Companies that list on both the NYSE and the Nasdaq use the same stock symbols on both markets—a one-to-three letter designation characteristic of NYSE-listed companies rather than the four or five letters associated with Nasdaq-listed companies.

INTRODUCING ECNs
Electronic communications networks (ECNs) are alternative securities trading systems that collect, display, and execute orders electronically without a middleman, such as a specialist or market maker. Trading on an ECN allows institutional and individual investors to buy and sell anonymously. That may help reduce the volatility that can be triggered by a bellwether investor making a major trade.

ECN trade execution can be faster and less expensive than trades handled through screen-based or traditional markets, and ECNs facilitate extended, or after-hours, trading. In the early years of ECNs, one limitation was that the trading volume was sometimes thin, which can translate into higher prices. However, as ECNs have consolidated and been acquired by the major stock markets—Archipelago by the NYSE and Instinet by the Nasdaq—to increase their electronic trading capability, the number of stocks traded on these systems has surged.

The Value of Stock

A stock's value can change at any moment, depending on market conditions, investor perceptions, or a host of other issues.

A stock doesn't have a fixed price but changes in response to supply and demand. When investors are buying the stock enthusiastically because they believe it is a good investment, the stock price typically increases. But if they think the company's outlook is poor, and either don't invest or sell shares they already own, the stock price will fall. But price is only one measure of a stock's value.

Return on investment—the amount you earn on the stock—is another. To assess the possibility, though not the guarantee, of a strong future return, you can look for a history of strong performance and steady growth.

THE UPS AND DOWNS AT BIGCO.

The peaks and valleys in the price of a stock dramatically illustrate how value changes.

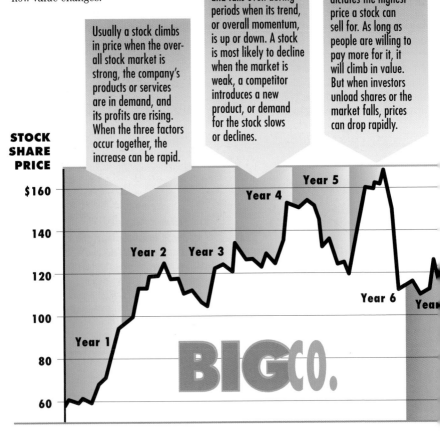

Usually a stock climbs in price when the overall stock market is strong, the company's products or services are in demand, and its profits are rising. When the three factors occur together, the increase can be rapid.

A stock's price rises and falls even during periods when its trend, or overall momentum, is up or down. A stock is most likely to decline when the market is weak, a competitor introduces a new product, or demand for the stock slows or declines.

Nothing ultimately dictates the highest price a stock can sell for. As long as people are willing to pay more for it, it will climb in value. But when investors unload shares or the market falls, prices can drop rapidly.

STOCK SHARE PRICE

$160 — 140 — 120 — 100 — 80 — 60

Year 1 · Year 2 · Year 3 · Year 4 · Year 5 · Year 6 · Year

THE MOVING AVERAGE

A moving average charts a stock or other security's changing price over a specific period. Every time it's modified—hourly, daily, or weekly, for example—the most current price is added and the oldest one is dropped. If the figure for the week beginning July 1 is the most recent entry in a 52-week moving average, for example, the figure for the week beginning July 8 of the previous year would be the oldest entry. The following week, the newest entry would be for the week of July 8, and the oldest for the previous July 15.

The moving average can provide a visual representation of the way the price is trending. The longer the interval—a weekly update rather than an hourly one—the smoother the curve and the stronger the indicator of market sentiment.

BETTING WITH THE ODDS

Investing involves taking some risks with your money, but it's not like betting on horses. A long shot can always win the race even if everyone puts money on the favorite. In the stock market, where the money goes influences the outcome. If lots of investors buy Atlas stock, Atlas's price will go up. The stock becomes more valuable because investors want it. The reverse is also true: If investors sell Zenon stock, it will fall in value. The more it falls, the more investors will sell.

MAKING MONEY WITH STOCKS

You can make money with stocks by selling your shares for more than you paid for them or by collecting dividends—or both.

The profit you make on the sale of stock is known as a **capital gain**. Of course, it doesn't all go into your pocket. You owe taxes on the gain as well as a commission on the sale, but if you've owned the stock for more than a year, it's a long-term gain. That means you pay the tax at a lower rate than you pay on your earned income.

Dividends are the portion of the company's profit paid out to its shareholders. A company's board of directors decides how large a dividend the company will pay, or whether it will pay one at all. Qualifying stock dividends are also taxed at your long-term capital gains rate.

If you're buying stocks for the quarterly income, you can figure out the **dividend yield**—the percentage of purchase price you get back through dividends each year. For example, if you buy stock for $100 a share and receive $2 per share, the stock has a dividend yield of 2%. But if you get $2 per share on stock you buy for $50 a share, your yield would be 4% ($2 is 4% of $50).

Purchase Price	Annual Dividend	Yield
$100	$2	2%
$ 50	$2	4%

Following a price collapse, a stock can recoup its value or continue to decline, depending on its internal strength and what the markets are doing. In this example, the price moved up and down for several years at about $100, the level it had reached several years before.

If a company is out of favor with its shareholders, has serious management problems, or is losing ground to competitors, its value can collapse quickly even if the rest of the market is highly valued. That's what happened here.

However, strong companies can cope with dramatic loss of value and can rebound if internal changes and external conditions create the right environment and investors' demand for stock increases.

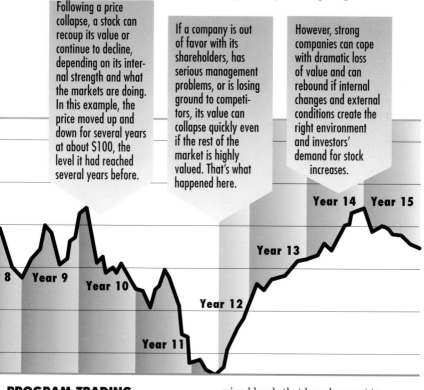

PROGRAM TRADING

Program trading, which means buying or selling either a **basket**, or group, of 15 or more stocks with a combined worth of more than $1 million, or all of the stocks in a particular index, can cause abrupt price changes in a stock or a group of stocks, or even dramatic shifts in an entire market.

Some program trades are triggered electronically when prices hit predetermined levels that have been set to limit losses. And, traders may initiate programmed buys to profit from large spreads they detect between offers to buy and prices asked by sellers.

To control potentially serious consequences, exchanges have instituted restrictions, called **circuit breakers**, to halt trading when markets fall too far too fast.

Market Cycles

Stock market ups and downs can't be predicted accurately—though they often can be explained in hindsight.

The market goes up when investors put their money into stocks, and it falls when they take money out. A number of factors influence whether people buy or sell stocks—as well as when and why they make decisions.

But most of the time the strength or weakness of the stock market as a whole is directly related to economic and political forces. For example, when earnings are strong and unemployment low, indexes tracking stock prices tend to rise. But when corporate earnings fail to meet expectations or investor confidence is shaken, stock prices drop, or the market is flat, or stagnant.

WHEN PEOPLE INVEST

Economic, social, and political factors affect investment. Some factors encourage it and others make investors unwilling to take additional risk.

Positive factors	Negative factors
Ample money supply	Tight money supply
Tax cuts	Tax increases
Low interest rates	High interest rates offering better return in less risky investments
High employment rate	High unemployment rate
Political stability or expectation of stability	International conflicts
	Pending elections

MOVING WITH THE CYCLES

Pinpointing the bottom of a slow market or the top of a hot one is almost impossible—until after it has happened. But investors who buy stocks in companies that do well in growing economies—and buy them at the right time—can profit from their smart decisions—or their good luck.

The S&P 500 1980–2004

Gold tops $850 a troy ounce

Biggest one-day stock market decline

Berlin wall comes down

Oil tops $40 a barrel

1980   1985

One characteristic of expanding companies is their ability to raise prices as the demand for their products and services grows. Increased income means more profit for the company and may also mean larger dividends and higher stock prices for the investor.

It's generally difficult to predict which companies will falter during a downturn and which ones will survive and prosper. No economic cycle repeats earlier ones exactly. So the pressures that companies face in one recession aren't the same ones they face in another. In most cases, though, long-term financial success depends more on the internal strength of the company and the goods or services it provides than on the state of the economy.

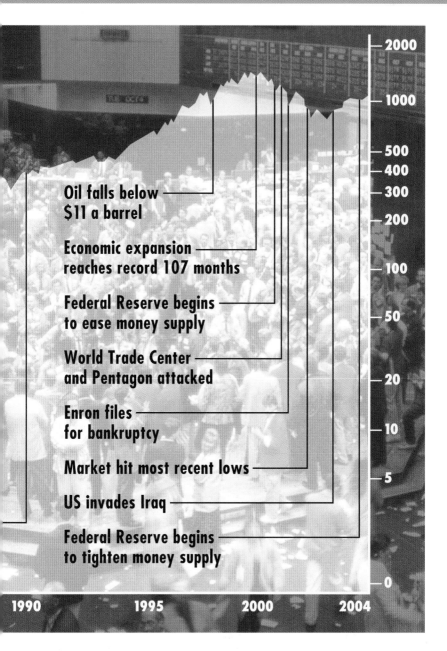

Oil falls below
$11 a barrel

Economic expansion
reaches record 107 months

Federal Reserve begins
to ease money supply

World Trade Center
and Pentagon attacked

Enron files
for bankruptcy

Market hit most recent lows

US invades Iraq

Federal Reserve begins
to tighten money supply

1990　1995　2000　2004

2000
1000
500
400
300
200
100
50
20
10
5
0

BULL AND BEAR MARKETS

The stock market moves up and down in recurring cycles, gaining ground for a period popularly known as a **bull market**. Then it reverses and falls for a time before heading up again. Generally, a falling market has to drop 20% before it's considered a **bear market**. Sometimes market trends last months, even years. Overall, bull markets have tended to last longer than bear markets.

But drops in the market tend to happen quickly, while gains take more time. It's much like the law of gravity: It takes a lot longer to climb 1,000 feet than to fall that distance. Markets also experience **corrections**, or across-the-board losses, that aren't as severe or sustained as a real bear.

UP

The bear market of the early 1970s hit bottom in 1974, with the DJIA at 570. Since its peak in January 2000, it has been as low as 7,286 in October 2002.

INVESTMENT ACTIVITY

When the DJIA closed above 1000 in 1972, it broke what had been considered a nearly absolute ceiling. In January 2000, it reached 11,722.

DOWN

Fundamental and Technical Analysis

There's more than one way to evaluate a stock.

Following the old adage, "Buy low, sell high," isn't as simple as it sounds. After all, the price of a stock selling at $50 per share could be either high or low, depending on whether that price is about to move up to $100 or spiral down to $20. But you can't know for sure until it happens.

While no investor can predict the future with absolute certainty, careful analysis of present conditions may provide an indication of how individual stocks are likely to behave, at least in the near term. To assess those conditions, investors rely on two types of analysis: **fundamental** and **technical**.

Fundamental analysts evaluate a company's financial strength and potential for increasing profits, while technical analysts anticipate investor demand for the stock by looking for patterns in price movement and trading volume. In practice, investors may use both types of analysis: fundamental to find companies worth buying (or selling) and technical to pinpoint the right time to make investment decisions.

IN GOOD COMPANY

Most investors begin with fundamental analysis, since long-term changes in a company's value derive ultimately from its business success. That success relies on a complex interplay of factors, internal and external. Internal factors include the quality of a company's management, business strategies, and operating efficiency, while external factors include the trends or events affecting the entire industry—including the company's competitors—and the economy in general.

As a starting point, fundamental analysts use information in a company's financial **balance sheet** and **income statement**, which are filed annually in Form 10-K with the SEC and updated quarterly.

WHO'S COUNTING THE EARNINGS?

Among the numbers that fundamental analysts focus on are **revenue**, or income, and **earnings**, or profits after expenses are paid. A pattern of steady increases in revenue and earnings often leads to a positive assessment.

There are many ways to measure a company's earnings, however, so it can be hard to draw meaningful conclusions from reported numbers. That's partly because the standards known as **GAAP**—for **generally accepted accounting principles**—give companies some leeway in how they report their earnings.

Pro forma earnings, for example, indicate what a company's results would have been if certain events had occurred earlier or hadn't occurred at all.

Another common measure, **earnings before interest, taxes, depreciation, and amortization (EBITDA)**, was designed to discount certain accounting items to give a clearer picture of the earnings of companies with expensive assets to write down over time.

With **free cash flow**, all cash expenses are subtracted from revenue, investments, and other sources of income to determine how much, if anything, is left over. Many analysts see free cash flow as a better measure of a company's health and future worth than EBITDA since it identifies money that can be used to pay dividends or can be reinvested. Some analysts also prefer free cash flow because it identifies the risk that may result from debt.

TECHNICAL

SPEED BUMPS

Technical analysts also focus on a stock's **volatility**, sometimes expressed as its **beta**.

Beta compares a stock's volatility to the stock market as a whole, which is set at 1. If the stock's price moves more dramatically than the market—typically gaining more on a percentage basis when the market is going up and losing more when the market is going down, that stock has a beta higher than 1, and is considered more volatile. In contrast, if a stock's price typically fluctuates less than the market, its beta is lower than one, and it's less volatile.

Volatility risk may play a large part in investment decisions. For example, you may have reasons to avoid a highly volatile stock even if a fundamental analyst gives it a strong buy recommendation. Conversely, you may have reasons to seek out highly volatile stocks in a rising market.

In an effort to increase transparency and consistency of corporate earnings reports, Standard & Poor's uses **core earnings**. This measure isolates the performance of the company's core operations, including the expenses of granting stock options, restructuring charges for ongoing operations, and pension obligations, while excluding the value of pension account gains, goodwill, and certain one-time sources of income, such as the sale of an asset.

IT'S ALL IN THE CHARTS

If you've ever looked at a chart showing the movement of a stock's price over a period of time, you might have wondered how anyone could make sense of its complex patterns. But to a practiced technical analyst, the patterns can provide vital clues of what's likely to happen to a stock's price based on supply and demand.

Technical analysts look for meaningful patterns or trends that have heralded price increases or declines in the past and that may signal price movements to come. For example, an upsurge in volume may mean that big institutional investors are starting to trade in a particular stock. Or a particular shape in the pattern of price movements may signal classic market behavior, such as a downward correction before a rise.

TOOLS OF THE TRADE

Point and figure charts, bar charts, and candlestick charts are some of the tools technical analysts use. Bar charts reveal trading volume. Point and figure charts establish price trends. Candlestick charts track high, low, and closing prices.

For example, analysts who use point and figure charts watch price patterns for signals of growing demand for a specific security. They recommend buying a stock when one of the signals they have identified as reliable indicates a strong probability, based on historical patterns, that the security's price will continue to go up. And they make sell decisions in a similar way.

Evaluating Companies

How can you tell if a company has the potential to be a good investment?

Evaluating a company means taking a close look at what that company makes or sells, how the company is managed, what it earns, the amount it owes, and how it performed during the ups and downs of the last full economic cycle. That information lets you evaluate its profitability, its growth potential, and its valuation.

✓ **Products**
✓ **Earnings**
✓ **Debt**
✓ **Performance**

PROFITS MATTER

Net earnings, or profits, are what a business has left after it pays operating expenses, taxes, and other bills. A profitable company can expand its business without increasing its debt or reducing the value of existing shares by issuing additional shares.

A profitable company may use a portion of its profits to make acquisitions or to buy back shares of its stock in the marketplace. Reducing the **float**, or number of shares available for purchase, can increase demand, and therefore the stock's price. If it chooses, the company can use a portion of those earnings to pay dividends.

DIVIDEND INVESTING

Dividends aren't only a source of current income, but can make a significant contribution to total return—adding more than 41% of the total return of the S&P 500 index from January 1926 through May 2005. In times of market weakness, stocks that pay dividends tend to outperform those that don't. And a long history of annual dividend increases sends a message that the company is prospering, which may stimulate demand for the stock.

IT'S ALL IN THE NUMBERS

One revealing statistic about any company is **earnings per share (EPS)**, computed by dividing the company's earnings by the number of outstanding shares. Since each share represents a slice of ownership in the company, EPS reports profitability of each slice during a specific period, making it easier to compare the results of companies of different sizes. But, remember that acceptable profit margins vary widely by industry and sector.

Other important measures of profitability are **return on assets (ROA), return on equity (ROE)**, and **return on invested capital (ROIC)**. The three also measure the efficiency with which capital is used. If a company's ROE is higher than its ROA, it may be a sign that it's using leverage to increase profits and profit margins.

$$\frac{\text{Earnings}}{\text{Outstanding shares}} = \text{Earnings per share (EPS)}$$

BigCo
MedCo
SmCo

WHAT'S THE POTENTIAL?

A pattern of annual percentage increases in sales and earnings is a key indicator of a company's potential success. Regular growth, especially when it's the result of new products or marketing strategies, is generally a better signal than a one-time spike resulting from price increases or other market conditions without an accompanying growth in sales.

Remember, though, that growth potential varies for different sized companies. Smaller, newer companies in an expanding industry may grow at a faster rate than larger companies in established industries.

LOOKING FOR THE LEADERS

Investors look for companies that are leaders in industries with promising futures. In those industries, the companies leading the pack often show distinct, sustainable advantages over their competitors, such as superior products or services, an effective marketing strategy, sound management, and operating efficiency. It's important to look for weak spots, though, especially if there are up-and-coming competitors.

No company evaluation would be complete without a thorough assessment of the risks it faces. That means asking what needs to happen for a company's business strategy to succeed, and what could throw that strategy off course. In making this assessment, analysts imagine a variety of scenarios, and then decide which are the most likely. The stock market bubble of the 1990s illustrates the dangers of ignoring warning signs.

WHAT'S ITS VALUE?

You can use various ratios, also called **multiples**, to measure a company's valuation, or its stock price in relation to the company's finances. One of the most widely cited multiples is the **price-to-earnings ratio (P/E)**, which is computed by dividing the stock's current price by EPS, telling you how much investors are currently willing to pay for each dollar of a company's earnings.

For example, a company with a P/E of 30 has a significantly higher multiple

currently willing to pay for it. But it could also mean that the company has serious problems that investors believe may limit its future success.

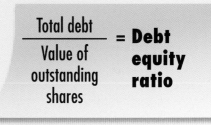

$$\frac{\text{Total debt}}{\text{Value of outstanding shares}} = \textbf{Debt equity ratio}$$

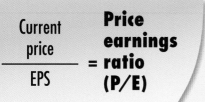

$$\frac{\text{Current price}}{\text{EPS}} = \textbf{Price earnings ratio (P/E)}$$

than a company with a P/E of 10. This may mean that investors believe that the company with the higher P/E is a promising investment whose price will continue to climb. But it may also mean that the stock is **overvalued**, or priced higher than future earnings may justify.

Similarly, it's possible that the company with the lower P/E is **undervalued**, and actually worth more than investors are

SAY AHHH!

A company's financial health is affected by how much debt it carries. A company that's taken on substantial debt and is not managing it well may find that its earnings potential is limited by its liabilities. In severe cases, heavy debt may even indicate that the company is veering toward insolvency.

One ratio commonly used to gauge financial strength is the **debt-to-equity** ratio, which divides total debt by the value of outstanding shares. The higher the resulting percentage, the greater the company's debt level. For companies in financial difficulty, another key measure is **current ratio**, which compares liquid assets—cash on hand or assets easily converted to cash—to the liabilities due within the year.

How much debt is too much? The answer varies, depending on the type of business, the company's ability to pay it back, how the debt is being used—to pay off other debts or to invest in new products or acquisitions—and the perspectives of the analysts who study the company.

When ROE is higher than ROA, it may indicate the use of leverage to boost profits.

Return on assets · ROA

Return on equity · ROE

Earnings

Choosing Stocks

You'll want to consider a stock on its own merits and how it fits into your portfolio.

When you invest in stocks, you can select among publicly traded US companies listed on the major stock markets plus public companies whose stocks are unlisted. You may also buy stocks issued by companies based in other countries, especially those listed directly on US markets or sold as American depositary shares (ADSs).

Given this variety, you need a strategy for choosing among them—or perhaps a number of strategies geared to specific market conditions. For example, you may take a different approach to selecting investments in bear markets than you do in bull markets, or in periods of higher as opposed to lower interest rates.

Whatever your approach, selecting appropriate stocks is usually a two-step process: first, finding stocks that are strong contenders on their own merits, and second, identifying those that will fit well into your investment portfolio.

TAKE YOUR PICK

Some stock-selection methods are simple, such as the value-oriented **dogs of the Dow** strategy. It advocates buying the ten companies in the Dow Jones Industrial Average with the highest yields at the beginning of each year, selling those that are no longer on the list 12 months later, and buying those that have been added.

Other systems can be more complex. Value Line, Inc., for example, ranks stocks for timeliness, safety, and technical indicators, and recommends buying, selling, or holding based on where stocks stand in those rankings. *Investor's Business Daily* measures **relative strength**, or momentum of the stock's price and the issuing company's earnings in relation to each other. Momentum means a trend—a steadily increasing price, for example—that is expected to continue at least in the short term.

Standard & Poor's **quality rankings** measure the historical performance of stock earnings and dividends in terms of stability and growth, though they aren't intended to predict future prices. Rankings are based on a computerized scoring system that covers a ten-year period for each company. There are seven grades from A+ to C, with B+ the average grade. D indicates a company in reorganization and NR means not ranked.

INTEREST RATES

PRIMARY BUSINESS
MARKET SHARE
GROWTH POTENTIAL
MARKET CONDITIONS

STANDARD &POOR'S

Recommendation: **STRONG BUY** ★ ★ ★ ★ ★

Sector: Energy
Sub-Industry: Integrated Oil & Gas
Peer Group: Supermajor Integrated Oil & Gas

Quantitative Evaluations

S&P Earnings & Dividend Rank: **A-**

D	C	B-	B	B+	A-	A	A+

S&P Fair Value Rank: **3+**

1	2	3	4	5
Lowest				Highest

Fair Value Calc.: **$59.00** (Fairly Valued)

S&P Investability Quotient Percentile

100%

XOM scored higher than 100% of all companies for which an S&P Report is available.

Volatility: **Average**

Low	Average	High

Technical Evaluation: **Bullish**
Since 8/05, the technical indicators for XOM have been Bullish.

Relative Strength Rank: **Moderate**

48

1 Lowest

THE STARS SYSTEM

The final step in STARS: The S&P Stock Appreciation Ranking System is determining a ranking to convey the equity analyst's forecast for the stock's price. The ranking is based on fundamental analysis, which takes into account the company's earning power and potential, as well as intangible elements such as its corporate governance and the regulatory environment. The highest rating is 5 STARS and the lowest is 1 STARS. For more information, visit www.standardandpoors.com.

At times when **domestic stocks** may falter in a general downturn in the US economy, **international stocks** may be enjoying booms elsewhere in the world.

Cyclical stocks from economy-sensitive industries, such as automobiles and travel, tend to lose ground when the economy is weak and gain when it's strong. In contrast, the performance of **defensive stocks** issued by companies supplying staples, such as food and medicines, is typically independent of turns in the general economy.

BUILDING A PORTFOLIO

If you buy stocks solely on the basis of their individual merits, rather than as part of a broader portfolio strategy, you risk committing too much of your principal to stocks that tend to behave the same way.

For example, if your entire portfolio is made up of blue chip stocks, cyclical stocks, or value stocks, you'll probably benefit in the years when that category is providing strong returns. But you may suffer through the years of weak or negative returns, which all types of investments, including those with strong fundamentals, provide from time to time.

One of the keys to maintaining a balanced portfolio is **diversification**. You diversify by investing in a variety of stocks that react differently to changing market conditions. That way, you can benefit from those that are flourishing at any point in the economic cycle and ride out the disappointing returns of those that are foundering.

One way to begin diversifying your portfolio is to recognize the different ways that stocks can be grouped.

Market capitalization, often shortened to market cap, is a measure of a company's size. The performance of **small-, mid-,** and **large-cap** stocks varies in a recurrent but unpredictable pattern, with each type providing better returns at some times and weaker returns in others.

DO YOU PAY FULL PRICE?

Another distinction is the difference between stocks identified as **growth** stocks and those identified as **value** stocks. You may look for growth in young companies in burgeoning industries poised to increase their earnings at a faster than average rate. However, established firms can also provide substantial if sometimes slower growth.

The general assumption about growth companies is that their future earnings will be significantly higher than they are now. As a result these stocks often trade at P/E values higher than the market average. In contrast, value stocks may be worth more than investors are currently willing to pay for them. Since these stocks often have P/Es lower than the norm, you might liken value investing to bargain shopping.

The classic value stock has been issued by a reputable company with quality assets, operating in an established industry, in which investor interest has lagged—sometimes deservedly so. Your expectation in buying a value stock is that the market will sooner or later realize the company's strengths and demand for the stock will increase again, pushing the stock price higher.

SWIMMING UPSTREAM

A **contrarian** goes against the flow—buying what other investors are selling and selling what other investors are buying. If others are unloading technology stocks, contrarians look for tech stocks to buy. If large-cap stocks are in demand, contrarians sell them. Bucking the trend has been a successful strategy for some investors, but it does have risks.

Finding Research

Where'd you get that research and what are you going to do with it?

Analysis comes in two basic varieties: buy-side and sell-side. As an individual investor, you never see buy-side analysis, which is created by and for institutional investors. But you may benefit if your mutual fund managers, pension fund managers, and similar professionals make profitable decisions based on this information.

Sell-side analysis—the kind you do see—is designed for individuals. It comes in two varieties: in-house and independent. In-house research is provided by brokerage firm analysts as a service to the firm's clients and as a way to stimulate activity. Independent analysis comes from companies devoted entirely to creating, collating, and selling research, including Standard & Poor's, Thomson Financial, Value Line, Lipper, Morningstar, and other firms.

THE GLOBAL SETTLEMENT

In the aftermath of the stock market bubble, regulators investigated research analysts at major firms with investment banking arms. The resolution was a $875 million global settlement that requires the firms to provide independent as well as in-house research through 2009. The firms must also ensure that their analysts and bankers operate totally independently, so an analyst's recommendation to buy will not be tainted by the banker's desire to secure the issuing company's business.

BUY, SELL, OR HOLD

The bottom line in an analyst's report, either literally or figuratively, is whether you should buy the stock if you don't own it—or buy more shares if you do—sell it, or just wait and see. When that recommendation is stated in the clearest possible terms, you're advised to buy, sell, or hold. If the analyst is really enthusiastic, there may be an additional option—strong buy. There may also be strong sell at the other end of the spectrum.

One of the complicating factors is that not all research reports use the same language for the actions they recommend. It's easy enough to see how *accumulate* means buy, but does *underweight* mean hold or does it mean sell? Research firms that provide **consensus information**, or a synthesis of what sell-side analysts are saying, attempt to handle these differences by grouping all the ways to say buy or sell under one term. But even then, a recommendation of buy/hold can leave you uncertain about what analysts think.

Another issue is that buy recommendations consistently outnumber sell recommendations, even in periods of market weakness. That's something to bear in mind as you evaluate the supporting details of an analyst's report in relation to its conclusion.

GOING TO THE WELL

PROS: The press can offer in-depth, accessible third-party coverage of industries and companies. Plus, many news websites offer customized email alerts for breaking news.

CONS: The press tends to be drawn to headline-ready subjects, rather than unexciting but potentially profitable industries. And by the time a company is profiled in a magazine, the best moment to buy may be past.

INDEPENDENT

ANALYSIS

BUYING WHAT YOU KNOW

Not all investors hunt long and hard to find good companies. Some prefer to buy stocks of companies they know—whose products they use, or whose offices are down the street. You may do pretty well investing in what you know. Or, you may miss some more lucrative opportunities.

One of the most perplexing decisions you may face is whether to buy stock in the company you work for—or hold onto stock you're granted by the firm or have the opportunity to buy at a favorable price.

Arguments in favor emphasize that you know a great deal about the company, both its strengths and weaknesses. And recognizing that your hard work will put you in a position to share in the company's successes may make going to the office early or staying late easier. Further, if you work for a strong company, whose shares split and whose prices rises over time, holding shares may be extremely profitable.

On the other hand, concentrating your portfolio in any one company makes you more vulnerable to losses than if you diversified across market capitalization, sector, and style. When that company is the one providing your paycheck, that risk is magnified. One solution may be to own some stock, but to pay careful attention to how much.

There's a wealth of sources for investor information in addition to what your brokerage firm provides. None of it is perfect, but if you're discriminating, much of it is very useful. Here's a snapshot of some of these sources:

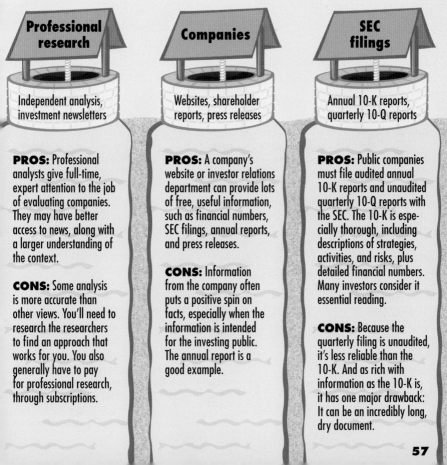

Professional research
Independent analysis, investment newsletters

PROS: Professional analysts give full-time, expert attention to the job of evaluating companies. They may have better access to news, along with a larger understanding of the context.

CONS: Some analysis is more accurate than other views. You'll need to research the researchers to find an approach that works for you. You also generally have to pay for professional research, through subscriptions.

Companies
Websites, shareholder reports, press releases

PROS: A company's website or investor relations department can provide lots of free, useful information, such as financial numbers, SEC filings, annual reports, and press releases.

CONS: Information from the company often puts a positive spin on facts, especially when the information is intended for the investing public. The annual report is a good example.

SEC filings
Annual 10-K reports, quarterly 10-Q reports

PROS: Public companies must file audited annual 10-K reports and unaudited quarterly 10-Q reports with the SEC. The 10-K is especially thorough, including descriptions of strategies, activities, and risks, plus detailed financial numbers. Many investors consider it essential reading.

CONS: Because the quarterly filing is unaudited, it's less reliable than the 10-K. And as rich with information as the 10-K is, it has one major drawback: It can be an incredibly long, dry document.

Stock Tables and Tickers

Stock tables and tickers keep investors up to date on what's happening in the market.

If you want current price and performance information about stocks in general or one stock in particular, you can find it daily in the financial press and updated regularly online at business, news, and research company websites.

Stock prices are quoted in dollars and cents. Decimal pricing has narrowed the **spread**, or gap, between the highest price bid by a buyer and the lowest price asked by a seller from 6.25 cents to 1 cent.

Percent yield tells you the amount of the dividend as a percentage of the current price. For example, the yield here is 1.8%. Percent yield also lets you compare your earnings on a stock with earnings on other investments. But it doesn't tell you your total return, which is the sum of your dividends plus increases or decreases in stock price. When there's no dividend, yield can't be calculated, so the column is left blank.

NEW YORK STOCK EXCHANGE

CLOSE	NET CHG	YTD % CHG	52-WEEK HI	52-WEEK LO	STOCK (SYM)	DIV	YLD %	PE	VOL 100s	CLOSE	N CH
13.38	0.52	11.8	31.94	10.77	PtrlBras ADS A **PBRA**	1.56e	5.2	...	6291	29.80	1.
37.58	0.28	16.8	43.50	18.75	PfeiffrVac **PV**	.60e	1.5	...	22	40.90	0.
29.38	.31	8.0	38.89	26.95	Pfizer **PFE** x	.68f	1.8	59	153386	38.15	0.
31.37	0.37	-7.6	75.44	31.93	PharmRes **PRX**		...	20	12285	60.18	1.
49.67	1.67	▲ 10.4	80.45	30.11	PhelpDodg **PD**		...	cc	48019	84.04	4.
40.16	0.02	0.2	25.97	25.00	PhilAuthInd **POB**	1.64	6.5	...	186	25.16	0.
17.85	0.63	-2.6	18.60	5.11	PhlpLngDst **PHI**		...	...	547	16.96	-0.
31.75	0.05	▲ 14.5	32.75	13.80	PhlpsEl **PHG**	.39e	1.2	...	15153	33.31	0.
15.89	0.13	2.3	18.31	11.16	PhillipsVanH **PVH**	.15	.8	40	542	18.14	-0.
16.40	...	13.3	14.25	6.03	PhoenixCos **PNX**	.16e	1.2	dd	7283	13.64	-0.
43.38	0.67	11.3	42.50	21.71	PhoenixCos un	1.81	4.3	...	2	42.00	0.
33.05	0.14	18.4	2.49	0.95	PhosphtRes **PLP**		...	dd	669	2.25	0.
33.21				33.22	PidmntNG **PNY**	1.66	4.0	...	813	41.52	0.
14.19						.32	1.41	7.00	10614	23.00	0.
15.50						.06	.3	14	5116	21.15	1.

Standard & Poor's Pocket Guide to Stocks

JPMorgan Chase (JPM)
★★★★

JPMorgan Chase is a leading global financial services firm with assets of $1.1 trillion and operations in more than 50 countries.

Recent Price:	$39.01	EPS:	
52 wk H/L:	$43.84 - $34.62		
P/E:	20.0		As Reported / S&P Core Earnings
Yield:	3.5%	2002	$0.80 / $0.65
5-Yr Annl Tot Ret:	-1.93%	2003	$3.24 / $3.12
Market Cap:	$139.00 Billion	2004 Est.	$3.07 / NA
Fiscal Year Ends: December 31		5-Yr Annl Growth: 2.74%	
		S&P Credit Rating: A+	

Jabil Circuit (JBL)
★★★

JBL manufactures circuit board assemblies for international OEMs in the PC, peripheral, communications and automotive markets.

Recent Price:	$25.58	EPS:	
52 wk H/L:	$32.40 - $19.18		
P/E:	29.1		As Reported / S&P Core Earnings
Yield:	Nil	2003	$0.21 / $0.04
5-Yr Annl Tot Ret:	-6.86%	2004	$0.81 / $0.59
Market Cap:	$5.10 Billion	2005 Est.	$1.22 / NA
Fiscal Year Ends:	August 31	5-Yr Annl Growth: 7.66%	
		S&P Credit Rating: BB+	

Janus Capital Group (JNS)

VOLATILITY
You can form an impression about how volatile a stock's price has been by looking at the range between highest and lowest prices over the past 52 weeks. The greater that difference, on a percentage basis, the more volatile the price. A year-to-date (YTD) percentage change will tell you how much of the change has occurred since January 1.

If you compare the current price to the 52-week highs and lows, you can also determine whether the stock is trading closer to its top or bottom.

Price/earnings ratio (PE) shows the relationship between a stock's price and the company's earnings for the last four quarters. It's figured by dividing the current price per share by the earnings per share—a number the stock table doesn't provide as a separate piece of information. Here, for example, the P/E ratio of 20 means its price is 20 times its annual per share earnings.

Since stock investors are interested in earnings, they use P/E ratios to compare the relative value of different stocks. But the P/E ratio reported in this chart, called a trailing P/E, reports past earnings, not future potential. Two companies with the same P/E may face very different futures: one on its way to posting higher earnings and the other headed for a loss.

Those differences may be revealed in a **forward P/E**, which stock analysts compute by combining earnings reports for the two most recent quarters with the earnings they expect for the next two.

Volume refers to the number of shares traded.

Cash dividends per share is an estimate of the anticipated yearly dividend per share in dollars and cents. The prices of stocks that pay dividends tend to be less volatile than the prices of stocks with no dividends. This dividend is estimated at .48 cents a share. If you owned 100 shares, you'd receive $48 in dividends, probably in quarterly payments of $12.

COMPOSITE TRANSACTIONS

YTD % CHG	52-WEEK HI	52-WEEK LO	STOCK (SYM)	DIV	YLD %	PE	VOL 100s	CLOSE	NET CHG	YTD % CHG	H
0.4	27.45	24.85	Safeco 8.072Corts **KNH**	2.02	7.5	...	3	27.10	...	-17.7	
29.5	6.25	1.16	SafegrdSci **SFE**		...	dd	75380	5.23	-0.77		
-0.5	25.83	16.20	Safeway **SWY**		...	dd	59361	21.79	-0.11		
1.2	21.84	16.20	SagaCom A **SGA**		...	30	245	18.75			
7.2	41.36	26.19	StJoe **JOE**	.48	1.2	31	10567				
22.3	75.60	40.69	StJudeMed **STJ**		...	41					
5.1	30.70	24.32	StMaryLand **SM**	.10							
8.3	43.40	29.00	StPaul **SPC**								
5.9	78.79	57.97	StPaul un								
14.4	17.30	6.66	Saks **SKS**							7.4	29.
-1.9	15.20	8.13								10.4	24.
-11.0	22.97								0.23	63	64
-3.3											

Change reports whether the price of the trade being reported is up (+) or down (−) from the previous price. When the previous trading day's closing price is provided, **net change** reports the difference between that number and the closing price on the previous trading day.

WHAT'S IN A NAME?
Every listed corporation has a symbol of one to five letters that's used to identify it when its trading data are reported. No two symbols are alike. There is a system though: Companies listed on the NYSE or the AMEX have a one, two, or three letter symbol. Those listed on the Nasdaq have four or five letters.

Some symbols are easy to connect to their companies, like GE for General Electric. Sometimes those that are less obvious result when two companies have similar names or when the logical abbreviation has already been used. Other times, the symbols make a comment about the company, like DNA for the biotechnology company Genentech.

Buying and Selling Stock

Buying stock isn't hard, but the process has its own rules, its own language, and a special cast of characters.

The professionals to whom you give buy and sell orders for stocks and other securities have different titles and do different jobs. You may have a personal relationship with your stockbroker—sometimes called a Financial Executive, Financial Adviser, or Account Executive—and depend on the broker's advice in making your investment decisions. But, in most cases, you have little or no connection to others who work in your broker's firm or handle the details of your transactions. But each of them fills a critical role.

The brokerage firm where you have an account is known as a **broker-dealer (BD)**. That means the firm has a license from the Securities and Exchange Commission (SEC) that entitles its employees to buy and sell securities for the firm's clients and for the firm's own accounts.

Brokers handle buy and sell orders placed by individual and institutional clients in return for a commission or an annual asset-based fee. A floor broker handles buy and sell orders on the floor of an exchange.

Dealers buy and sell securities for their own accounts or the firm's account rather than for a client. For example, if you tell your broker to sell shares of a particular stock, a dealer working for the same firm might buy those shares for the firm's account. Dealers make their money on the difference between what they pay to buy a security and the price they get for selling it.

Traders, also called registered or competitive traders, buy and sell securities for their own portfolios. The term traders also describes employees of broker-dealers who handle the firms' securities trading.

A **broker**, originally, was a wine seller who broached—broke open—wine casks. Today's broker has a less liquid but often heady job as a financial agent.

CUSTOMERS
Invest in stocks

As an **individual investor**, you buy and sell securities for your personal portfolios. You can invest through regular taxable accounts, special purpose accounts that are either tax deferred or tax free, or both types. For example, you might have a retirement savings plan at work, an individual retirement account (IRA), a Coverdell education savings account (ESA), a 529 college savings plan—or all four.

Institutional investors are organizations, such as financial services companies, pension funds, and money managers, that invest their own assets or assets they hold for their clients or members. Because they have so much money to invest and are committed to investing those assets, institutional investors trade regularly and in great volume. In fact, to be considered an institutional transaction, a stock trade must be for 10,000 or more shares.

If you invest in an equity **managed account**, an institutional investor—the account's professional money manager—handles the transactions, but you and other individual investors own the stocks in the individual yet similar portfolios the manager runs. This hybrid approach may be appealing if you're seeking investment expertise and yet want to own stock individually rather than through a mutual fund.

WHERE THE COMMISSION GOES

A commission you pay to buy and sell stocks is divided—by prearranged contract—between your broker and the brokerage firm. Commissions and any additional fees are set by the firm, but your broker may be able to give you a break if you trade often and in large volume. Generally, the higher the commission rate the firm usually charges, the more room there is for negotiation.

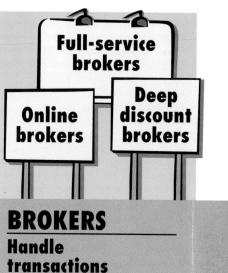

Give brokers orders, or instructions

When you tell your broker to buy or sell a stock at the current price, called the **market price**, you're giving a **market order**. The price you pay or receive depends on how quickly it's handled and how actively traded the stock is.

A **stop order** instructs your broker to trade once the stock hits a specified target price, called the **stop price**. You typically use stop orders to limit potential losses or protect profits by selling when the price seems likely to fall.

When the stock hits the stop price, your order becomes a market order. If the price of the stock changes between the time the stop price is reached and the time your trade is executed—say because of heavy volume—you could sell for much less or pay much more than you intended.

A **limit order**, on the other hand, instructs your broker to buy or sell a stock at a specific price, called the limit price. A limit order doesn't become a market order, so you won't pay more or sell for less than you want. The risk is that if the price changes quickly, your order may not be executed even if the stock reaches the limit price because it can't be done fast enough.

You might also give a **stop-limit order** to buy or sell when the stock hits the stop price but not to pay more or accept less than the limit price. A stop-limit order can protect you against a rapid price increase, but there's still some risk that your order won't be filled.

BROKERS
Handle transactions

Some brokers, usually called **full-service brokers**, provide a range of services beyond executing buy and sell orders for clients, such as researching investments and developing long- and short-term investment goals.

Discount brokers carry out transactions for clients but typically offer more limited services. Their fees, however, are usually lower than full-service brokers'.

The cheapest way to trade securities, however, is usually with an **online brokerage account**. Many established brokerage firms offer substantial discounts to their customers who buy and sell securities online, and some firms exist exclusively online.

Firms in each category come in a range of sizes, from huge national firms sometimes called **wirehouses** to small one- or two-broker firms. The term wirehouse predates the information age, when large firms with private communications systems enjoyed quicker access to market data. The name survives, though the advantage doesn't.

ALL IN THE TIMING

When you give a stop order or a limit order, your broker will ask if you want a **good till canceled (GTC)** or **day order**. A GTC stands until it is either filled, you cancel it, or the firm's time limit expires. A day order is canceled automatically if it isn't filled by the end of the trading day.

Buying on Margin

Buying on margin lets investors borrow some of the money they need to buy stocks.

If you want to increase the potential return on a stock investment, you can **leverage** your purchase by **buying on margin**. That means borrowing up to half of the purchase price from your broker. If you can sell the stock at a higher price than it cost, you can repay the loan, plus interest and commission, and keep the profit. But if the stock drops in value, you still have to repay the loan. And if you must sell the shares for less than you paid, your losses could be larger than if you had owned the stock outright.

MARGIN ACCOUNTS
To buy on margin, you set up a **margin account** with a broker and transfer the required minimum in cash or securities

How It Works

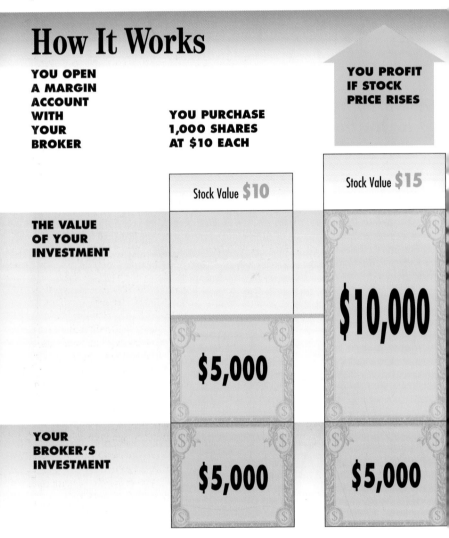

YOU OPEN A MARGIN ACCOUNT WITH YOUR BROKER

YOU PURCHASE 1,000 SHARES AT $10 EACH

YOU PROFIT IF STOCK PRICE RISES

Stock Value **$10**

Stock Value **$15**

THE VALUE OF YOUR INVESTMENT

$10,000

$5,000

YOUR BROKER'S INVESTMENT

$5,000

$5,000

CLOSING THE BARN DOOR
During dramatic drops in the market, investors who are heavily leveraged because they've bought on margin may not be able to meet their margin calls. The result is panic selling to raise cash and further declines in the market. That's one reason the SEC instituted Regulation T, which limits the leveraged portion of any margin purchase to 50%.

LEVERAGING YOUR STOCK INVESTMENT

Leverage means investing with money borrowed at a fixed rate of interest in the hope of earning a greater rate of return. Like the lever, the simple machine for which it is named, leverage lets you use a small amount of cash to exert a lot of financial power.

Companies use leverage—called **trading on equity**—when they issue both stocks and bonds. Their earnings per share may increase because they expand operations with the money raised by bonds. But they must use some of the earnings to repay the interest on the bonds.

to the account. Then you can borrow up to 50% of a stock's price and buy with the combined funds.

In the example shown here, if you buy 1,000 shares at $10 a share, your total cost would be $10,000. But buying on margin, you put up $5,000 and borrow the remain-ing $5,000. If you sell when the stock price rises to $15, you get $15,000. You repay the $5,000 and keep the $10,000 balance (minus interest and commissions). That's almost a 100% profit. Had you paid the full $10,000 with your own money, you would have made a 50% profit, or $5,000.

MARGIN CALLS

Despite its potential rewards, buying on margin can be very risky. For example, the value of the stock you buy could drop so much that you could lose the entire amount you invested and perhaps more.

To protect brokerage firms from losses, the New York Stock Exchange (NYSE) and NASD, formerly the National Association of Securities Dealers, require you to maintain a margin account balance of at least 25% of the purchase price of any stock you buy **long**, which means to hold in your account. Individual firms can require a higher margin level, say 30%, but not a lower one.

If the market value of your investment falls below its required minimum, the firm issues a **margin call**. You must either **meet the call** by adding money to your account to bring it up to the required minimum, or sell the stock, pay back your broker in full, and take the loss.

For example, if shares you bought on margin for $10 a share declined to $7 a share, your equity would be $2,000, or 28.6% of the total value of the shares ($7,000 − $5,000 = $2,000 ÷ $7,000 = 0.286 or 28.6%). If your broker has a 30% margin requirement, you would have to add $100 to bring your margin account up to $2,100 (30% of $7,000).

When the margin call comes, there's still a cushion protecting your broker's share—in this case, $5,000. Because your shares will be sold if you don't meet the call or sell the shares yourself, your money is at risk. In fact, your broker could sell other stock in your margin account to recoup a loss that selling the shares didn't cover.

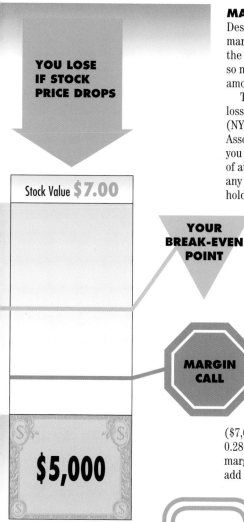

YOU LOSE IF STOCK PRICE DROPS

Stock Value **$7.00**

YOUR BREAK-EVEN POINT

MARGIN CALL

$5,000

$2,000 MINIMUM

MARGIN MINIMUMS

To open a margin account, you must deposit a minimum of $2,000 in cash or securities that your broker could liquidate quickly. All margin trades are conducted through this account, though you can't use the $2,000 as part of your share of the purchase.

Selling Short

Some stock investors take added risks in the hope of greater returns.

Not all stock trades are straightforward buys or sells. There are several strategies you can use to increase your gains, though they also increase your risk of incurring losses. Among these strategies are **selling short** and **buying warrants**. Both are based on a calculated wager that a particular stock will change in value, either dropping quickly in price—for a short sale—or increasing, for a warrant.

How Selling Short Works

While most investors buy stocks they think will increase in value, others invest when they think a stock's price is going to drop, perhaps substantially. What they do is described as **selling short**.

To sell short, you borrow shares you don't own from your broker, order them sold, and pocket the money. Then you wait for the price of the stock to drop. If it does, you buy the shares at the lower price, turn them over to your broker (plus interest and commission), and keep the difference.

For example, you might sell short 100 shares of stock priced at $10 a share. When the price drops, you buy 100 shares at $7.50 a share, return them to your broker, and keep the $2.50-a-share difference—minus commission. Buying the shares back is called **covering the short position**. In this case, because you sold them for more than you paid to replace them, you made a profit. And you didn't have to lay out any money to do it.

YOU BORROW 100 SHARES AT $10 PER SHARE FROM YOUR BROKER	**YOU SELL THE 100 SHARES AT THE $10 PRICE, GETTING $1,000**
	Stock Value **$10**
SHARES YOU OWE YOUR BROKER	**100** Shares
YOUR COST TO PAY BACK THE SHARES	
YOUR PROFIT— OR LOSS	

SHORT INTEREST HIGHLIGHTS

Short interest is trading activity in stocks that have been sold short on the New York Stock Exchange and the American Stock Exchange and not yet repurchased. The volume of short interest gives you a sense of how many investors expect prices to fall and the stocks they expect to be affected.

Selling short often increases when the market is booming. Often, short sellers believe that a **correction**, or drop in market prices, has to come, especially if the overall economy does not seem to be growing as quickly as stock values are rising. But short selling is also considered a bullish sign, or a predictor of increased trading, since short positions have to be covered.

WHO'S THE LENDER?

You might wonder where brokers find the stocks to lend their clients who want to go short. They may tap their firm's inventory of shares, but it is much more likely that they borrow from other investors' margin accounts or from shares held in institutional accounts, such as mutual fund portfolios or pension funds.

There's a certain lack of transparency, in the sense that the actual shareowners may never be aware that their shares have been loaned. On one hand, that's not really a problem because their ownership is not at risk. That's because brokers who act on short-sale orders hold the proceeds from the sales in escrow on behalf of the lender until the shares are returned.

BUYING WARRANTS

Like a short sale, a warrant is a way to wager on the future price of a stock—though a warrant is definitely less risky. Warrants guarantee, for a small fee, the opportunity to buy stock at a fixed price during a specific period of time. Investors buy warrants if they think a stock's price is going up.

For example, you might pay $1 a share for the right to buy DaveCo stock at $10 within five years. If the price goes up to $14 and you **exercise**, or use, your warrant, you save $3 on every share you buy. You can then sell the shares at the higher price to make a profit ($14 − ($10 + $1) = $3), or $300 on 100 shares.

Companies sell warrants if they plan to raise money by issuing new stock or selling shares they hold in reserve. After a warrant is issued, it can be listed in the stock columns and traded like other investments. A **wt** after a stock table entry means the quotation is for a warrant, not the stock itself.

If the price of the stock is below the set price when the warrant expires, the warrant is worthless. But since warrants are fairly cheap and have a relatively long life span, they are traded actively.

YOU PROFIT IF STOCK PRICE DROPS	YOU LOSE IF STOCK PRICE RISES
Stock Value **$7.50**	Stock Value **$12.50**
100 Shares	**100** Shares
$750	**$1,250**
$250 Profit	**$250** Loss

WHAT ARE THE RISKS?

The risks in selling short occur when the price of the stock goes up—not down—or when the drop in price takes a long time. The timing is important because you're paying your broker interest on the stocks you borrowed. The longer the process goes on, the more you pay and the more the interest expense erodes your potential profit.

An increase in the stock's value is an even greater risk. If the price goes up instead of down, you will be forced sooner or later to pay more to cover your short position than you made from selling the stock. In fact, sometimes you can have a major loss.

SQUEEZE PLAY

Sometimes short sellers are caught in a squeeze. That happens when a stock that has been heavily shorted begins to rise. The scramble among short sellers to cover their positions results in heavy buying, which drives the price even higher.

But while the shares are safe, there is a potential downside to being a lender that may take you by surprise. Any dividends paid on your shares during the time they are on loan are taxed at your regular federal tax rate rather than the lower long-term capital gains rate that applies to qualified dividends. You may also be unable to vote on corporate issues with other company shareholders if that vote occurs when your shares are on loan.

These rules have prompted some investors to limit their use of margin accounts if they aren't doing a lot of margin buying or short selling, or to be careful to deposit only nondividend-paying stocks to meet the minimum required for being able to buy through the account.

THE LONG AND THE SHORT

Going long on a stock is the opposite of selling short. But rather than being a strategy to take advantage of what seems to be a sign of weakness, going long is what most investors do. It means buying stock to hold in your portfolio until you're ready to sell, either to realize a profit or to prevent further losses. The same idea is sometimes expressed as being long or as a long position.

In a related use of language, when you buy options on equities or other investment products, you are the long and investors who sell options are the shorts. In options trading, unlike stock trading, the number of longs must equal the number of shorts.

Clearance and Settlement

A lot happens between the time you place an order and the time you own the stock.

Once your broker executes your order to buy or sell a stock, your decision-making is over—but the trade has just begun. The process of completing an order is called **clearance and settlement**. It takes place through a streamlined, electronic system that finalizes the transfer of ownership and payment for more than a billion transactions initiated each trading day. By law, those tasks must be completed in no more than three business days after the trade date.

THE ROLE OF THE MIDDLEMAN

Once upon a time, the end of a day's active trading signaled the beginning of a mass migration of papers. Stock certificates representing thousands of shares were carted from the firms that sold them to firms that bought them, where they were exchanged for the checks that paid for them. But with 1.62 billion shares currently trading daily on the NYSE alone, a physical exchange of securities and checks each evening would prove a filing and accounting nightmare, if it were physically possible at all.

Fortunately, mountains of paper are no longer necessary now that most trades in North America are cleared and settled electronically by an organization known as the **Depository Trust & Clearing Corporation (DTCC)**. One DTCC subsidiary, the **National Securities Clearing Corporation (NSCC)**, is the oldest and largest clearing corporation in operation. Another subsidiary, the **Depository Trust Company (DTC)**, facilitates the trades that NSCC clears. Part of DTC's job is to act as a bank, holding and transferring money and securities for NSCC and for the brokerage and clearing firms involved in the transactions.

Getting Settled

Clearance and settlement is basically a three-step process:

1 **Shares bought must equal shares sold**
Matching shares is the essence of the clearing process. Any discrepancies must be resolved before clearing can be completed.

2 **Money paid must equal money received**
A trade is settled when the account of the firm selling a security is credited with the purchase price paid by the firm buying that security.

3 **Shares and money must move**
Shares must be transferred from sellers to buyers, and money from buyers to sellers.  In practice, these exchanges take place electronically, when accounts and records are updated to show new ownership and new account balances.

THE PAPERLESS CHASE

Certificates are paper documents representing stock ownership. Once ubiquitous, they're slowly vanishing, and many in circulation are not really in circulation at all: They're **immobilized**, or stored, in vaults at DTC. When shares are sold, the transfer is recorded electronically.

More recently issued securities may be **dematerialized**, which means they're never issued in paper form at all. The records are strictly electronic.

Stocks held in **street name** are registered in your brokerage firm's name at DTC, but the firm records you as the **beneficial owner**, or stock-

Netting Down

The clearance and settlement process begins when the details of the transaction are **compared**, or matched, at the point of execution. Each security has a CUSIP number, a unique nine-digit identifier assigned by the Committee on Uniform Securities Identification Procedures, which is used to ensure an accurate match.

The next step is **netting down**, or reducing, the number of transactions that need to be forwarded to NSCC by offsetting each firm's own buy and sell orders.

For example, if at the end of the day a brokerage firm's clients have bought 1,000 shares of a particular company and sold 1,000 shares of the same company, those orders offset each other—they net down. The firm simply needs to shift money and shares among its own clients' accounts.

Of course, there's little chance that buy and sell orders at any firm will match up perfectly, though some clearing and settlement may be handled among affiliated firms. All remaining transactions—on average about 3% of a day's trades—are forwarded to NSCC, which acts as the **counterparty** to both buyer and seller in each transaction.

HOW THE PROCESS WORKS

2 Firms that owe shares have them debited from their DTC accounts and credited to NSCC's DTC account.

1 NSCC nets down trades and issues settlement instructions to firms, either to send shares or money.

4 NSCC then distributes money to the firms that delivered shares.

5 NSCC also distributes shares to the DTC accounts of firms that paid money.

THE FIRMS

3 Firms that owe money have it wired to NSCC's DTC account.

holder, in its own books. Owning in street name makes trading easier, since the firm can transfer shares directly without having to wait for you to sign and deliver paper certificates.

Some companies register ownership of securities you purchase from them using a **direct registration system (DRS)**. This means that the company holds the stock for you and keeps records of your ownership.

WHO'S COUNTING?
More than 5.5 million stock certificates worth more than $20 trillion are immobilized in the DTC vaults. They represent about 83% of the outstanding shares listed on the NYSE and about 72% of those listed on the Nasdaq Stock Market.

PROTECTING YOUR TRADE
How do NSCC and DTC ensure that each firm involved in a transaction can meet its settlement obligations? For example, what would happen if a firm were to go bankrupt sometime between the trade (T) and settlement (T+3) dates?

To address such an event, NSCC requires that member firms deposit securities in a DTC account as **collateral**, which can be liquidated to settle transactions if a firm is unable to meet its obligations. Furthermore, NSCC limits the amount each firm is allowed to owe on unsettled trades. This ensures that DTC always has enough assets on hand to settle the trades that NSCC clears.

Bonds: Financing the Future

Bonds are loans that investors make to corporations and governments. The lenders earn interest, and the borrowers get the cash they need.

A bond is a loan that pays interest over a fixed **term**, or period of time. When the bond **matures** at the end of the term, the **principal**, or investment amount, is repaid to the lender, or owner of the bond.

Typically, the rate at which interest is paid and the amount of each payment is fixed at the time the bond is offered for sale. That's why bonds are also known as **fixed-income securities**. It's also why a bond seems less risky than an investment whose return might change dramatically in the short term.

A bond's interest rate is competitive, which means that the rate it pays is comparable to what other bonds being issued at the same time are paying. It's also related to the cost of borrowing in the economy at large, so when bond rates are lower, for example, mortgage rates also tend to be lower.

TYPES OF BONDS

You can buy bonds issued by US companies, by the US Treasury, by various cities and states, and various federal, state, and local government agencies. Many overseas companies and governments also sell bonds to US investors. When those bonds are sold in dollars rather than the currency of the issuing country, they're sometimes known as **yankee bonds**. There is an advantage for individual investors: You don't have to worry about currency fluctuations in figuring the bond's worth.

ISSUERS PREFER BONDS

When companies need to raise money, they often prefer issuing bonds to issuing stock. New stock tends to **dilute**, or reduce, the value of existing stock. And some privately owned companies prefer to remain private. What's more, companies may raise more money through a bond offering, plus enjoy some tax advantages.

Unlike companies, governments can't issue stock because they have no equity to sell. Bonds are the primary way they raise money to fund capital improvements like roads or airports. Money from bond issues also keeps everyday operations running when other revenues, such as taxes, tolls, and other fees aren't available to cover current costs.

MAKING MONEY WITH BONDS

There are two ways to make money with bonds: income and capital gains. Conservative investors use bonds to provide a steady income. They buy a bond when it's issued and hold it, expecting to receive regular, fixed-interest payments until the bond matures and the principal is paid back. Then, they can invest in a new bond.

THE INDIVIDUAL AS LENDER

INVESTORS WILLING TO LEND MONEY

$

INVESTOR GETS PAR VALUE AT MATURITY

INVESTOR GETS INTEREST PAYMENTS AT SPECIFIC INTERVALS

THE LIFE OF A BOND

The life, or **term**, of any bond is fixed at the time of issue. It can range from **short-term** (usually a year or less), to **intermediate-term** (two to ten years), to **long-term** (more than ten years). Generally speaking, the longer the term, the higher the interest rate that's offered to make up for the additional risk of tying up your money for so long a time. The relationship between the interest rates paid on short-term and long-term bonds is called the **yield curve**.

It's also possible to sell bonds at a profit when interest rates fall. For example, investors may be willing to pay more than the face value of an older bond paying 8% interest if new bonds are paying 5%. An increase in the price of a bond, or **capital appreciation**, may produce more profits than holding bonds to maturity.

More aggressive investors **trade** bonds, or buy and sell as they might with stocks, hoping to sell them at a profit.

But there are risks in bond trading. If interest rates go up, you can lose money if you want to sell an older bond paying a lower rate of interest. That's because potential buyers will typically pay less for the bond than you paid to buy it.

DOES IT FLOAT?

When a company or government wants to raise cash, it tests the waters by **floating a bond**. That is, it offers the public an opportunity to invest for a fixed period of time at a specific rate of interest. If investors think the rate justifies the risk and buy the bond, the issue floats.

Another risk is rising inflation. Since the dollar amount you earn on a bond usually doesn't change, its value can be eroded by inflation. For example, if you have a 30-year bond paying $50 annual interest, the income will buy less at the end of the term than at the beginning.

THE INSTITUTION AS BORROWER

CORPORATE BONDS

Corporations use bonds:
- To raise capital to pay for expansion, modernization
- To cover operating expenses
- To finance corporate takeovers or other changes in management structure

US TREASURY BONDS

The US Treasury floats debt issues:
- To pay for a wide range of government activities
- To pay interest on the national debt

MUNICIPAL BONDS

States, cities, counties, and towns issue bonds:
- To pay for a wide variety of public projects, such as schools, highways, stadiums, bridges
- To supplement their operating budgets

BOND MATURES

ISSUING BONDS

For corporations, issuing a bond is a lot like making an initial public offering. An investment firm helps set the terms and underwrites the sale by buying the bonds from the issuer. In cooperation with other companies, together known as a syndicate, the investment firm then offers the bonds for public sale.

When bonds are issued, they are typically sold at **par**, or face value, usually in units of $1,000. The issuer absorbs whatever sales charges there are. After issue, bonds trade in the **secondary market**, which means they are bought and sold through brokers, similar to the way stocks are. The issuer gets no money from these secondary trades.

US Treasury issues are available directly to investors through a federal program called Treasury Direct or through brokers. Most agency bonds and municipal bonds are sold through brokers, who buy bonds in large denominations ($25,000 or more) and sell pieces of them to individual investors.

The Language of Bonds

A bond is an IOU, a record of the loan and the terms of repayment.

Unlike stockholders, who have **equity**, or part ownership, in a company, bondholders are **creditors**. The bond is an IOU, or a record of the money you lent and the terms on which it will be repaid.

Until 1983, all bondholders received certificates that provided the terms of the loan. Some of these **bearer bonds** had coupons attached to the certificate. When it was time to collect an interest payment, the **bearer**, or investor, detached the coupon and exchanged it for cash. That's why a bond's interest rate is known as its **coupon rate**.

Today most new bonds, known as **book-entry bonds**, are registered electronically, the way stock purchases are, rather than issued in certificate form. But there are still thousands of investors holding certificates that haven't yet matured.

US SAVINGS BONDS

To many people, bonds mean the US savings bonds you buy through a regular savings program at work or online at www.savingsbonds.gov, where you establish a Treasury Direct account.

Savings bonds share some similarities with other bonds. You earn interest on your investment principal and can redeem the bonds for cash at maturity.

But they also differ in several important ways. Perhaps the most significant difference is that savings bonds are not marketable, which means you can't sell them to another investor and there's no secondary market where they are traded. You simply buy them and hold them until you cash them in.

You can find helpful information at www.savingsbonds.gov about how the different types of savings bonds work, the interest they pay, the way that interest is taxed, and the different ways to buy them. It also explains how you may be able to use the interest you earn on Series I and some Series EE bonds to pay higher education expenses without owing any income tax on those earnings if you qualify.

Dr. Martin Luther King, Jr.

UNITED STATES SAVINGS BOND

THE UNITED STATES OF AMERICA
ONE HUNDRED DOLLARS

WHAT'S AVAILABLE

There are different types of savings bonds, each with some distinctive features:

Series EE bonds. You buy electronic EE bonds at face value and paper EE bonds at half of face value and earn a fixed rate of interest for the 30-year life of the bond. Series EE bonds are guaranteed to double in value in 20 years.

Series I bonds. You buy I bonds at par value and earn a real rate of return that's guaranteed to exceed the rate of inflation during the term of the bond.

Series EE bonds issued before May 2005 continue to earn interest to maturity at variable rates, which are reset twice a year. Existing Series HH bonds also earn interest to maturity. No new HH bonds are being issued.

The **indenture** is the legal agreement between the issuer and the bondholder, spelling out the terms of the bond.

The **issuer** is the corporation, government, or agency that sells the bond. Publicly held corporations can issue both stocks and bonds. Some privately held corporations issue bonds as well.

Interest rate is the fixed percentage of par value that is paid to the bondholder annually. For example, a $1,000 bond with a 6.5% interest rate pays $65 a year.

Term is the length of time between the date of issue and the date of maturity. The term helps determine the interest rate.

Par value, or the dollar amount of the bond at the time it was issued, is the amount that will be repaid at maturity. Most bonds have a par value of $1,000.

A **baby bond** has a par value of less than $1,000. Bonds of $500, or even less, can be issued by municipal governments to involve a larger number of people in the fund raising process.

Maturity date is the date the bond comes due and must be repaid in full. A bond may be bought and sold in its life-time and re-registered in the new owner's name. Whoever owns the bond at maturity is the one who gets par value back.

22222
REGISTERED

CUSIP 121212 AA 0
SEE REVERSE FOR CERTAIN DEFINITIONS

CUC INTERNATIONAL INC.

tional Inc., a Delaware corporation (the "Issuer"), for value received hereby promises to pay to

DOLLARS

ose in New York, New York on June 6, 1996 in such coin or currency of the United States of America as at the time of payment shall be legal tender for the payment of public and private debts. bear interest except in the case of a default in payment of principal upon acceleration, redemption or at maturity and in such case the overdue principal of this Security shall bear interest at the payment of such interest shall be legally enforceable), which shall accrue from the date of such default in payment to the date payment of such overdue principal has been made or duly provided asis of a 360-day year of twelve 30-day months. Interest on any overdue principal shall be payable on demand. Payment of the principal and any such interest on this Security will be made at the ... ... New York.

...t including without limitation provisions subordinating the payment of principal of and interest on overdue principal, if any, on the Securities to the payment in ..."Indenture") between the Issuer and Morgan Guaranty Trust Company of New York, as Trustee (the "Trustee"), and provisions giving the holder hereof the ..."Common Stock"), of the Issuer on the terms and subject to the conditions and limitations referred to on the reverse hereof, as more fully specified in the

...hough fully set forth at this place.
...hentication hereon shall have been duly signed by the Trustee acting under the Indenture.

...caused this instrument to be duly executed under its corporate seal.
CUC International Inc.

Attest: By:

BEARERS STILL
Eurobonds, which are bonds denominated in a major currency, such as pounds or yen, that are issued and traded in countries outside of the country whose currency is being used, are still bearer bonds. They're not registered with any regulatory authority, and the certificates can be traded or redeemed by the bearer. You're not likely to own one, though, since they're sold in very large denominations. Typical buyers are corporations and governments.

Figuring a Bond's Worth

The value of a bond is determined by the interest it pays and by what's happening in the economy.

In most cases, once a bond is issued, its interest rate doesn't change, even though current interest rates do. If the bond is paying more interest than new bonds with the same credit rating, you, as an investor, may be willing to pay more than its face value to own it. If the bond is paying less, the reverse is true.

Interest rates and bond prices fluctuate like two sides of a seesaw. As the table below illustrates, when interest rates drop, the price of existing bonds usually goes up. When rates climb, the price of existing bonds usually falls.

HOW IT WORKS

Generally, when inflation is up, the money supply is tightened and interest rates go up. And conversely, when inflation is low, interest rates drop because more money is available. It's the change in market interest rates that causes bond prices to move up or down. Those price fluctuations produce much of the trading that goes on in the bond market.

Suppose that a corporation floats a new issue of bonds paying 6% interest, and if it seems like a good investment, you buy some bonds at the full price, or par value, of $1,000 a bond. Two years later, interest rates are up. If new bonds pay 8% interest, no buyer will pay full price for a bond paying 6%. To sell your bonds you'll have to offer them at a **discount**, or less than you paid. If you must sell, you might have to settle for a price that wipes out most of the interest you've earned.

But consider the reverse situation. If, three years later, new bonds offer only 3% interest, you'll be able to sell your 6% bonds for more than you paid—since buyers will pay more to get a higher interest rate. That **premium**, combined with the interest payments for the last three years, provides your profit, or total return.

SELLER   BUYER

Original bond issuer is selling bond
AT PAR VALUE

Par value:	$1,000
Term:	10 years
Interest rate:	6%

6% Prevailing interest rate

At Issue

BUYING AT PAR VALUE
- Pay par value at issue and keep to maturity
- Receive 10 annual interest payments of $60
- Receive par value—$1,000—at maturity

If bondholder sells two years after issue when interest rates are high, the bond is

SELLING AT A DISCOUNT

Market value	$800
Interest (x2)	+ 120
	920
Less original cost	− 1000
LOSS	**−$80**

8% Prevailing interest rate

2 Years Later

BUYING AT A DISCOUNT
- Pay $200 less than par value
- Receive 8 annual interest payments of $60
- Receive par value—$1,000—at maturity

If bondholder sells three years after issue when interest rates are low, the bond is

SELLING AT A PREMIUM

Market value	$1,200
Interest (x3)	+ 180
	1380
Less original cost	− 1000
RETURN	**$380**

3% Prevailing interest rate

3 Years Later

BUYING AT A PREMIUM
- Pay $200 more than par value
- Receive 7 annual interest payments of $60
- Receive par value—$1,000—at maturity

BONDS

THE YIELD CURVE

The relationship of the yields on bonds of the same credit quality but different terms is an interesting story. It's told by the **yield curve**, a graph that's created by

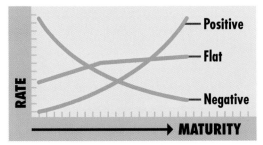

plotting the yields on US Treasury issues. Their advantage, in this situation, is that they're considered free of credit risk.

If the relationship is normal, and longer-term bonds are providing a higher yield, the result is a **positive curve**—higher to the right. But if short-term rates are higher, the curve moves the other way—higher to the left. That's a **negative** or **inverted curve**, and it's quite unusual. In other cases, the line is essentially flat. That happens when there is very little difference in rates between the shortest and the longest maturities.

The structure of the current yield curve is one of the market indicators that bond analysts evaluate in trying to determine where interest rates are headed.

YIELD AND RETURN

Yield is what you earn, expressed as a percentage of what you invested. There are several ways to measure yield, so it's important to know which one you're looking at when you compare bonds.

Coupon yield is the most basic type of yield. It's calculated using the face value of the bond as the price, and the yield is always the same as the bond's interest rate, or **coupon**. So for example, the coupon yield for a bond with a par value of $1,000 that's paying annual interest of $60 is 6%.

FIGURING YIELD

$$\frac{\text{Annual interest}}{\text{Price}} = \text{Yield}$$

You can use this ratio to find coupon yield and current yield.

But if you buy a bond in the secondary market, you probably won't pay par.

Current yield is based on the current, or market, price of the bond.

One measurement of yield, which is widely quoted by bond tables and brokers, is a more complicated calculation known as **yield to maturity (YTM)**. As the name suggests, YTM accounts for all a bond's earnings, on a percentage basis, from the time of the calculation until it matures. YTM includes the money you'll gain or lose (based on the price you paid) when par value is returned, all the interest the bond pays over its lifetime, and **interest-on-interest**—what you'd earn by **reinvesting** payments at the same coupon rate.

Because YTM assumes both that you reinvest every single payment at the same rate and that you hold the bond to maturity, your chances of actually realizing the YTM rate are slim. But it's a way to get an idea of a bond's total earnings potential. For example, you might compare YTM for two bonds you are considering as possible investments.

Securitization

How does a bundle of individual loans turn into one big bond issue?

It's fairly easy to understand corporate, municipal, and Treasury bonds: You lend money to the issuer, who pays you interest and repays your principal at maturity. **Asset-backed bonds**, or **debt securities**, are a different story. Instead of representing the debt of a single large issuer, an asset-backed bond represents a pool of many loans taken by smaller borrowers.

The most common type, a **mortgage-backed security (MBS)**, represents a pool of mortgages that have been **securitized**, which means they have been packaged by a securities firm into bonds that are sold to investors. Many kinds of payment streams can be securitized—

credit card debt, student loans, and car loans, to name a few. As debtors pay off the underlying loans, the money is passed through to bondholders—which is why these bonds are also called **pass-throughs**.

Among the reasons that asset-backed bonds may be attractive to borrowers is that they tend to pay a somewhat higher interest rate than federal bonds with similar terms, but the composite nature of these securities means they behave differently than other bonds do. They involve different risks and have different payment schedules. And the way they work can be complicated, making them harder to predict and understand.

HOW SECURITIZATION

BORROWERS

SERVICER

FEE

LOAN PAYM

1 A securities firm known as the **servicer** bundles a pool of loans or payment streams that share similar features. For example, a pool could comprise a group of 30-year mortgages at 6% interest, totaling $1 million or more.

2 The servicer divides the pool into pieces and sells each piece to an investor as a bond. Each bond represents a percentage of the pool.

CASH FLOWS...AND EBBS

Because of the way asset-backed bonds are put together, their **cash flows** differ substantially from the coupons paid by other bonds. For example, because mortgages are paid monthly, mortgage-backed securities pay bondholders monthly, too. Each bond payment contains some interest and some principal, just like the underlying mortgage payments.

So there's no big return of principal at the end—it is paid back bit by bit over time.

Since each MBS represents a pool of specific, individual loans, no two behave exactly alike. Some people pay mortgages on schedule over the 15 to 30 years of the original term. But many homeowners end their mortgages early by making extra payments, selling their homes, or refinancing. These **prepayments** initially

ASSESSING CREDIT RISK

Mortgage payments sometimes come in late or not at all, but most mortgage-backed bonds have backup to ensure bondholders get paid on time. Mortgage-backed bonds may be issued by an agency of the federal government, by a **government-sponsored enterprise (GSE)**, or by private firms. Debt of a government agency is considered credit-risk free, and the debt of a GSE is generally considered to have a high credit quality.

But when mortgage-backed bonds are packaged by private issuers, their credit quality varies, and some may expose you to more risk. You can find credit ratings on these bonds from rating agencies, such as Standard & Poor's or Moody's Investors Service.

SLICE IT UP, S'IL VOUS PLAIT

To address investor concerns about the unpredictability of prepayments, securities firms have created another class of

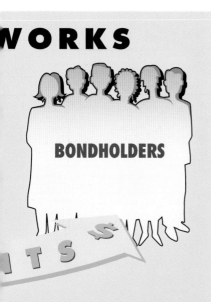

BONDHOLDERS

3 Payments that come in from the loans are passed through to bondholders after the servicer takes a fee (usually 0.5% to 1%).

bulk up the cash flow, but ultimately they shrink the bond's yield and lifetime. So an MBS based on 30-year mortgages actually behaves more like an intermediate-term bond.

Because of prepayments, it's impossible to know exactly how long any particular asset-backed bond will pay out, or how much. This unique risk factor is called **prepayment risk**.

THE MAN WHO SOLD THE WORLD

One of the more ingenious securitizations has been a bond based on artist royalties. The artist gets money up front rather than having to wait decades for a slow payout, and bondholders receive royalties as they come in. Rock musician David Bowie was the first to try it in 1997, giving the bonds the nickname of **Bowie bonds**. Since then, other musicians and owners of other types of intellectual property have arranged financing this way.

mortgage-backed security: **collateralized mortgage obligations (CMOs)**.

CMOs take a larger pool of mortgages and slice the payments into different streams known as **tranches**. (*Tranche* is French for *slice*.) The tranches are designed to offer more defined cash flows.

For example, the basic **sequential** structure uses tranches that mature at specific intervals. In the first interval, all tranches get interest payments, but prepayments are funneled only to the first tranche. After the first interval ends, the first tranche matures, and the next tranche receives prepayments over the next interval.

Institutional investors have advantages over individuals in the CMO market for a number of reasons. First, these investments can be complicated and are often designed specifically with institutional investors in mind. Second, brokers tend to give first pick of tranches to their best customers—in other words, larger investors.

INTEREST RATE RISK

Because of prepayments, asset-backed securities fare worse than other bonds when interest rates change.

Normally, when rates drop, bond prices rise. But people tend to refinance their debt when rates drop, causing a spike in prepayments. Prepayments decrease an asset-backed bond's potential yield, making it less attractive to investors and preventing its market price from going up.

On the other hand, when rates rise, bond prices fall—and the prices of asset-backed bonds fall even more. That's because prepayments slow down when rates are high, lengthening the lifespans of asset-backed bonds. Investors feel they'll be stuck with their bond for longer than they expected, and may have to pass up higher-paying investment opportunities that come along.

Rating Bonds

Investors want to know the risks in buying a bond before they take the plunge. Rating services measure those risks.

Just as potential lenders turn to credit bureaus as a way to check the risk they'd be taking on if they extended credit to you, potential bond investors turn to bond rating services for an assessment of the risk they'd be assuming in buying a particular bond.

The best-known are **Standard & Poor's, Moody's Investors Service, Inc.**, and **Fitch Ratings**. These companies carefully investigate the financial condition of a bond issuer rather than the market appeal of its bonds. They look at other debt the issuer has, how fast the company's revenues and profits are growing, the state of the economy, and how well other companies in the same business (or municipal governments in the same general shape) are doing. Their primary concern is to alert investors to the credit risks of a particular issue.

WHAT IS RATED?

The rating services evaluate municipal bonds, all kinds of corporate bonds, and international bonds. US Treasury issues are not rated. The assumption is that they're free of **default risk**, since they're obligations of the federal government, backed by its full faith and credit. This means the government has the authority to raise taxes to pay off its debts.

What rating services can't evaluate is **market risk**, or the impact that changing interest rates will have on the market price of a bond that you sell before maturity. Even the highest rated bonds and US government issues are vulnerable to loss of market value as interest rates rise.

Rating System

Each rating service focuses its investigation a little differently and uses a slightly different grading system. Standard & Poor's uses

Standard & Poor's

AAA

AA

A

BBB

BB

B

CCC

CC

C

D

Safeway Inc.—Financial Summary

Industry Sector: Supermarkets

Rating history	—Fiscal year ended Dec. 31—				
	BBB/Stable/A-2	BBB/Stable/A-2	BBB/Stable/A-2	BBB/Stable/A-2	BBB/Stab
	2004	**2003**	**2002**	**2001**	
(Mil. $)					
Sales	35,822.9	35,727.2	32,399.2	34,301.0	31
Net income from cont. oper.	560.2	(169.8)	568.5	1,253.9	1
Funds from oper. (FFO)	1,815.1	1,983.0	2,337.3	2,392.6	1.
Capital expenditures	1,190.5	913.9	1,339.5	1,767.3	1,
Total debt	9,296.8	10,382.0	10,528.3	9,972.2	8,
Common equity	4,306.9	3,644.3	3,627.5	5,889.6	

THE RISK OF DOWNGRADING

One danger bondholders face—and one they can't anticipate—is that a rating service may substantially **downgrade**—from investment grade to speculative grade—its assessment of a bond issuer during the life of a bond, creating a **fallen angel**. That happens if the issuer's financial condition deteriorates, or if the rating service feels a business decision might have poor results.

If downgrading occurs, investors usually demand a higher yield for the existing bonds. That means the price of the bond falls in the secondary market. It also means that if the issuer wants to float new bonds, the bonds will have to be offered at a higher interest rate to attract buyers.

combinations of the capital letters A through D, indicating small variations within categories with a plus (+) or (−).

Moody's system combines capital and small letters, with Aaa as the highest rating and C as the lowest. It doesn't assign a rating to bonds in default. The company indicates small variations within rankings with the numbers 1, 2, and 3.

Meaning		
Best quality, with the smallest risk. Issuers exceptionally stable and dependable		
High quality, with slightly higher degree of long-term risk	**INVESTMENT GRADE BONDS**	
High-medium quality, with many strong attributes but somewhat vulnerable to changing economic conditions		**Investment grade** generally refers to any bonds rated BBB or higher by Standard & Poor's. The comparable Moody's ratings are Baa and higher.
Medium quality, currently adequate but perhaps unreliable over long term		
Speculative element, with moderate security but not well safeguarded	**SPECULATIVE GRADE**	
Able to pay now but at risk of default in the future		
Poor quality, clear danger of default		
Highly speculative quality, poor prospects of repayment though may still be paying		
Lowest-rated, often in default		
In default		

JUNK BONDS

Junk bonds are the lowest-rated corporate and municipal bonds. There's a greater-than-average risk of default. But investors may be willing to take the risk of buying these low-rated bonds because the yields are much higher than on other, higher-rated bonds. However, the prices are volatile as well, exposing investors to increased market risk.

RANKINGS INFLUENCE RATES

Credit ratings influence the interest rate an issuer must pay to attract investors. In bonds with the same maturity, typically the higher the bond's rating, the lower its interest and yield.

Upgrades and downgrades of investment-grade bonds—for example, moving from AA to A—tend to result in relatively small adjustments to yield. But if a bond's credit rating is moved up to investment grade or down to junk, there's a massive change in demand and therefore in yield.

TIME IS MONEY

When bonds have the same rating but different terms, those with longer terms typically pay higher rates to encourage investment for an extended period, which means greater potential for inflation, interest rate, and default risk.

Bond Prices

A bond's price starts changing as soon as it's out of the gate.

What you pay for a bond, and the amount you collect when you sell it, depends on when those transactions occur.

The only time a bond's purchase price is predictable is at issue, when you pay **par value**—usually $1,000, which is also the amount you expect to get back if you hold the bond to maturity. After issue, however, bonds trade at prices above and below par, in response to current interest rates, predictions about future rates, the specific credit risk involved, and shifts in investor demand.

When a bond trades at a price above par, it's said to trade at a **premium**. When a bond trades below par, it trades at a **discount**. In the shorthand of bond pricing, a bond at par value is said to be priced at 100. Figuring the dollar price of a bond is easy: Just multiply by 10. So a bond listed at 98.7 has a price of $987.

INTEREST RATE CHANGES CAUSE BOND PRICE CHANGES

Interest rates
UP
Bond prices
DOWN

BONDS TRADE AT PRICES ABOVE OR BELOW THEIR PAR VALUE

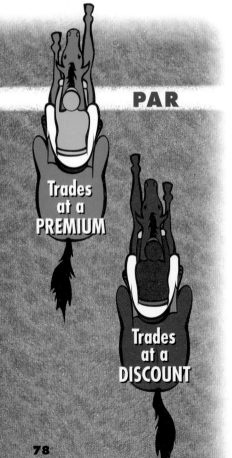

PAR

Trades at a PREMIUM

Trades at a DISCOUNT

WHY PRICES MOVE

Change—or the expectation of a change—in the current interest rates exerts the strongest influence on bond prices. When interest rates rise, the prices of existing bonds drop. That's because demand for existing bonds decreases when newer bonds that are paying higher rates attract more investors with their better yield.

Corporate and municipal bond prices are also subject to changes in their issuers' credit ratings. Small changes in credit rating tend to result in small price changes. But if a bond drops out of investment grade, rises into investment grade, or rapidly jumps several ratings categories, the change could translate to a massive shift in price.

Treasury bonds that have already been issued may also change in price to reflect market sentiment. For example, they may cost more and yield less when there's uncertainty in the equity markets or as a result of political pressures. If sentiment changes, Treasurys could drop in price, providing a higher yield.

All three types of bonds have a par value of $1,000. But unlike corporate and municipal bonds, which are priced in dollars and cents, Treasury prices are stated in 32nds, with 1/32 equal to 31.25 cents (0.3125). For example, if a note is quoted at 100:12, or 100 and 12/32 (3.75), the price is $1,003.75.

Interest rates **DOWN**
Bond prices **UP**

TRACING A TRADE

Stock prices are everywhere, crawling across tickers and being updated as soon as they change. Bond prices are less transparent.

The vast majority of bonds trade over-the-counter—as private arrangements between individual dealers. Because of the one-on-one nature of the bond business, bond prices have been much harder to track. But that's changing.

The NASD Trade Reporting and Compliance Engine (TRACE), founded in 2002, started reporting details on 99% of over-the-counter corporate bond trades in 2005, with over 80% of trades reported within five minutes. TRACE data is available free to the public, with a time delay, at www.nasdbondinfo.com, and is available in real time to subscribers.

The pricing of municipal bonds also became more transparent in 2005, when the Municipal Securities Rulemaking Board began offering free real-time pricing information on municipal bond trades at the website of the Bond Market Association, www.investinginbonds.com.

These new systems are a vast improvement over the former practice, when investors had to call several dealers to compare quotes, making it hard to determine a fair price.

Reporting the prices hasn't solved all bond pricing questions, though. Most of the trading in the bond market involves a relatively small number of bonds. For bonds that trade infrequently, it's still difficult to gauge fair pricing.

MEET THE MARKUP

One way that bond pricing differs substantially from stock pricing is in the way dealers charge commissions. On a stock trade confirmation, you see the actual price of the stock and the price of the commission. In contrast, the bond price on a confirmation includes the commission, which is figured as a loosely regulated percentage of the bond's price.

The difference between the price the dealer pays and the price you pay is the **markup**. Markups may be substantial— up to 4% or 5% for some bonds—which could be a whole year's interest. The harder a bond is to sell, the higher the markup tends to be. If you're buying or selling a bond with a lot of active trading, such as a Treasury security, the markup will be much lower than it would be with a high-yield corporate bond that trades infrequently. (Markups on Treasurys generally stay under 0.5%.) Also, if interest rates are rising, older bonds with lower rates become harder to sell, which means higher markups. Smaller trades also involve higher markups, which can greatly affect the bond's yield.

If the broker you buy from doesn't have the bond in inventory, there may actually be two markups embedded in the bond price. That's because the broker must buy the bond from another dealer, who charges a separate markup.

Corporate Bonds

From plain vanilla to bells and whistles—corporate bonds run the gamut.

When corporations need to raise money, they can borrow the cash from investors by issuing bonds. There's a substantial market for these bonds—as evidenced by the $4 trillion of corporate debt that's currently outstanding.

But investing in corporate bonds can require making a number of potentially complex decisions. For starters, the companies that issue debt range from large, well-known blue chips to small, new startups that are not publicly held.

What's more, corporations can craft a bond to control the cost of borrowing and to encourage investors to purchase. As a result, two bond issues from the same corporation may be very different investments.

Corporate bonds also involve risks that don't apply to government or agency bonds. Some of these risks are linked to the specific fortunes of a company, some to the state of the economy, and some to the special features of the bonds themselves.

To make up for these added risks, corporate bonds generally pay higher interest rates than Treasurys or municipals with comparable maturities. But there's a catch. Interest you earn from corporate bonds is taxed as ordinary income at federal, state, and local levels.

BIG HAS ITS BENEFITS

Large institutional investors have advantages over individual investors in purchasing corporate bonds. That's because institutional investors trade in larger lots—a minimum of $100,000 per transaction—so their markups tend to be lower. In addition, since broker-dealers cultivate institutional investors, they tend to give them preference on the most attractive bond offerings.

ONE MAN'S JUNK

Many institutional investors are required to limit their bond holdings to highly rated issues known as investment grade bonds. So investment grade pickings can be slim for individuals shopping for bonds, since the supply is limited, and the big investors tend to have the advantage.

In the market of bonds that fall below investment grade, however, individual investors find more opportunities. These bonds—known as **speculative grade**, high-yield, or less flatteringly as junk—carry a higher risk of default than investment grade bonds, but they yield considerably more. Investing in high-yield bonds, however, requires a different strategy from investing in investment-grade bonds.

The most important difference is this: While the value of investment grade debt depends mostly on shifts in interest rates, the value of junk bonds depends mostly on the credit risk of the companies that issue them. As a result, junk bond markets tend to act more like stock markets, rising and falling with company performance.

If you invest in a junk bond, and your assessment of the company's financial health turns out to be right, you could end up with a substantial return, based on what the bond pays coupled with the gains you could realize if the credit rating rises and pushes up the price. If you're wrong and the company defaults, however, you could lose your principal.

NOT DEAD YET

Defaulted bonds aren't always worthless, since bondholders are fairly high on the priority list of who gets paid if a company emerges from bankruptcy or is reorganized. Bondholders may eventually get some, if not all, of their investment back. So some investors actually buy up defaulted bonds for pennies on the dollar, speculating on the eventual payout.

CORPORATE BONDS

Plain Vanilla

Equity Warrants

Put Options

Debenture Bonds

Bells & whistles

THE PAPER ROUTE

Sometimes a company needs to borrow money not to finance a huge long-term project or a major expansion but to meet short-term bookkeeping needs—for example, to keep up inventories and make provision for the uncertain timing of accounts receivable. If the company has a high credit rating, it's often cheaper and easier to borrow from investors than from a bank. This highly rated, short-term, unsecured corporate debt is known as **commercial paper**. It's mostly issued by large financial companies, like banks, which need a lot of short-term loans to manage their cash flows.

Like other short-term debt, the paper trades at a discount and pays par at maturity, which is usually around 30 days from issue and no more than 9 months. Unlike longer-term corporate debt, commercial paper doesn't have to be registered with the SEC. It's considered very safe and highly liquid in both the US and international markets. That low risk typically translates into low yield.

Who buys commercial paper? Mostly, other companies do. That's because the paper comes in denominations of $100,000 and up—and sometimes over $1 million. Individual investors usually get exposure to commercial paper through **money market funds**, which invest heavily in short-term issues.

NO SPRINKLES?

The simplest, most straightforward corporate bonds are described as plain vanilla. A **plain vanilla** bond pays the same fixed rate over a set period of time.

All the special features and add-ons that issuers use to boost the appeal of their bonds are called **bells and whistles**. A typical example is **equity warrants**, which give bondholders the right to buy the company's stock at a certain price at a date in the future. Another is **put options**, which allow the bondholder to redeem the bond for par value before maturity.

GOT COLLATERAL?

Some corporate issuers back up their bonds with collateral, which can be liquidated to repay bondholders if the company should default. For example, **collateral trust bonds** are backed by securities, usually those issued by wholly owned subsidiaries of the issuer. If a corporate bond has no collateral backing it up, it's known as a **debenture** or **note**.

Municipal Bonds

Munis offer investors a less taxing way to earn bond income.

Municipal bonds, widely known as **munis**, are a way for governments below the federal level, such as states, cities, and counties, to raise money. Their major appeal for investors is their tax treatment. In most cases, muni interest isn't subject to federal income tax, though there are some exceptions.

If you invest in your own state's munis, the income is usually free of state tax, too. The same goes for the munis of your own city or county. So even though munis may offer a lower coupon rate than comparable taxable bonds, the tax break can push their value higher, especially if you're in a higher tax bracket.

You do take certain risks when you buy munis, however. Bonds with longer maturities are vulnerable to **interest rate risk**, which would mean a lower market price, and **inflation risk**, which would reduce the buying power of the interest they pay. Also, some munis can be **called**, or redeemed by the issuer before maturity.

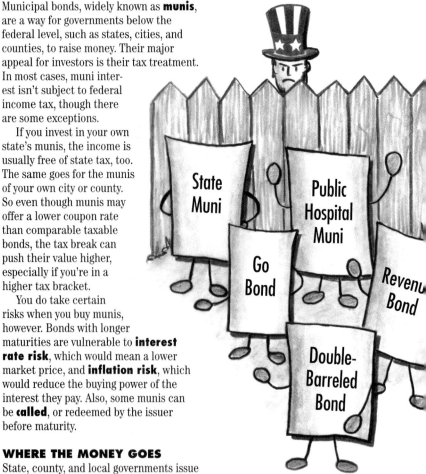

WHERE THE MONEY GOES

State, county, and local governments issue bonds to fund ongoing activities, new projects, and improvements. So do other public enterprises and authorities, such as public hospitals, toll roads and bridges, universities, and public utilities.

When these municipalities or municipal agencies issue bonds, they release a **prospectus** to investors, containing all the details about the bond—including how the issuer plans to raise the cash to pay its debt. If the interest will be paid out of tax revenues, the muni is a **general obligation (GO) bond**. If the bond will be paid with specific fees collected by the issuer—such as the tolls on a bridge—it's called a **revenue bond**. Sometimes an issuer uses a combination of taxes and fees to pay for a bond, known as a **double-barreled bond**.

Although some investors consider GO bonds safer than revenue bonds, it's rarely wise to generalize. Interest on many revenue bonds is paid with regular, predictable fees for services that are in constant demand, such as bridge tolls or airport departure fees. And some GO bonds are issued by governments in dire fiscal circumstances that can't raise enough in taxes to meet their obligations. Before you invest, it's best to review each bond on its own merits.

WHO INVESTS IN MUNIS?

Big institutional investors like pension funds, mutual funds, and life insurance companies don't dominate the muni market as they do other bond markets. So muni underwriters tend to cater more to individual investors, in part by making it possible to make an investment in the $5,000 to $10,000 range. Another advantage is that muni prices tend to be relatively stable, since individuals are less likely than institutions to trade munis before maturity.

TAX EXCEPTIONS

Not all munis are tax exempt. Some, called **taxable munis**, are subject to federal income tax. They're issued by governments on behalf of private enterprises that don't provide qualifying public services. For example, proceeds from a taxable muni may be used to build a sports stadium or a shopping mall.

Other munis that are exempt from ordinary federal income tax are subject to the **alternative minimum tax (AMT)**. Almost 9% of munis fall into this category, because the tax law defines them as **private-purpose** bonds. They're used to fund non-governmental projects like housing, airports, and student loans.

Furthermore, you'll have a taxable **capital gain** if you sell the bond at a higher price than you paid to buy it. The same is true if you buy a muni at a discount and redeem the bond at par. If you've held the bond for more than a year, you can figure the tax at your long-term capital gains rate, which is a maximum of 15%.

THE SMOKING BOND

In 1998, states won a multi-billion dollar settlement from tobacco companies, forcing the companies to cough up a portion of their proceeds to the states. So some states released **tobacco bonds**, backed by those settlement payments.

GETTING A GUARANTEE

Better credit quality means more investor demand and lower coupon rates, so municipalities have found ways to improve the credit rating of their bonds. One way is through **bond insurance**, which guarantees coupon and principal payments. If the issuer defaults, the insurer makes the payments.

The companies that insure municipal bonds carefully assess the credit quality of the issuer before agreeing to the coverage. In that sense, bond insurance can also be seen as an expert second opinion on credit risk. But though bond insurance protects you from credit risk, it doesn't apply to interest rate risk.

THE RATINGS GAME

The credit quality of municipal bonds tends to be high. Just 1% of issues were rated below investment grade in 2005, according to Standard & Poor's. And there were no defaults of AAA or AA rated debt between 1986 and 2005.

That's not to say that munis are absolutely free of **credit risk**. Defaults have happened—in the 1970s, for example, when New York City delayed an interest payment on its debt, and in the 1990s, when Orange County, California, went bankrupt.

When rating agencies are assessing municipal credit risk, one element they look at is a ratio known as **debt coverage**—how much money an issuer has available for its debt divided by the amount it owes. If that ratio is below 1 then the rater concludes that the issuer doesn't have the money to cover the debt. A debt coverage ratio of 2 is considered good, and of 4 or higher, excellent.

STANDARD & POOR'S

Publication date: 18-Jul-2005
Reprinted from RatingsDirect

Maryland

Primary Credit Analyst(s): Kenneth
Secondary Credit Analyst(s): Robi

Credit Profile

US$20 mil GO state & local facs loan bnds (taxable) ser 2005B due 08/01/2012
AAA
Sale date: 20-JUL-2005

US$430 mil GO state & local facs loan ser 2005A due 08/01/2020
AAA
Sale date: 20-JUL-2005

AFFIRMED
Outstanding GO bnds
AAA

Outstanding GO bnds state & local facs loan
AAA

OUTLOOK: STABLE

US Treasury Issues

Investors line up to make loans to the US government.

Because the federal government needs to raise funds to pay for the difference between what it spends and what it collects in taxes and other revenues, the US Treasury borrows money from the public by issuing debt securities.

The Treasury is considered the perfect creditor. Its debt is backed by the "full faith and credit" of the government. This means a Treasury security, unlike any other debt investment, involves no credit risk. You're assured that if you hold it to maturity, you'll collect all the interest and principal owed you.

The market for US Treasurys is like no other bond market. For starters, it's enormous, with about $4.5 trillion in Treasury debt held by a variety of investors in 2005. It's also extremely liquid, with a dependable supply of buyers and sellers to keep trading fast and efficient and to push transaction costs down.

The Treasury market is also distinguished by the fairness of its issuing process. Competitive bids determine an issue's coupon rate and yield, and individuals and institutions get the same access and yield. The secondary market is similarly transparent, since price and yield data are readily available.

Treasury debt held by investors in 2005:

$4.5

TYPES OF TREASURYS

Treasury bills (T-bills)
Maturities: 26 weeks or less
Coupon: No coupon payments as bills are sold at discount and redeemed at par
   These short-term Treasurys pay low coupon rates and are considered cash equivalents.

Treasury notes (T-notes)
Maturities: 2, 3, 5, and 10 years
Coupon: Semiannual fixed-rate payments
   The 10-year note is tracked in the financial press as a benchmark for bond performance.

Treasury bonds (T-bonds)
Maturities: Over 10 years, up to 30
Coupon: Semiannual fixed-rate payments
   The Treasury stopped issuing T-bonds in 2001, but older bonds are still actively traded. Sale of these bonds will resume in February 2006.

Treasury Inflation-Protected Securities (TIPS)
Maturities: 5, 10, and 20 years
Coupon: Semiannual fixed-rate payments based on inflation-adjusted principal
   Principal is adjusted twice a year according to changes in the **Consumer Price Index (CPI)**.

SAVINGS BONDS

Bills, notes, and bonds are transferable—you can sell them to whomever you want. The Treasury also offers nontransferable bonds called **savings bonds**, which accumulate interest for up to 30 years. You can choose between savings bonds that pay a fixed interest rate (Series EE) or those whose rate is indexed for inflation (Series I).

HOW PRICES AND YIELD CHANGE

Because Treasurys aren't affected by credit risk, changes in their prices and yield are governed largely by interest rates and by demand sparked by political or economic events. As with any debt security, Treasury prices rise when interest rates drop and fall when rates rise. The longer the issue's maturity, the more sensitive it is to interest rate changes.

Treasurys are also affected by investor speculation on the next rate move.

For example, if the market expects rates to rise, demand might drop for long-term bonds. But if a drop in rates is expected, demand for these issues might shoot up as investors try to lock in the higher rate.

BONDS ON THE RUN

On-the-run Treasurys are the latest issues in a particular maturity. For example, all the notes sold in the most recent auction of 10-year notes would be the on-the-run 10-year issue. Any 10-year notes issued previously would become **off-the-run**.

When the financial press talks about Treasurys, it's generally talking about on-the-run issues, because they're the most in demand and the most frequently traded. So they're often more expensive than off-the-run issues, even if the coupon and maturity are almost identical. This makes off-the-run issues a potential bargain.

WHEN TREASURYS STRIP

STRIPS are zero-coupon Treasury securities. Rather than pay semiannual coupons over the life of the security, STRIPS accrue interest and pay it all at once, along with principal, at maturity.

The odd name is an acronym for Separate Trading of Registered Interest and Principal of Securities. You can't buy or sell STRIPS through Treasury Direct, though, because they're creations of broker-dealers, who separate Treasury holdings into income and principal streams, called **tranches**, which they then repackage and sell to investors.

As with all zero-coupon bonds, you buy STRIPS at a discount and receive par at maturity. STRIPS are more susceptible to interest-rate risk than unstripped Treasurys, and prices can vary widely from dealer to dealer. And even though you don't get coupon payments from STRIPS, you owe income tax each year as if you did unless you hold them in a tax-deferred account.

THE REPO MARKET

One way to increase potential return on a Treasury security, though with added risk, is to use **leverage**, or buy the Treasurys with borrowed money. Full service brokers can help investors leverage Treasury purchases by lending them the money. The interest on the loan is charged either at the broker loan rate paid by stock investors buying on margin, or at the lower rates offered by the **repo market**—an overnight loan market for financing Treasurys that's used primarily by institutions.

The repo rate is lower than the broker loan rate because Treasurys are less volatile than stocks. Minimum investments for repo purchases are fairly high, however, and brokers don't automatically offer this option to individual investors.

Agency Bonds

You may want to meet Ginnie, Fannie, Freddie, Sallie, and their friends.

Agency bond is an umbrella term that covers different types of securities. The Rural Electrification Program, for example, issues bonds through the Federal Financing Bank, a unit of the US Treasury that helps government agencies raise capital. Bonds issued by most federal agencies carry the same risk-free credit guarantee as Treasury issues.

Another category, Ginnie Mae securities, is also free of credit risk, though these government guaranteed bonds are actually issued by private companies.

Finally, positioned somewhere between the federal government and wholly private corporations are entities that are a little bit government, a little bit corporate. These **government-sponsored enterprises (GSEs)** issue a variety of agency bonds that offer investors higher yields than Treasurys but are guaranteed only by the GSEs themselves.

GINNIE MAE
- Public corporation
- Zero credit risk
- Subject to interest rate and prepayment risk

TYPES OF AGENCY BOND ISSUES

Discount notes mature in less than a year. Like Treasury bills, discount notes don't pay a coupon. Instead, as the name implies, you buy them at a discount and cash them in at par at maturity. The interest earned is the difference between the original price and par.

Bonds mature in two years or more and pay a regular coupon.

Zero-coupon bonds or **zeros** pay no coupon and are created by securities firms out of agency bonds. Interest accrues unpaid at a fixed compounded rate. At maturity, you get one payout consisting of both principal and interest.

Interest-only bonds are created by securities firms by splitting up mortgage-backed agency bonds into different tranches. These pay bond-holders only the interest portion of mortgage payments.

Principal-only bonds, like interest-only bonds, are created by securities firms out of mortgage-backed agency bonds. They're sold at a discount and pay the bondholder principal payments but no interest.

GINNIE MAE, GOVERNMENT AGENT

Ginnie Mae, formerly the **Government National Mortgage Association**, sometimes shortened to GNMA, is a corporation that's part of the federal government—the Department of Housing and Urban Development (HUD). The corporation doesn't actually issue bonds, though you're likely to hear about Ginnie Maes or GMNAs. Rather, it guarantees that investors who buy either **mortgage-backed securities (MBSs)** created from federally insured loans made by the Federal Housing Administration or federally guaranteed loans from the Department of Veterans Affairs (VA) that are issued by private firms will receive timely payment of principal and interest.

Even though the bonds Ginnie Mae guarantees have zero credit risk, they're still vulnerable to **interest rate risk**, so their market prices change as interest rates change. They're also subject to **prepayment risk**—the risk that home-owners will pay off their mortgages ahead of schedule, interrupting an anticipated income stream. To compensate investors for this risk, Ginnie Maes yield more than Treasurys, though generally less than GSE bonds.

The minimum investment for Ginnie Maes is high: $25,000. That price tag means that individuals tend to invest in these securities through mutual funds, rather than directly.

FLOOD CONTROL

The Tennessee Valley Authority (TVA) is a public power utility that's owned by the federal government. Unlike a public company or GSE, it can't issue stock, but it can issue bonds to provide capital for its electricity generating programs. TVA bonds, some of which are targeted at individual investors, are backed entirely by revenues from the sale of the power it generates.

ON HER OWN

Until the end of 2004, Sallie Mae, formerly the Student Loan Marketing Association (SLMA), was a stockholder-owned GSE like Fannie Mae and Freddie Mac. But in 1996, Congress gave the company authorization to privatize, ending its federal charter.

GSEs
- Run as corporations
- Some publicly traded
- Implicit zero credit risk

FANNIE MAE & FREDDIE MAC
- Private corporations
- Publicly traded
- Specialize in mortgage-backed securities

PUBLIC   **PRIVATE**

A FOOT IN EACH CAMP

GSEs are organized and run as corporations. Some, like Farmer Mac, are publicly owned companies listed on the New York Stock Exchange. Others, including the Federal Home Loan Bank, are not publicly traded. But all GSEs enjoy a special relationship with the government, which defines their roles, oversees their activities—and provides an implicit guarantee for their debt.

The implicit guarantee of GSEs is not as solid as the "full faith and credit" guarantee of Treasurys. But investors—and the financial markets—generally assume that a GSE default would be so disastrous to the economy that the government would use Treasury funds to bail it out.

That's not a rash assumption. The government has come to the assistance of a GSE in the past, when the Farm Credit System faced financial trouble during the 1980s. Most GSEs also have backup for their debt in the form of lines of credit that authorize borrowing from the Treasury to pay their obligations, if need be.

FANNIE AND FREDDIE

The largest issuers of agency debt are two giants of the mortgage industry, **Fannie Mae**, formerly the Federal National Mortgage Association (FNMA), and **Freddie Mac**, formerly the Federal Home Loan Mortgage Corporation (FHLMC). Both are private corporations with publicly traded stock. Both were created by Congress to fill needs in the US housing market and are governed by federal charters.

Fannie Mae and Freddie Mac specialize in **mortgage-backed securities**. But unlike Ginnie Mae, Freddie and Fannie actually create securities backed by mortgages they purchase and then offer these bonds for sale. They also draw on a larger, more geographically diverse mortgage pool than Ginnie Mae does and engage in a range of more complex financial transactions.

Because Fannie Mae is the largest agency bond issuer in the United States, it has the largest secondary market, meaning it's easier to find buyers or sellers for Fannie Maes than for other agency bonds.

Bond Variations

The fine print can have a big impact on the value of a bond.

Like the word **security**, which once meant the written record of an investment, the word **bond** once referred to the piece of paper that described the details of a loan transaction. Today the term is used more generally to describe a vast and varied market in debt securities.

The language of bonds tells potential investors the features of the loan: the time to maturity, how it's going to be repaid, and whether it's likely to be **called**, or repaid ahead of schedule.

Bonds with Strings Attached

Callable bonds don't always run their full term. The issuer may call the bond, which means pay off the debt before the maturity date. The process is called redemption. The first date a bond is vulnerable to call is named at the time of issue. Callable bonds come with either a **call schedule**, which lists specific dates and prices at which a bond can be called, or a date beyond which the issuer could call the bond at any time.

Issuers may want to call a bond if interest rates drop. If they pay off their outstanding bonds, they can float another bond at the lower rate. (It's the same idea as refinancing a mortgage to get a lower interest rate and make lower monthly payments.) Sometimes only part of an issue is redeemed, rather than all of it. In that case, the bonds that are called are chosen by lottery. In some cases, a bond is issued with a **sinking fund**, which is a cash reserve set aside specifically to retire portions of the bond issue before maturity.

Callable bonds can be less attractive for investors than noncallable ones because an investor whose bond has been called is often faced with reinvesting the money at a lower, less-attractive rate. To protect bondholders expecting long-term steady income, call provisions usually specify that a bond can't be redeemed before a certain number of years, usually five or ten. And sometimes issuers offer to redeem called bonds at a premium, or price higher than par, to make the bonds more attractive to investors. That could result in a capital gain, if the **premium** price is higher than the price you paid to buy.

Bonds with Conditions

A subordinated bond is one that will be paid after other loan obligations of the issuer have been met. **Senior bonds** are those with stronger claims. Corporations sometimes sell senior and subordinated bonds in the same issue, offering more interest and a shorter term on the subordinated ones to make them more attractive.

Floating-rate bonds promise periodic adjustments of the interest rate—to persuade you that you aren't locked into what seems like an unattractively low rate.

Prerefunded bonds are corporate or municipal bonds, usually AAA rated, whose repayment is guaranteed by a second bond issue. The money the issuer raises with the second bond is usually invested in US Treasury securities, timed to mature at the first bond's initial call date. Prerefunded bonds typically offer a lower than average coupon rate and are called at the first opportunity.

Insured bonds are backed by bond insurance. If the issuer can no longer make timely interest payments, the insurer pays. But the reduced risk generally means the bonds are offered at a lower than average coupon rate.

Bonds with equity warrants are corporate bonds that give investors the right to buy the issuer's stock at a certain price on a specific date.

Put bonds give investors the right to redeem the bond before maturity at par value. In general, put bonds are issued at a lower-than-average coupon rate because they have what amounts to an escape clause that fixed-rate bonds don't provide.

MONDAY

9AM *T-bills offered on Thursday for Monday sale*

10AM

① The US Treasury offers 13-week and 26-week T-bills for auction every Monday.

② Across the country, institutional investors (such as pension funds and mutual funds) who want to buy the major part of the issue ready their competitive bids. Their bids must arrive at the Treasury by 1:00 p.m. Monday, the auction deadline.

11AM
Bidders state the rate they are willing to accept on the bills. In a hypothetical example, one fund might bid 2.205%, another, 2.210%, a third, 2.215%, and a fourth, 2.220%.

③ At the same time, individual investors can submit noncompetitive tenders, or offers, through Treasury Direct. Investors decide how much they want to put into T-bills, and either send

NOON
a check or authorize a debit for that amount. For example, someone might commit $30,000.

1PM *—Deadline for all bids!*

④ The Treasury accepts bids, from the lowest to the highest rate, until the quota is filled.

1:10—1:15 Results announced

2PM

⑤ Within minutes, the Treasury announces the auction results, and bidders learn what the auction rate is and the price they will pay to buy the bills. Using the sample bids above, that rate might be 2.215%. All the competitive bidders who bid rates lower than the cutoff bid have their orders filled at the auction rate. However, the institution whose bid is the cutoff,

3PM
or auction rate, may not be able to invest as much as it had wanted if the quota has already been filled.

⑥ Individuals and small institutions that have submitted non-competitive bids get the auction rate that's been determined by the competitive auction. They can invest as much as they wish, up

4PM
to $1 million.

⑦ If an individual has submitted a check for the purchase amount, the Treasury refunds the difference between the par value and the auction price. But if the investor has authorized a debit, the amount of the purchase is taken out of the designated account. For example, if the auction rate on a 26-week bill was 2.028%,

5PM
the price for each $1,000 investment would be $989.86 because six months of interest would be $10.14, or half the annual yield. Someone who had written a check for $30,000 would get a refund of $304.20, or $10.14 on each $1,000. But if a debit had been authorized, $29,695.80 would have been taken out of the account.

⑧ At maturity, noncompetitive bidders with Treasury Direct accounts can roll over their T-bill investment at the new auction rate, or they can redeem their investment at par value.

The World of Bonds

	Type of bond	Par value	Maturity period
	CORPORATE BONDS Corporate bonds are readily available to investors. Companies use them to finance expansion and other activities.	$1,000	**Short-term:** 1 to 5 years **Intermediate-term:** 5 to 10 years **Long-term:** 10 to 20 years
	MUNICIPAL BONDS More than one million municipal bonds have been issued by states, cities, and other local governments to pay for construction and other projects.	$1,000 (but may vary)	From 1 month to 40 years
	T-BONDS The Treasury suspended new long-term bonds issues in October 2001, though they may be offered in the future. There's an active secondary market in existing bonds.	$1,000	Over 10 and up to 30 years
	T-NOTES and BONDS These debt issues of the federal government are a major source of government funding to keep operations running and to pay interest on national debt.	$1,000 (also issued in amounts up to $1 million)	2 years 3 years 5 years 10 years 30 years
	T-BILLS Treasury bills are the largest component of the money market—the market for short-term debt securities. The government uses them to raise money for immediate spending at lower rates than bonds or notes.	$1,000 (also issued in amounts up to $1 million)	4 weeks 13 weeks 26 weeks
	AGENCY BONDS The issues may be floated by US government agencies or government sponsored enterprises.	$1,000 (often sold in lots of $10,000 to $25,000)	From 30 days to 20 years

BONDS

Trading details	Rated	Tax status	Call provisions	Interest and safety
Through brokers, either on an exchange or over-the-counter (OTC)	Yes	Taxable	Callable	**Riskier** than government bonds, but potentially **higher yields**. Default risk depends on issuer
Through brokers, OTC	Yes	Exempt from federal income taxes and state and local income taxes under certain conditions	Sometimes callable	**Lower interest rates** than comparable corporate bonds because of **tax exemption**
New issues: Through Treasury Direct when available **Outstanding issues**: Through brokers, OTC	Not rated, considered free of default risk	Exempt from state and local income taxes	Sometimes callable	**Maximum safety** from default because backed by federal government Long maturities increase **interest rate risk** and **inflation risk** **Low** interest rates
New issues: Through Treasury Direct **Outstanding issues**: Through brokers, OTC	Not rated, considered free of default risk	Exempt from state and local income taxes	Sometimes callable	**Maximum safety** from default since backed by federal government, but relatively **low** interest rates New T-bond issue beginning February 2006
New issues: Through Treasury Direct **Outstanding issues**: Through brokers, OTC	Not rated, considered free of default risk	Exempt from state and local income taxes	Not callable	**Short-term investments**, with no periodic interest payments. Instead, interest consists of the difference between a discounted buying price and the par amount paid at maturity
By brokers, OTC, or directly through banks	Some issues rated by some services	Some issues taxable and others exempt from state and local income taxes	Sometimes callable	Marginally **higher risk** and **higher interest** than Treasury bonds

Tracking Securities Markets

You get a clear picture of what's up and what's down, thanks to market indexes and averages.

Indexes and averages track day-to-day changes in stock, bond, and mutual fund performance as well as longer-term trends in financial markets. The best-known US indicators, such as Standard & Poor's 500 Index (S&P 500) and the Dow Jones Industrial Average (DJIA), are often used as snapshots of the country's economic health.

Both individual and institutional investors—such as mutual fund companies—use indexes and averages as **benchmarks**, or standards, to gauge the performance of a specific investment or portfolio of investments. Indexes are also the basis for a variety of investment products, including index mutual funds, exchange traded funds (ETFs), options contracts, and futures contracts.

MEASURE FOR MEASURE

Since each index or average is constructed differently, it conveys different information about the markets and provides a slightly different answer to the question "How's the market doing?".

For instance, some indexes measure stock performance, while others follow bonds. There are indexes for growth stocks and value stocks, and long-term and short-term bonds, to name a few.

While some indexes are very broad, tracking thousands of global securities, others are narrowly focused on a specific sector of the US economy—technology companies, financial companies, or healthcare companies, for example.

INDEX OR AVERAGE?

You've probably wondered why some market benchmarks are called indexes while others are called averages. The differences aren't always clear—in part because some measurements that are called averages are essentially indexes, and some indexes are really averages.

A true average is an arithmetic mean. To find an average, the prices of the securities included in the measurement are added together and divided by the total number of securities represented. For example, you could find the average price of 25 stocks by adding their individual prices and dividing by 25.

An index, on the other hand, is a statistical measure usually expressed as a percentage change from an established base value as of a certain date. For instance, an index might have a base value of 100 as of December 31, 1996.

The best-known financial average, the DJIA, is actually a hybrid. It's computed by adding the closing prices of its 30 stocks and then dividing not by 30, but by a much smaller number that has been adjusted over the years to account for mergers and stock splits, as well as the changing roster of component stocks. Its movement is reported as point changes and as a percentage—the same way changes in an index are. So for example you might hear that the DJIA was up 65 points, or 0.6%, on a day the average was 10,500.

value of each company in an index has the same impact on the value of the index. The S&P Equal Weight Index (S&P EWI), for example, tracks the same 500 stocks as the S&P 500, but gives them equal weight.

WEIGHING IN ON THE WEIGHTINGS

Weighting can, in some respects, create a more accurate measurement. What happens with larger, less volatile companies with recognizable brand names may be a truer measure of the marketplace than the fluctuations of smaller, less established companies.

But weighting can also give a skewed picture of the markets when a handful of large-cap or highly priced stocks behaves differently than smaller or lower-priced stocks. For example, the upward trend of the S&P 500 in the late 1990s was driven by the market capitalization of several high-flying stocks. In fact, in early 2000, roughly 30 stocks, rather than the more typical 40 to 50, accounted for 50% of the results. Their momentum overshadowed the fact that many other stocks remained flat or lost value during the same period.

Similarly, the price-weighted DJIA may rise based on the performance of its most expensive stocks, even if the majority of the stocks are falling in price, or vice versa.

WEIGHTING THE OUTCOME

Most stock indexes and averages are weighted, which means that some stocks in the index are assigned greater value in the calculation than others.

Capitalization-weighted indexes are designed to reflect the economic

impact of companies with the highest **market capitalization**, which is calculated by multiplying the number of shares by their current market price. The majority of indexes are capitalization weighted, including the S&P 500 and the Nasdaq Composite Index.

Price-weighted indexes are more affected by changes in the prices of higher priced stocks than by changes in the value of lower priced stocks. The DJIA is a price-weighted index as is Japan's Nikkei.

Equal-weighted indexes and **averages** give equal attention to the relative, or percentage, changes in the price of all the stocks they measure, so the percentage change in the

ARITHMETIC vs. GEOMETRIC

While equally weighted indexes may address some imbalances, they may also understate or overstate the combined performances of the stocks they track. That's because the return of an equal-weighted index depends on whether the index is calculated as an arithmetic or geometric mean.

Indexes computed as an arithmetic mean, or simple average, tend to report higher returns than indexes computed as a geometric mean. A geometric mean is a compounded rather than averaged return and accounts for the timing and severity of drops in the index.

For example, the Value Line Geometric Index increases less in value during any one time period than the Value Line Arithmetic Index—despite the fact that the indexes include exactly the same stocks.

Constructing an Index

Crafting an index begins with making some critical decisions.

An index doesn't just happen. One of the companies that provides indexes must create it, typically to meet one or more objectives, such as tracking a market or market segment, providing a benchmark, or serving as the basis of a financial product, such as an index mutual fund.

While each index is a bit different, the process used to create one typically involves the same kinds of decisions, including:

- Defining the index's focus and scope
- Identifying the securities that will form its portfolio
- Determining how the index will be weighted
- Setting the criteria for changing the components of the index and how those changes will be made
- Fixing its baseline value

☑ *Focus*
☑ *Portfolio contents*
☑ *Weighting?*
☑ *Criteria for change*
☑ *Baseline value*

MAKING A LIST

While the scope of an index helps determine the number of securities the index includes, it doesn't determine the method for selecting the portfolio. There's choice there as well, as the same three indexes demonstrate.

The S&P 500 list, which has existed in its current form—though not with the same components—since 1957, is determined by an eight-person index committee. The committee weighs individual stocks, which might be eligible for inclusion based on certain criteria that have been set, while maintaining a balance among sectors and industries that make the index representative of the economy as a whole. The same committee also constructs the other S&P indexes.

The Russell company portfolios, including the Russell 2000, are determined statistically, using market capitalization data. The Nasdaq 100 and a range of other indexes are determined this way as well.

FINDING A FOCUS

There are limitless possibilities for what an index might track, and the companies that could be included in its roster. An example of this diversity is provided by three different indexes, each looking at the US stock market from a different perspective:

The Standard & Poor's 500 Index (S&P 500) is a broad-based index whose portfolio includes 500 widely owned large-capitalization US companies chosen to represent the sectors and industries that make up the economy.

The Russell 2000, on the other hand, has a much larger portfolio of small-capitalization stocks that includes, as its name suggests, 2,000 stocks. They are also included in the Russell 3000, a broad-market index.

The Dow Jones Industrial Average (DJIA) has a much narrower scope. Its portfolio includes just 30 large-capitalization stocks, each of them a household name.

The original DJIA portfolio, which was created by Charles Dow in 1896, is modified from time to time by the editors of *The Wall Street Journal* as they think appropriate to provide a picture of the US economy.

And in yet another variation, some socially responsible index portfolios are created using a series of qualifying screens to eliminate companies that don't meet certain financial or ethical requirements.

CHECKING IT TWICE

Index companies change their portfolios in a variety of ways and on different schedules. Some indexes are modified only when it seems appropriate to those making the decision, while others are updated regularly on an annual schedule. Between those extremes, there are a number of variations.

Providing a mechanism for change enables an index to keep up with the markets it tracks, as illustrated by the addition, in 1999, of technology stocks to the traditional manufacturing and energy base of the DJIA.

The flip side of choosing securities for inclusion in an index is identifying those that should be deleted. It's not an issue in the open-ended indexes such as the Dow Jones Wilshire 5000, where the number of securities in the index is larger than the name of the index indicates. But in order to add a company to one of the Standard & Poor's indexes, to the DJIA, or to the Russell 2000, another one has to go.

The most obvious disappearing acts are by companies that have been merged or acquired out of existence. Also excluded are formerly public companies that have been taken private. Some companies may be deleted because they no longer meet the defining terms, such as minimum market capitalization. In some cases, being deleted from an index is in effect a promotion—when, for example, a company moves up to the S&P 500 from the S&P MidCap 400.

FIXING A BASELINE

When an index company creates an index it also decides what the **baseline**, or starting point, will be. That's the value against which future changes in the index, typically expressed as a percentage, are measured. For example, the S&P 500 baseline was set at 10 for the period 1941-1943, while the baseline for the S&P Composite 1500 was set at 100 as of December 31, 1994.

The fact that different indexes start from different baselines helps explain their different readings, even when they track a similar market. For example, on a day in July 2005 when the S&P 500 closed at 1229.35, the DJIA closed at 10,646.56, and the Russell 2000 closed at 668.86.

In fact, the baseline is arbitrary. But with an established starting point, you can evaluate market performance in an historical context even though that record doesn't predict what will happen in the future.

NEW INCARNATIONS

Once an index has been created, it may be used to create a number of smaller, more focused indexes. Or it may be combined with one or more other indexes to create a broader index, or subdivided to create style-based indexes.

Decoding an Index

There's more to an index than meets the eye.

Whether a market index is up or down at the end of the trading day may be all you want to know. But if you're curious about where that closing number comes from, you'll need to understand how changes in an index are calculated.

DOING THE MATH

One of the principles underlying an equity index is that it provides a snapshot—or more precisely a constantly updated snapshot—of a specific market. Though indexes measure the markets they track in different ways, each calculation depends on similar pieces of information:

- Prices of the stocks in the index at a series of particular moments—for example, the S&P 500 is updated every 15 seconds during the trading day
- Number of shares for each company in the index
- Weighting factor, which is assigned to each stock in the index
- A divisor, or scale factor

Essentially, the index level is calculated by multiplying the prices, numbers of shares, and weighting factors to find the total value of the stocks. That number is divided by the divisor to yield the index level. Both the weighting factor and the divisor are unique to the index provider, though one or both may be public information.

A MATTER OF SCALE

An index divisor is set at the time the index is introduced and modified over time to keep the index smooth as changes are made to the index portfolio. For example, if the market value at the end of one trading day is $14 billion and the index level is 20, the divisor was 0.7 billion (If $14 ÷ x = 20, then x = 0.7). If changes are made after the market closes so that the market value of the new portfolio is $14.25 billion, and the index level remains 20, the divisor on the next day will be 0.7125 billion (If $14.25 ÷ x = 20, then x = 0.7125).

With a capitalization-weighted index, the divisor is modified each time its portfolio is changed. With a price-weighted equity index, the divisor must also be adjusted to account for stock splits since the lower price (and corresponding greater number of shares) will affect the stock's weighting. That isn't an issue in a capitalization-weighted index, since the capitalization remains the same whether there are more shares at a lower price or fewer shares at a higher price.

Price × Number of Shares

FINDING TOTAL RETURN

The total return of a stock index like the S&P 500, which is widely quoted as a benchmark for stock performance, is a calculation that depends on the change in the index, either positive or negative, plus reinvested dividends. Since an index is not an investment, but a statistical computation, however, the reinvestment occurs only on paper—or more precisely, in a software program. Rather than reinvesting dividends in the stocks that pay them, the index provider reinvests all dividends in the index as a whole.

Total return on an index is calculated daily, though the results are more typically provided as monthly, annual, or annualized figures, expressed as a percentage.

BEYOND THE OBVIOUS

The S&P 500 and other market indexes provide much more than a daily report on changing prices. They capture the market's history, which enables you to compare the present with the past. While the past can't predict the future, it can—and does—provide a context for thinking about what is possible.

Dividend **yield**, or the amount of the dividend divided by the stock price, is one measure that may have particular relevance for stock investors. Though the role of dividends as an indicator of business success tends to shift over time—they were de-emphasized in the long bull market starting in 1982 and re-emphasized with the reduced tax rate on qualifying dividends in 2003—they are a key element in total return.

Comparing the dividend yield of a specific company with the average yield of the industry to which the company belongs can be helpful in making

MAKING A CHANGE

Standard & Poor's completed the switch from outstanding shares to floating shares in September 2005. The company adjusts the number of shares quarterly unless a company's share count changes by 5% or more. Those changes are generally made weekly but in specific instances are handled more quickly.

investment decisions. An unusually high yield, for example, may be an important danger sign, either of an impending dividend cut or an imploding company.

Other details you can mine from an index include earnings growth, price/earnings and other relevant ratios, price momentum, relative strength, and total return.

$$\times \text{ Weight Factor} \div \text{Divisor} = \text{Index Level}$$

FLOATING SHARES

An equity index provider must determine the number of shares for each stock in its indexes to determine the market capitalization, which in most, though not all, indexes determines weighting. There are two ways to calculate the number of shares: An index may use **outstanding shares** or **floating shares**.

Outstanding shares are all of the shares that have been issued and are held by shareholders. Floating shares are the outstanding shares that are available for public trading. Shares that are closely held by founding partners or other groups with a controlling interest and aren't available for trading are not included. Neither are shares held in the company's pension fund, employee stock ownership plan, or similar programs.

The chief argument for using a float-adjusted index is that the value of the index is a more accurate reflection of the value of the security in the public marketplace.

OUTSTANDING SHARES

FLOATING SHARES

Indexes as Benchmarks

You can use indexes and averages as yardsticks to measure your investments.

Investors use indexes and averages as **benchmarks**, or yardsticks of investment return. These benchmarks can help you evaluate the performance of the overall market, particular market sectors and industries, individual securities, mutual funds, and ETFs.

For example, you can measure the performance of a large-cap stock fund against the S&P 500— the standard benchmark for large-cap equity

performance because it includes many of the stocks that this type of fund holds in its portfolio. You can also measure the fund against one of the Lipper large-cap mutual fund indexes—Growth, Core, or Value, depending on the fund's investment objective—and against a number of other indexes, including those provided by Morgan Stanley Capital International (MSCI) and Morningstar, Inc. Of course, the fund's return can also be measured directly against the performance of funds that are its primary competitors.

PORTFOLIO A

S&P 500 INDEX

S&P up	15%
Your portfolio up	8%
UNDER-PERFORMING BY	**7%**

PORTFOLIO B

S&P 500 INDEX

S&P down	10%
Your portfolio steady	
OVER-PERFORMING BY	**10%**

DIFFERENT BENCHMARKS

Not all benchmarks are indexes or averages. Long-term bond yields, for instance, are commonly measured against the yield of the 10-year US Treasury bond. Similarly, the benchmark for cash equivalent investments is the return on the 13-week US Treasury bill.

WHAT A BENCHMARK SHOWS

Since there's no absolute measure of investment performance, comparing your investments to benchmarks is really the only way to evaluate your results. For example, suppose your portfolio of large-cap stocks gained 8% in a particular year. That might seem fine. But if the S&P 500 gained 15%, that means your portfolio of large-cap stocks underperformed its benchmark by a wide margin.

Of course, you may want to give your large-cap portfolio a year or two to live up to your expectations. But if your investment mix underperforms its benchmark year after year, it may be time to rethink your strategy. On the other hand, if your portfolio of mid-sized company stocks held steady in a year that the S&P MidCap 400 lost 10%, you might decide that you've done well under the circumstances, even though your portfolio didn't realize any gains.

APPLES TO APPLES

One thing you want to avoid is measuring the performance of one **asset class** or **subclass** against the benchmark of another. For instance, let's say you are trying to evaluate the performance of your small-cap portfolio. In that case, an index that tracks small-company stocks, such as the S&P 600 or the Russell 2000, would be a much more accurate yardstick than a large-cap benchmark, such as the S&P 500.

From one year to the next, large-cap and small-cap stocks may report significantly different returns. For instance, in 2001 large-company stocks lost almost 12% of their value, while small-company stocks gained almost 23%. In 1998, on the other hand, large caps gained over 28%, while small caps lost more than 7%.

PORTFOLIO PERFORMANCE

The same caution applies when you evaluate bond performance against a benchmark. For example, the annual return on long-term US Treasury bonds tracked by a Lehman Brothers index is likely to be very different from the return on high-yield corporate bonds or 12- to 22-year general obligation (GO) municipal bonds, both tracked by Merrill Lynch.

THE BIGGER PICTURE

Just because an investment outperforms its benchmark in a particular year doesn't necessarily mean it's right for your portfolio. You still want to evaluate each investment in light of your risk tolerance, time horizon, and overall investment strategy. Similarly, an investment that misses its benchmark from time to time may still be a smart addition to your portfolio if it helps you diversify.

A TWO-WAY STREET

Just as you use benchmarks to measure performance, you can use them to evaluate the suitability of an asset class or subclass you're considering adding to your portfolio.

Let's say you want to diversify a stock portfolio that contains predominately large-cap stocks and you're considering adding a small-cap mutual fund or ETF. As part of your research, you can compare the performance of the individual small-cap funds you're investigating to the historical performance of this class overall as recorded by the S&P 600 or the Russell 2000. The benchmark will show where a particular fund fits in the universe of similar funds. (Keep in mind, however, that past performance is no guarantee of future results.)

You can also gauge how the particular characteristics of small-caps—for instance, their **risk-return profile** and **volatility**—compare to the behavior of equities included in a broader index, such as the Russell 3000 or S&P Composite 1500. Those indexes track a combination of small- and large-caps. The Russell 2000 is part of the Russell 3000 and the S&P 600 is included in the S&P Composite 1500.

Remember, too, that when you're evaluating a specific mutual fund, it's smart to compare its past performance to its target index over a number of years, rather than focusing on a single year in which the fund might have fared significantly better or worse than its benchmark.

INSTITUTIONAL BENCHMARKS

Institutional investors use benchmarks as well: When an actively managed mutual fund aims to "beat the market," its goal is to outperform the index that best matches its investment portfolio.

Some benchmarks are designed specifically for institutional investors, who use them to compare international markets, evaluate asset allocation models, determine standards for returns-based style analysis, and perform a number of other analyses. These indexes are governed by a strict set of rules that cover, among other things, the market capitalization of the stocks that may be included in a particular index.

Index Investing

You can ride the ups and downs of the market with an index-based investment vehicle.

An index might seem to be an ideal investment—a convenient way to "buy the market." The catch is that you can't invest in an index. It's a statistical calculation, not a security. And there are no shares for sale.

But you can invest in a wide range of index-based investment vehicles. These include index mutual funds and exchange traded funds (ETFs) in particular, as well as options contracts and futures contracts.

INVESTMENT PRODUCTS

Indexes aren't securities, and they aren't investments. So you're likely to hear them called investment products, investment instruments, or investment vehicles. That's the same language you use to describe derivatives such as futures and options.

CONTRACTUAL ISSUES

You can buy or sell contracts on index-based options or index-based futures, which allow you to hedge your portfolio or speculate on future changes in the value of a specific index within a particular time frame. Each contract is based on a specific index, and what it is worth at any time before it expires is determined by a variety of factors, including investor demand. Your profit or loss depends on how the index changes and the position you've taken on that outcome.

EXCHANGE TRADED FUNDS (ETFs)

Mutual funds, which own portfolios of securities and sell shares to investors, may be actively or passively managed. In an actively managed fund, the manager decides what to buy and sell and when to make those trades. In a passively managed fund, such as an **index fund**, the fund holdings are determined by the index that the fund tracks and change only when the securities in the underlying index change.

An **exchange traded fund (ETF)** is a flexible hybrid product that's part index mutual fund and part stock. An ETF portfolio contains the securities included in a particular index, just as an index fund does. But the fund is listed on a stock market and trades throughout the day as a stock does. In 2005, all ETFs in US markets are passively managed, though actively managed ETFs have been proposed and may become available.

SUPPLY AND DEMAND

The appeal of index-based investing has produced an interesting by-product. Not only has the number of investment possibilities increased, but so, too, has the number of indexes. The creation of new indexes is a direct response to increased demand from financial institutions that want to offer a greater number and wider variety of index-based products.

In order for a financial institution to offer an index fund or ETF that tracks a specific

BEATING AN INDEX

Of course, there are investors and money managers who do outperform the market, though only a few have done so consistently over long periods of time. Beating the indexes may be more likely in a sluggish or falling market, when an experienced manager may be able to avoid companies that are the biggest drag on an index and focus on those that are outperforming their peers. And as a rule, index funds that track small companies have produced spottier results than funds that invest selectively in small companies.

THE MARKET
Index-based
Investments

MODEL T FUND

In 1975, John Bogle, one of the pioneers of index investing, proposed a new category of mutual fund with what was, for the time, a radical investment objective: The fund wouldn't aim to beat the market as measured by the S&P 500, but would attempt to match it. That fund, the Vanguard 500 Index Fund Investor Shares (VFINX) is now the largest stock mutual fund in the United States. And, there are dozens of funds based on nearly all the major indexes, plus a number of funds linked to some of the smallest or most specialized indexes, both domestic and international.

sector, a particular investment style, or a socially responsible position, there must be an index that tracks that sector, style, or position.

Index providers, including Standard & Poor's, Dow Jones, Morgan Stanley, Lehman Brothers, and others, create and maintain indexes, which they license to financial institutions, giving them the right to use those indexes as the basis for their investment products. And financial institutions are willing to pay for the licenses because index-based products are both an important source of revenue and a key to staying competitive in the marketplace.

Dow Jones Indexes, for example, partners with over 300 licensees who offer more than 1,500 investment products based on its indexes. And Standard & Poor's has more than 550 license agreements with major financial institutions around the world.

BEING EFFICIENT

Despite its growing popularity, index investing had a difficult time gaining critical acceptance in the financial community. In no small part, that struggle can be attributed to the still-controversial **efficient market theory (EMT)**.

Proponents of the efficient market theory believe that a stock's current price accurately reflects all the information an investor can possibly know about the stock. They also maintain that you can't predict a stock's future price based on its past performance.

Their conclusion—which is vigorously contested, by **technical analysts** in particular—is that because it's impossible to predict market performance, it's also impossible for an individual or institutional investor to outperform the market as measured by an index like the S&P 500. Their investment strategy is based on the same principle that underlies index investing—namely, buying and holding the entire market, or more precisely, the market as represented by a broad-based index.

Index Mutual Funds

Index investing can be an economical way to diversify your portfolio.

Index mutual funds are designed to produce the same return that you would get if you owned all the stocks in a particular index. While you could buy and hold all of the thousands of stocks included in the Dow Jones Wilshire 5000, in the same proportion as they're weighted in the index, it's infinitely easier—and significantly cheaper—to invest instead in a fund that tracks that index.

There are index funds linked to almost every known stock index for large, mid-cap, and small companies—as well as bond market indexes and international indexes. And there are a number of index funds based on specialty indexes that track narrower market segments. In fact, you can create a truly diversified portfolio without venturing beyond index funds.

WHEN AN INDEX

FULL REPLICATION

Most index funds do what's known as full **replication**. That means they buy all of the securities in the funds they track. Others optimize their portfolios. For example, they may use complex mathematical models to identify securities from among those in the index or look for price inconsistencies on which they can capitalize.

ENHANCED

An **enhanced index fund** chooses selectively from a particular index portfolio in order to produce a slightly higher return. The goal is to narrowly beat the index by anywhere from a fraction of a percent to two percentage points but not more, since a wider spread would classify the enhanced fund as an actively managed mutual fund rather than an index fund.

Enhanced index fund managers may achieve higher returns by identifying the undervalued stocks in the index, adjusting

FEES TO AN END

The average **expense ratio** for an actively managed fund—which includes the management fees and operating expenses expressed as a percentage of the fund's net asset value (NAV)—is around 1.5%. On the other hand, the Vanguard 500 Index Fund Investor Shares (VFINX), the oldest and largest index fund, has an expense ratio of only 0.18%, almost nine times less.

That means the average actively managed fund must consistently outperform the Vanguard 500 Fund by 1.32 percentage points—or 132 basis points—just to deliver the same results. That's not impossible, but it's not always easy either. And what if the actively managed fund performs poorly? The higher expense ratio stays the same.

SHARES FOR RENT

To keep their expense ratios low, index fund managers may also use a variety of methods to offset the costs of running the fund—for example, by lending the fund's securities to investment firms for short sales. Those tactics are described in the fund prospectus.

FUND APPEALS

One reason for the popularity of index-based funds is that they tend to cost investors less than actively managed funds. That's because index-based fund portfolios are determined by the relevant indexes, and not by professional managers. In addition, the fund holdings are traded only when the index changes—sometimes only once a year or even less often than that.

Investors also like the **transparency** that index funds provide. Transparency, in this context, means that the fund holdings, and the percentage of the fund's portfolio that each of the holdings comprises, is clear at all times.

Many index funds also offer the additional advantage of risk-reduction that comes with having a widely diversified portfolio. Indexes do vary, however, and some are more diversified than others. Indexes that track securities that are limited to a narrow segment of the market, will obviously be less diversified than those that track a broad-based index.

GOES TO MARKET

holdings to include a larger proportion of securities in higher-performing sectors, or using other investment strategies, such as buying derivatives. While enhanced index funds may expose you to the risk of greater losses than their plain-vanilla counterparts, they may also offer an opportunity for higher returns.

QUANT

Quant funds are named for their quantitative investment style. They also aim to beat the index funds they imitate by relying on statistical analysis to decide which securities will top the benchmarks. For example, instead of buying all the stocks in the S&P 500, a quant fund would buy selected stocks—perhaps 350 of them—that their analyses indicate will turn a higher profit.

Each index fund's prospectus explains its approach to selecting investments, in addition to its expense ratio, historical returns, risk profile, and other information about the fund that must be reported.

It's important to keep in mind, however, that index funds that replicate the same index may vary in performance if their expense ratios differ. The higher the ratio, the lower your return will be, even when funds are making the same investments. In addition, some fund companies levy a **load**, or sales charge, on their index funds, though most companies don't, even when they levy loads on their other funds.

THE POP EFFECT

Since S&P 500 index funds alone own approximately 10% of the outstanding shares of each company in the index, changes in the index have historically had a positive, if temporary, effect on the prices of the stocks being added to an index. There's also been a comparable negative effect on the prices of stocks that were dropped. That's because all the funds tracking the index must update their portfolios. The impact of the changes is reduced, though, when the funds spread their updating process over several weeks rather than creating an artificial and temporary demand.

IN

OUT

Exchange Traded Funds

ETFs are an increasingly popular way to buy and sell investments.

One of the distinguishing features of modern trading is the speed at which information can be processed and shared. That speed, combined with innovative technology, has made it possible to invest in new ways. The prototypic exchange traded fund (ETF), the SPDR (pronounced Spider), debuted on the American Stock Exchange (AMEX) in 1993. Since then, more than 100 ETFs have been introduced in response to investor demand for these products.

IS IT A STOCK?
IS IT A MUTUAL FUND?
NO, IT'S AN ETF!

ETFs are hybrid investment vehicles that are part individual security and part mutual fund. With an ETF, you buy and sell shares in the collective performance of an entire portfolio of securities—sometimes described as a basket of securities—in the same way you buy and sell shares of a single stock.

Because of their growing popularity, you can find ETFs for nearly every published index, no matter how narrow a segment of the market it may track. In the United States, in most cases, there's only one ETF tracking each index—the exception is that both the SPDR and the iShares S&P 500 Index Fund hold all the stocks in the S&P 500. That helps to avoid potential liquidity problems, which may occur with multiple ETFs tracking the same index.

ASSESSING THE DIFFERENCES

Apart from its distinctive brand name and stock symbol, what distinguishes one ETF from another?

One difference is the fees, which are listed in the ETF prospectus as the fund's **expense ratio**, or percentage of the assets invested. For example, if an expense ratio is 0.8% and you've invested $10,000, only $80 is deducted from your dividends annually to cover your share of the cost of managing the ETF. The ETFs with the lowest fees tend to be the ones that invest in the most sought after, broadest-based indexes, a characteristic they share with index mutual funds.

Generally, you also pay a brokerage commission to buy or sell shares of an ETF. That cost varies, depending on the firm where you have an account, and can add up if you trade frequently or use a dollar cost averaging investment strategy that requires regular purchases. So you may want to consider cost carefully in in choosing between an ETF and a no-load index mutual fund and in choosing the firm through which you trade.

	Exchange traded funds	Index funds
Real-time quotes	Yes	No
Intraday trading	Yes	No
Commissions or sales charges	Yes	Sometimes
Shareholder services	No	Yes
End of day NAV = Trading price	No	Yes
Sales charges to reinvest earnings	Yes	Sometimes
Buy on margin or sell short	Yes	No

KISSING COUSINS

Unit investment trusts (UITs) have a strong family resemblance to ETFs and they've been around longer. Like ETFs, they're investment vehicles that purchase a fixed portfolio of investments and sell units, or shares, to investors. Those shares trade in the secondary market after issue. Bond UITs are set up to expire when the bonds in its portfolio mature, and equity UITs expire on a specified date in the future, though they may be rolled over, or extended.

One of the best-known trusts, the SPDR, trades under the ticker symbol SPY on the American Stock Exchange and tracks the S&P 500. Another is the DIAMONDS trust that tracks the Dow Jones Industrial Average. But, in fact, both are widely considered ETFs.

CREATING AN ETF

Before you can buy shares in an ETF, the fund must be created. The fund sponsor, usually a major money management firm, seeks approval from the Securities and Exchange Commission (SEC) and then accumulates a basket of securities that are included in a particular fund—stocks for a stock ETF or bonds for a bond ETF. The basket is equal in value to a fixed number of ETF shares.

The sponsor forwards the securities to a custodian, usually a bank, for safe-keeping. The custodian, in turn, sends the ETF shares to the sponsor, who offers them for sale. After the initial sale, investors buy and sell shares through a brokerage firm, just as they do stocks. In fact, three ETFs—the Nasdaq 100, the SPDR, and the iShares Russell 2000—are among the ten most actively traded stocks on the composite data for the Nasdaq Stock Market and the American Stock Exchange.

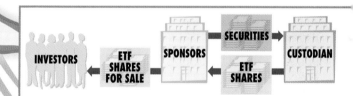

INVESTORS — ETF SHARES FOR SALE — SPONSORS — SECURITIES — CUSTODIAN — ETF SHARES

SECTOR BY SECTOR

One way to think of the global marketplace is as a set of building blocks, called sectors. Every asset that's traded on any of the world's markets belongs to a particular sector. Add up all the sector building blocks and you've got the total market. And you can find ETFs that correspond to just about every one.

WITH THE SPEED OF THE INTERNET!

DISTINCTIVE DIFFERENCES

Despite certain similarities to mutual funds, ETFs are different in a number of ways. Of course, in either case, you risk potential loss of value if securities prices decline or if you sell in a falling market.

- ETFs trade throughout the day at current market price, while mutual funds shares trade only once, at the end-of-day price

- ETFs don't have to buy and sell shares to accommodate shareholder purchases and redemptions, minimizing portfolio turnover and the potential tax consequences of capital gains or losses

- ETFs can be bought on margin or sold short, even on a downtick, which is useful in hedging or other risk management strategies

The Ins and Outs of ETFs

The more you know about ETFs, the more you may want to know.

Like mutual funds, each ETF has a **net asset value (NAV)**, that reports what a single share is worth at a particular point in time.

The NAV is determined by the total market capitalization of the securities the ETF holds, plus dividends or interest minus fund expenses, divided by the number of fund shares. In other words, the NAV is not a fixed value, and moves up or down as the price of the underlying investments change and the number of outstanding shares increases or decreases.

PREMIUMS AND DISCOUNTS

Unlike no-load mutual funds, though, you don't pay the NAV when you buy shares, and you don't receive that value when you sell. Instead, an ETF trades at the market price, which is determined by supply and demand as well as other market forces, just as it is when you're trading individual stocks. If other investors are buying when you buy, creating greater demand, you may pay more than the NAV. And if you buy when the majority is selling, you may pay less than the NAV.

If the price of an ETF is higher than the NAV, you're buying or selling at a **premium**. And if the price is lower than the NAV, you're buying or selling at a **discount**. The amount of the premium or discount is usually very small—and the more popular the ETF is, the lower the spread between market price and the NAV tends to be. You can find a particular ETF's premium or discount through the exchange on which it trades, from your financial adviser, or online at financial websites.

This price difference allows ETF sponsors, also called the authorized participants or market makers, to make a profit of a few cents per share each time they buy or sell shares. Since ETF shares

VALUE OF AN ETF SHARE

Market capitalization
of fund shares

+ Dividends or interest

− Fund expenses

÷ Number of fund shares

= NAV

NAV CHANGES AS:
- Share prices change
- Number of shares changes

IDENTITY SHIFT

In the past, closed-end mutual funds, which issue a fixed number of shares and are listed on a stock market, were often described as exchange traded funds. Unlike an index-based ETF, though, a closed-end fund typically builds a portfolio focused on a particular country or asset category.

tend to trade in extremely high volume, the small profits add up. In return, the ETF market gets the benefit of **liquidity**, which means it's easy for individual investors to find a buyer or seller at any time, especially when they're trading the most active ETFs.

A unique feature of ETFs is that institutional investors may buy or redeem large blocks of shares at the NAV with in-kind baskets of the fund's securities. This helps ensure that ETF prices don't deviate significantly from their NAVs and provides a buffer against potentially large premiums and discounts often associated with closed-end mutual funds.

ASSET ALLOCATION MADE EASY

Since the holdings in an ETF's portfolio are made public every day, and since those securities also appear in the index that the fund tracks, the asset class to which the ETF belongs is crystal clear.

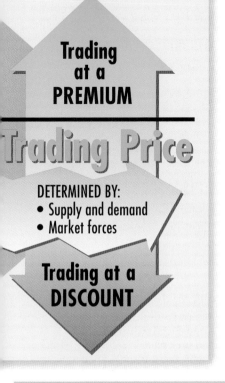

NAV vs. TRADING PRICE

Trading at a PREMIUM

Trading Price

DETERMINED BY:
- Supply and demand
- Market forces

Trading at a DISCOUNT

The advantage to an investor is that ETFs may simplify the process of building a portfolio that corresponds to a specific asset allocation model.

For example, the SPDR trust owns shares of the 500 large-capitalization stocks in the S&P 500, making it a large-cap equity ETF. You can similarly find mid-cap and small-cap equity ETFs, long-term corporate bond ETFs, and ETFs invested in a specific, sometimes narrow, sector—say companies that manufacture semiconductors.

That is not always the case with actively managed mutual funds. While mutual funds focus on a particular asset class, they may actually shift the makeup of the fund in some circumstances. For example, under certain market conditions some funds may hold a substantial percentage of their assets in cash. Others may seek to improve their returns by buying securities in different asset classes to take advantage of what's happening in the markets.

While those actions are perfectly legal, they might leave you underweighted in the asset class you have selected, and overweighted in another. For example, if you purchase a small-cap mutual fund that holds 50% of its assets in cash, you have only half the exposure to small-cap stocks that you had anticipated. Of course, you can also buy individual securities in different asset classes as you allocate your portfolio. That requires more research and many more transactions than simply purchasing an ETF.

GETTING DIVERSIFIED

ETFs, like other funds, simplify portfolio diversification since you don't have to evaluate individual securities and then buy them in sufficient numbers to protect yourself against portfolio risk.

For example, if you own shares of the Nasdaq 100 ETF (QQQQ), made up of the 100 largest nonfinancial companies listed on the Nasdaq Stock Market, you might reasonably anticipate—though nothing is guaranteed—that even if some of the stocks falter as part of the normal market fluctuation, other stocks will boom.

Since ETFs trade throughout the day, an added

advantage is the speed with which you can gain exposure to an underlying index and diversify your holdings. If, for example, your research indicates that there might be a surge in a certain sector's performance—particularly a sector in which you might be underweighted—you can make a tactical bet and buy an ETF based on that sector's index.

UNWRAPPING THE BUNDLE

ETFs have a high degree of transparency because the fund's sponsor, or provider, announces the contents of the ETF's portfolio at the beginning of each business day, generally through the National Securities Clearing Corporation (NSCC).

ETFs: Strategies, Taxes, and Risk Management

ETFs can play many parts in your investment strategy.

Although buying and holding is a viable strategy for ETFs, as it is for individual securities and open-end mutual funds, the recent boom in ETF popularity can partly be explained by their flexibility as an investment vehicle—they can be shorted, bundled, hedged, and optioned.

PAIRS TRADING

Pairs trading is a strategy that exploits both the similarities and differences between ETFs and stocks. Here's how it works: Suppose your research indicates that XYZ company has strong growth prospects but is in a sector that appears to be sluggish at best. One way to capitalize on the difference between the performance of XYZ stock and its entire sector is to buy the stock and short the sector ETF.

Shorting means borrowing shares of the ETF through your broker and selling them in the marketplace, expecting them to drop in price. If they do, you buy back the shares at the lower price, return them to your broker, and pocket the difference between what you sold them for and what you had to pay to rebuy them, minus interest and commissions.

Or, if the circumstances are reversed—the sector looks strong but XYZ company is struggling—you could do the exact opposite—namely, buy the ETF and short the stock. It's important to remember, however, that this strategy comes with obvious risks. If both the stock and the sector ETF produce results different from what you anticipated, your losses can be compounded.

DRYING OUT THE WASH

As part of a tax planning strategy, you may sell investments that have lost value during the year and use that loss to offset taxable capital gains on other investments. But it's crucial to the strategy's success to avoid what's known as a **wash sale**. That happens when you sell an investment that has lost value, realize that loss to offset other gains, and then rebuy what securities law describes as a substantially identical investment within 30 days.

To avoid a wash sale, you might sell an investment that has lost value to offset other gains, and then buy an ETF that is similar to the investment you sold, but not substantially identical to it—and thereby avoid hanging yourself out to dry. After 30 days, you may buy back your original investment and then decide whether to hold or sell the ETF.

TAX EFFICIENCY OF ETFs

OPTIONS FOR RISK MANAGEMENT

As ETFs have grown more popular, individual investors have grown more creative in using them to manage portfolio risk and hedge against potential losses in their portfolios. The most frequent tool is an options contract.

Two basic strategies for using ETF options conservatively involve **covered calls** and **protective puts**. Say, for example, you own shares in an ETF and would like to protect your unrealized gains against a potential downswing in the market. By **writing**, or selling, a covered call, you can do just that. You collect a premium for the call and if the option holder exercises the contract, you sell your ETF shares at the strike price. Keep in mind, however, that in doing so you also limit your potential earnings if the ETF trades at a price higher than the strike price of the call you wrote.

Another way to protect your ETF holdings against a steep drop in price is to purchase a protective put. That way, you have the right to sell your shares if the price falls below the strike price.

Buying a protective put means you'll be able to limit your loss if the price falls during the term of the contract, either by exercising your right to sell your ETF shares or by selling the contract itself. As a general rule, the more the ETF decreases in price, the more valuable the put may become. And if prices don't fall and your option expires unused, the typically small premium you pay may have provided some valuable peace of mind.

LOTS OF OPTIONS

The first options contract on an ETF was listed in 1998, on the S&P MidCap SPDR. In 2005, options on the SPDR tracking the S&P 500 were offered for the first time, to significant demand.

ETFs are relatively tax-efficient investments, especially when compared to actively managed mutual funds. One reason is that ETFs do not have to redeem shares for cash when you want to sell, as open-end mutual funds must do. That reduces turnover, limiting more costly short-term gains and eliminating what are known as **phantom gains**, which are fund earnings on which you may owe tax but which were paid before you purchased your shares.

Of course, if you own an ETF in a taxable account, you may owe tax on any capital gains you realize if you sell your shares. You'll also owe tax on any investment income, though dividend income from qualifying stock may be taxed at the lower long-term capital gains rate. You may also realize capital gains when the fund updates its portfolio to reflect changes in the index it tracks.

With both ETFs and mutual funds, you can decide when to sell your shares. For example, you may want to sell shares late in the year and use a potential capital loss to offset gains. Or you might decide to postpone a sale on which you'll realize gains until the next tax year.

Indexes Plus

Indexes take aim at a long list of moving targets.

Although many of the best-known indexes, such as the S&P 500 and DJIA, track the US stock and bond markets, they're only part of the picture.

There are multiple indexes reporting the activity of the world's major markets, including the London FTSE 100-share and 250-share measures of the London Stock Exchange, the Paris CAC 40, and the Tokyo Nikkei Stock Average, as well as smaller markets in Chile, Singapore, and Turkey,

to name just a few. In addition, index companies provide worldwide indexes that report composite results for dozens of markets.

In addition to securities indexes, there are dozens of others—some compiled by US government agencies and some by independent companies—which provide snapshots of the economy at a specific point in time.

INDEXES AROUND THE GLOBE

Morgan Stanley Capital International (MSCI) has developed one of the world's most comprehensive indexing systems, tracking both developed and emerging securities markets in various geographic regions. The MSCI-EAFE® is probably the best known, and the one against which US activity, as tracked by the S&P 500 and the comparable MSCI index, are most frequently compared. It covers stock markets in Europe (E), Australasia (A), and the Far East (FE). As is the case with other major indexes, there are both index funds and ETFs available on the EAFE.

The comprehensive S&P/Citigroup Global Equity Index Series tracks global stock market performance in all countries

that are considered investable. It includes companies with a free float market capitalization of US $100 million or greater, with a minimum annual trading liquidity of US $20 million.

Standard & Poor's also provides indexes of emerging markets that it has developed with the International Finance Corporation, a division of the World Bank. These S&P/IFC Indexes provide benchmarks that investors can use to evaluate the performance of newer markets that are eager to attract international capital.

Dow Jones Indexes track both country and world markets, including the Dow Jones China 88, Russian Titans 10, and the Euro STOXX 50.

SPEAKING THE SAME LANGUAGE

In 1999, MSCI and Standard & Poor's jointly developed the Global Industry Classification Standard (GICS) to establish a global standard for categorizing companies into sectors and industries based on their primary business activity.

The goal is to ensure that investors, asset managers, and investment researchers can make meaningful comparisons among the results that local, regional, and global indexes report. The two companies update the standard every year to keep the categories timely.

RIPPLE EFFECTS

Among the lessons that indexes teach is how interconnected the world's markets actually are. What happens in London and Toyko while US stock markets are closed—as reported by the FTSE and the Nikkei—is the driving force behind the prices of futures contracts traded before the opening bell on the New York Stock Exchange (NYSE). While the markets don't march in lockstep, when the FTSE is down, prices for futures contracts on the S&P 500 and the DJIA are usually down as well. And if the FTSE is up, those futures prices are generally up.

As the trading day develops, the expectation of gains or losses doesn't always materialize. But it happens often enough to influence investor behavior.

COMMODITIES INDEXES

What happens in the commodities marketplace has both an immediate and a long-range impact on the economy. For example, when indexes tracking those markets are significantly up or down in comparison to the previous year, it may indicate that a period of volatility is likely.

The best-known commodities indexes, including the Reuters Commodity Research Bureau Futures Price Index (CRB), the Goldman Sachs Commodity Indexes, and the S&P Commodity Indexes, each track somewhat different elements. For example, the CRB tracks 19 commodities—aluminum, cattle, cocoa, coffee, copper, corn, cotton, crude oil, gold, heating oil, hogs, natural gas, nickel, orange juice, silver, soybeans, sugar, unleaded gasoline, and wheat.

TAKING THE ECONOMIC PULSE

There are also a number of indexes that economists and lawmakers use to help them understand and predict changes in the economy.

- The **Index of Leading Economic Indicators** is the primary tool for forecasting changing patterns in the economy. Its ten components, which currently include the S&P 500, the average work week, and average initial claims for unemployment, are adjusted from time to time to help improve the accuracy of the index.

LEADING INDICATORS

109
108
107
106
105

Year 1   Year 2

- The **Consumer Price Index (CPI)** is compiled monthly by the US Bureau of Labor Statistics (BLS) and is used to gauge inflation by measuring changes in the prices of basic goods and services. The CPI, though widely acknowledged to be less than a perfect measure, is used as a benchmark for making adjustments in Social Security payments, wages, pensions, and tax brackets to keep them in tune with the buying power of the dollar.

Producer Price Index
In billions of dollars
$260
255
250   ■ New Orders
245   ■ 18-month moving avg.
240
225
220

Employment Cost Index
Weekly claims in thousands
400
375   Weekly
        4-Week
350   Average
325
300
275
     M J   N D J F

- The **Producer Price Index (PPI)** is also compiled monthly by the BLS and measures price change from the perspective of the seller, not the buyer. Since manufacturers often pass on the higher prices of wholesale items to their consumers, analysts use the PPI to anticipate changes in the CPI.

- The **Employment Cost Index (ECI)** is published quarterly by the BLS and measures the growth of employees' compensation, or the cost of labor, in private industry, as well as state and local government. Many economists look to the ECI for inflationary warning signs. A greater than expected increase in the index is often seen as an indicator of rising inflation, since employees' wages tend to increase before consumer prices.

Major US Equity Indexes

Equity indexes are reliable barometers of stock market performance.

Index providers make it possible for you to measure the performance of the US equity markets from multiple perspectives. Each provider offers a range of indexes, each with a slightly different focus, and defines the criteria for inclusion in each one.

Index	Number of stocks	Index weighting	Eligible securities
Standard & Poor's	**www.indices.standardandpoors.com**		
S&P 500	500	Capitalization-weighted	US companies with capitalization over $4 billion
S&P 500	500	Equal-weighted	Same as S&P 500
S&P 100	100	Capitalization-weighted	Drawn from S&P 500
S&P MidCap 400	400	Capitalization-weighted	$1 to $4 billion in market capitalization
S&P SmallCap 600	600	Capitalization-weighted	Less than $1 billion in market capitalization
S&P Super Composite 1500	1500	Capitalization-weighted	Combination of S&P 500, S&P MidCap 400, and S&P SmallCap 600
S&P Global 1200	1200	Capitalization-weighted	Global large caps comparable to S&P 500
Dow Jones Averages	**http://averages.dowjones.com**		
Industrial	30	Price-weighted	Blue chip stocks
Transportation	20	Price-weighted	Airline, railroad, and trucking companies
Utility	15	Price-weighted	Gas, electric, and power companies
Composite	65	Price-weighted	Industrial, Transportation, and Utility Averages
MSCI Indexes	**www.msci.com**		
US Large Cap 300	300	Capitalization-weighted	Large-cap US stocks
US Broad Market Index	2500 + microcap	Capitalization-weighted	Large-, mid-, small-, and micro-cap US companies
EAFE®	21 country indexes	Capitalization-weighted	Stocks of 21 developed countries excluding US and Canada

Index	Number of stocks	Index weighting	Eligible securities
Dow Jones Indexes	www.djindexes.com		
Dow Jones Wilshire 5000	More than 7000	Capitalization-weighted	All US company stocks with readily available prices
Dow Jones Wilshire 4500	Around 6500	Capitalization-weighted	DJ Wilshire 5000 excluding the S&P 500
US Large-Cap	More than 200	Capitalization-weighted	Large-cap companies
US Mid-Cap	More than 500	Capitalization-weighted	Mid-cap companies
US Small-Cap	More than 800	Capitalization-weighted	Small-cap companies
US Total Market	More than 1600	Capitalization-weighted	Combination of US Large-Cap, US Mid-Cap, and US Small-Cap
Frank Russell Company	www.russell.com		
Russell 3000	3000	Capitalization-weighted	3000 largest US companies
Russell 1000	1000	Capitalization-weighted	Largest 1000 of Russell 3000
Russell 2000	2000	Capitalization-weighted	Stocks 1001 to 3000 in Russell 3000 (Small-cap)
Russell MidCap 800	800	Capitalization-weighted	Smallest 800 stocks in Russell 1000 (Mid-cap)
Market Indexes	www.nasdaq.com, www.nyse.com, www.amex.com		
Nasdaq Composite	More than 3000	Capitalization-weighted	All stocks listed on The Nasdaq Stock Market
Nasdaq 100	100	Capitalization-weighted	100 largest nonfinancial companies listed on The Nasdaq Stock Market
NYSE Composite	More than 2000	Capitalization-weighted	All common stocks listed on the NYSE
NYSE US 100	100	Capitalization-weighted	100 largest US companies listed on the NYSE
NYSE International 100	100	Capitalization-weighted	100 largest non-US companies listed on the NYSE
AMEX Composite	More than 700	Capitalization-weighted	All stocks listed on the AMEX
Value Line	www.valueline.com		
Value Line (Arithmetic) Index	Around 1700	Equal-weighted	Stocks in Value Line Survey
Value Line (Geometric) Index	Around 1700	Equal-weighted	Same stocks as Arithmetic Index

Mutual Funds: Putting It Together

A mutual fund buys investments with money it collects from selling shares in the fund.

The idea of diversification is that it's smarter to own a variety of stocks and bonds than to risk attempting to meet your financial goals based on the successful performance of just a few. But diversifying can be a challenge because buying a portfolio of individual stocks and bonds can be expensive. And knowing what to buy—and when—takes time and concentration.

Mutual funds offer one solution: When you put money into a fund, it's pooled with money from other investors to create much greater buying power than you would have investing on your own. As a fund investor you own the fund's **underlying investments** indirectly rather than outright, as you do when you buy stock. Instead, you own shares of the fund.

Since a fund may own dozens of different securities, its success isn't dependent on how one or two holdings do. And the fund's professional managers keep constant tabs on the markets, trying to adjust the portfolio for the strongest possible performance.

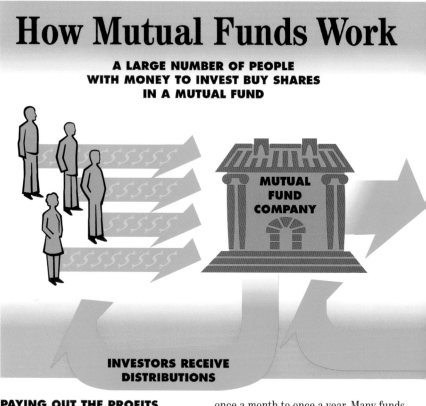

How Mutual Funds Work

A LARGE NUMBER OF PEOPLE WITH MONEY TO INVEST BUY SHARES IN A MUTUAL FUND

MUTUAL FUND COMPANY

INVESTORS RECEIVE DISTRIBUTIONS

PAYING OUT THE PROFITS

A mutual fund may make money in two ways: by earning dividends or interest on its investments and by selling investments that have increased in price. The fund distributes, or pays out, these profits (minus fees and expenses) to its investors.

Income distributions are paid from the income the fund earns on its investments. **Capital gains distributions** are paid from the profits from selling investments. Different funds pay their distributions on different schedules—from once a month to once a year. Many funds offer investors the option of reinvesting all or part of their distributions to buy more shares in the fund.

You pay taxes on the distributions you receive from the fund, whether the money is reinvested or paid out in cash. But if a fund loses more than it makes in any year, it can use the loss to offset future gains. Until profits equal the accumulated losses, distributions aren't taxable, although the share price of the fund may increase to reflect the profits.

HOW A MUTUAL FUND IS CREATED

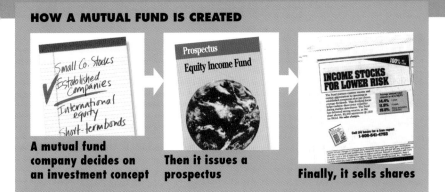

A mutual fund company decides on an investment concept

Then it issues a prospectus

Finally, it sells shares

A FUND SNAPSHOT

Investment companies, also called mutual fund companies, brokerage firms, banks, and insurance companies offer mutual funds for sale to individuals and institutional investors, such as money managers or pension funds. Most fund sponsors offer a range of fund types, while others specialize in one category of funds.

Each actively managed fund has a professional manager, an investment objective, and an investment program it follows in building its portfolio. The manager invests to produce a **return**, or profit, that's stronger than the return of the broad market from which the fund's investments are chosen and than competing funds with similar objectives.

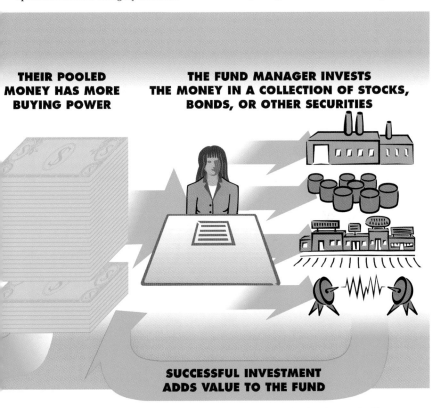

THEIR POOLED MONEY HAS MORE BUYING POWER

THE FUND MANAGER INVESTS THE MONEY IN A COLLECTION OF STOCKS, BONDS, OR OTHER SECURITIES

SUCCESSFUL INVESTMENT ADDS VALUE TO THE FUND

OPEN- AND CLOSED-END FUNDS

Most mutual funds are **open-end funds**. That means the fund sells as many shares as investors want. As money comes in, the fund grows. If investors want to sell, the fund buys their shares back. Sometimes open-end funds are closed to new investors when they grow too large to be managed effectively—though current shareholders can continue to invest money. When a fund is closed this way, the investment company may create a similar fund to capitalize on investor interest.

Closed-end funds more closely resemble stocks in the way they are traded. While these funds do invest in a variety of securities, they raise money only once and offer only a fixed number of shares that are traded on an exchange or over the counter. The market price of a closed-end fund fluctuates in response to investor demand as well as to changes in the value of its holdings.

The Mutual Fund Market

Mutual funds never invest at random. Each shops for products that fit its investment strategy.

There are three main categories of mutual funds:

- **Stock funds**, also called equity funds, invest primarily in stocks
- **Bond funds** invest primarily in corporate or government bonds
- **Money market funds** make short-term investments in an effort to keep their share value fixed at $1

THE PART DIVERSITY PLAYS

Most funds diversify their holdings by buying a wide variety of investments that correspond to their category. A typical stock fund, for example, might own stock in 100 or more companies providing a range of different products and services. The charm of diversification is that losses on some stocks may be offset—or even outweighed—by gains on others.

But some funds are extremely focused:

- **Precious metal funds** trade chiefly in mining stocks
- **Sector funds** buy shares in a particular industry, such as healthcare, electronics, or utilities
- **High-yield bond funds** seek high income from risky bonds

The appeal of focused funds is that when they're doing well, the returns can be outstanding. The risk is that a change in the economy or in the sector can wipe out any earlier gains in a period when the fund posts major losses.

A TEAM APPROACH

A fund's manager works with teams of **analysts** who evaluate fund holdings, assess the financial markets, and identify companies that may be appropriate additions to the fund portfolio.

A fund also employs **traders**, who stay tuned to the market and buy or sell specific securities when the price is within the range the manager has set, based on the analysts' research. The fund's back office manages the logistics of these transactions, which may involve buying and selling millions of dollars of securities each day.

At the close of the trading day—4 p.m. in New York—the fund determines its price per share, and all the money investors have put into the fund during the day is invested to buy shares at that price.

STOCK FUNDS

The name says it all: Stock funds invest in stocks. But stock fund portfolios vary, depending on the fund's investment objectives. For example, some stock funds invest in well-established companies that pay regular dividends. Others invest in younger, more growth-oriented firms or companies that have been operating below expectation for several years.

Unlike individual investors, who might buy several different types of stocks to diversify their portfolios, a fund typically concentrates in one area, like blue chips or small-company stocks. A fund's prospectus identifies its major holdings and its investment goals—though funds sometimes buy more widely to try to provide stronger returns.

CONSCIENCE FUNDS

Socially responsible funds attract investors whose strong political, social, or religious convictions make them unwilling to put money into companies whose business practices are at odds with their beliefs. A fund might avoid companies with poor environmental records, with specific employment practices, or those selling certain products. In its prospectus, each fund explains the criteria, called **screens**, it uses to find acceptable investments.

BOND FUNDS

Like bonds, bond funds provide income. Unlike bonds, however, these funds have no maturity date and no guaranteed repayment of the amount you invest, in part because the fund's holdings have different terms.

On the plus side, you can automatically reinvest your distributions to buy more shares. And you can buy shares in a bond fund for much less than you would need to buy a bond portfolio on your own—and get a diversified portfolio to boot. For example, you can often invest $1,000 to open a fund, and make additional purchases for smaller amounts.

Bond funds come in many varieties, with different investment goals and strategies. There are investment-grade **corporate bond funds** and riskier junk bond funds often sold under the promising label of high-yield. You can choose long- or short-term **US Treasury funds**, funds that combine issues with different maturities, and a variety of tax-free **municipal bond funds**, including some limited to a particular state.

IT'S ALL IN THE FAMILY

Mutual fund companies usually offer a variety of funds—referred to as a family of funds—to their investors. Keeping your money in the family can make it easier to transfer money between funds, but like most families, some members do better than others.

MONEY MARKET FUNDS

Money market funds try to maintain their value at $1 a share, so they're often described as cash equivalent investments. Typically, you earn interest on the investments the fund makes. Since these funds are considered stable in value, some investors prefer them to stock or bond funds. But the interest the funds pay is low when interest rates are low.

As an added appeal, most money market funds let investors write checks against their accounts. There's usually no charge for check-writing—although there may be a per-check minimum.

BOND FUNDS
- SAFER OR RISKY
- SHORT-TERM OR LONG-TERM

HIGH-YIELD TAXABLE FUNDS

INTERMEDIATE NDS

GENERAL UNICIPAL DEBT

GINNIE MAEs

TAX-FREE FUNDS

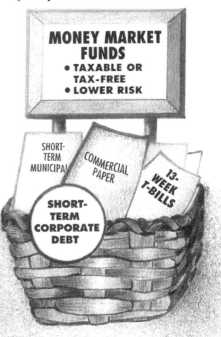

MONEY MARKET FUNDS
- TAXABLE OR TAX-FREE
- LOWER RISK

SHORT-TERM MUNICIPAL

COMMERCIAL PAPER

13-WEEK T-BILLS

SHORT-TERM CORPORATE DEBT

BALANCED FUNDS

Rather than choosing stock funds and bond funds to build a diversified portfolio, you may prefer a **balanced fund**. A balanced fund invests in both stocks and bonds, allocating a percentage to each—such as 60% to stocks and preferred stocks and 40% to bonds. You can find the specific guidelines in the fund's prospectus. A balanced fund may provide a less volatile return than a fund investing in a single asset class.

TARGET-DATE FUNDS

If you're investing in mutual funds in a retirement savings plan, you may want to consider a **target-date fund**, sometimes called a lifecycle fund. For example, if you plan to retire in 2035, you might choose XYZ Fund Retirement 2035. The XYZ fund company will invest primarily in stocks for a number of years, and then move more money into bonds and perhaps cash as 2035 gets closer, with the goal of achieving growth now to provide income later.

The Language of Mutual Funds

Mutual funds don't keep performance secrets from their shareholders.

You can find a mutual fund's current price—and often much more information about the fund—in a newspaper or other financial publication, on financial news websites, or on an investment company's website. Unlike a stock or an exchange traded fund (ETF), whose price changes constantly throughout the day as investors buy and sell shares, a mutual fund's **net asset value (NAV)** is fixed at the end of each trading day. That price remains in effect until the close of trading on the next day.

FIGURING THE PRICE

After the markets close, each mutual fund:

- Multiplies the final prices of each of their underlying investments by the number of shares of that investment the fund owns

- Adds those amounts to figure total value and subtracts fees and expenses

- Divides the total value by the number of fund shares that investors own to calculate the fund's new NAV

This information is forwarded to NASD, formerly the National Association of Securities Dealers, which passes it to financial reporting firms.

These companies calculate each fund's performance based on the most recent data. Some of them, including Standard & Poor's, Lipper, and Morningstar, evaluate the funds using many different criteria, such as returns over specific time periods, performance compared to other funds with the same objective, and the suitability of funds for specific investor goals. This information is available in newspapers, on financial websites, and from financial advisers.

NEWSPAPER REPORTS

The information in a mutual fund table is organized alphabetically by investment company. Beneath each company name, the funds it sponsors are listed alphabetically by fund name. If a company offers

more than one group, or family, of funds, or different classes of funds, the groups are listed alphabetically under the company name and followed by the specific funds within that group.

Daily reports are usually limited to the most recent NAV and percentage change from the previous trading day. But the monthly and quarterly reviews provide more detail about fund cost and performance.

NAV$	FUND NAME	INV OBJ
Performance Fds		
22.98	EqCon p	LC
23.05	EqIns	LC
10.19	INGI I	IG
15.22	MCGr p	MC
15.32	MCpGrl	MC
8.57	SmCap I	SC
10.01	STGI I	SU
Luna Funds		
18.90	New Fund	XC
18.23	Full Fund	MP
29.63	Waning Fund	SB
Smith Funds		
7.40	Asia A	PR
9.84	GlSmCA p	GL
9.42	GlSmCB p	GL
9.50	IntlA	IL
8.92	IntlB p	IL
8.37	WldOpA p	GL
7.77	WldOpB p	GL
9.07	CoreBondA	AB
21.50	LgCapGA p	LG
17.39	LgCapV A p	SE
20.49	LgCpCoA p	SE
12.48	MaMuA p	GL
20.51	MdCpCoA p	GL
12.43	MgGvA p	AB
15.26	MgMuA p	LG
13.07	MuFI A	

NAV$ is the price per share of the fund before sales charges, if any, are added. A fund's NAV changes to reflect the changing value of its underlying investments and the number of outstanding shares. NAV isn't necessarily an indication of the strength or weakness of the fund.

Name, followed by an **A, B**, or other letter, indicates a class of shares, and lower case letters report that the fund charges a distribution fee (p), a redemption fee (r), or both fees (t).

Year-to-date percent return (YTD) is the total return since the beginning of the current year. For example, Smith Asia fund has 3.1% return. This means the value of an investment that's been in the fund since January 1 has increased 3.1%, after fund operating expenses are subtracted, assuming that all distributions were reinvested.

Fund objective describes the fund's investment goal using a two-letter symbol such as **LC** for large-cap core or **IL** for international funds. Examples of that category are the Smith International funds. Symbols may differ from paper to paper, so check each paper's explanatory notes to interpret these and other abbreviations in the charts.

Fund performance, calculated as **total return**, is reported for several different time periods. The results are figured assuming that all distributions have been reinvested, and are reduced for annual operating expenses but not sales or redemption charges.

The longer the fund's history, the more clearly you can see how it has performed in different market conditions.

The figure for **1 year** reports on the previous 12 months. The reports for **3, 5, and 10 years**, when they're available, are annualized to give you the average figure per year. That helps to explain why the 5-year or 10-year returns for some funds are much stronger than for 1 or 3 years. Luna's New fund is one example.

Ranking compares a fund with other funds of the same general type or the same objective, or both. The ranking may use letters—with A being the highest and E the lowest—or numbers, typically from 1 to 5. Be sure to check the footnotes to find out whether 1 or 5 is the highest ranking.

You'll find that some charts provide one ranking per fund, as this one does, and others provide two, such as ⅓ or ⅔. The notes will explain what the numbers mean.

	TOTAL RETURN & RANK †ANNUALIZED				MAX INIT CHRG	EXP RATIO
YTD	1 YR	3 YR†	5 YR†-	10 YR†		
+6.3	−15.3 D	+2.1 D	+13.4 C	NS ..	5.25	1.12
+6.3	−15.1 D	+2.3 D	+13.7 C	NS ..	0.00	0.87
−0.6	+11.9 B	+5.4 D	+6.4 C	NS ..	0.00	0.75
+9.0	−1.3 D	+1.8 D	+12.0 D	NS ..	5.25	1.36
+9.1	−1.1 D	+2.0 D	+12.3 D	NS ..	0.00	1.11
+6.7	−1.5 D	−6.2 E	NS ..	NS ..	0.00	1.27
+0.4	+9.3 C	+6.0 B	+6.0 C	NS ..	0.00	0.70
10.8	+0.1 A	+10.7 A	+15.7 B	+17.1 B	0.00	1.73
+3.5	+5.5 A	+2.1 D	+3.7 E	+5.1 E	0.00	1.47
+0.3	+4.9 E	+4.3 E	+4.2 E	+3.9 E	0.00	1.02
+3.1	−14.6 A	+3.7 C	NS ..	NS ..	5.75	2.10
+2.7	−12.8 B	+7.3 B	NS ..	NS ..	5.75	2.10
+2.6	−13.8 C	+6.4 B	NS ..	NS ..	0.00	2.85
+4.3	−22.4 C	−1.9 E	+6.7 B	+7.1 C	5.75	1.53
+4.2	−23.0 D	−2.6 E	+5.9 C	NS ..	0.00	2.29
+4.0	−9.6 B	+4.8 B	+10.7 B	+12.0 B	5.75	1.56
+3.9	−10.3 B	+4.0 C	+9.9 C	NS ..	0.00	2.31
−0.6	+10.2 D	+4.4 D	+5.8 D	+6.5 E	4.75	1.17
+6.7	−13.6 A	−1.3 E	NS ..	NS ..	5.75	1.25
+6.3	−15.3 D	+2.1 D	+13.4 C	NS ..	5.25	1.12
+6.3	−15.1 D	+2.3 D	+13.7 C	NS ..	0.00	0.87
−0.6	+11.9 B	+5.4 D	+6.4 C	NS ..	0.00	0.75
+9.0			+12.0 D	NS ..		

Max(imum) init(ial) charge reports the front-end load, if any, but not back-end loads. Some papers list the maximum initial and exit charges. If the fund is a no-load, an N/A, NO, or 0.00 appears in the sales charge column. That's the case with Luna funds and five of the Performance funds. Three Smith funds are B shares.

Exp(ense) ratio is the percentage of the fund's current income that's deducted each year to cover your share of the fund's operating expenses. Here, they vary from less than 1% to 2.85%.

ONLINE QUOTES

Looking for mutual fund quotes online is fast and efficient. If you want fund price and return information, you can find it for free on the investment company's website or on a range of financial and general news sites.

To get the fund's price, you enter the fund's name or its trading symbol.

The next screen almost always includes a fund's current NAV, daily and year-to-date returns, and returns over several years. It may also include a ranking for the fund.

If you want more comprehensive fund analysis, you can find that, too. Many sites provide a history of the fund's distributions and a list of the fund's top **holdings**, by company and by sector. Some sites may provide graphs of a fund's performance and links to news stories about the fund.

Evaluating Mutual Funds

All mutual funds may be created equal, but some are more equal than others.

You may be looking for a mutual fund to help diversify your portfolio or meet a specific objective, such as long-term growth or current income. With several thousand funds to choose from, how do you narrow the choice?

EVALUATING A FUND

The important elements in any mutual fund evaluation include:

- **The cost of investing, based on the fund's expense ratio and turnover rate**
- **Its performance history**
- **Its risk profile**
- **Its management team**

The **cost** of investing in a fund has a predictable effect on the fund's performance. The higher the fund's **expense ratio**, which is the percentage of your account's value that you pay in annual fees, the lower your long-term return. That's because every dollar you pay in fees reduces both the present value of your account and the amount available for reinvestment.

Turnover rate is a measure of how frequently the fund buys and sells investments. Funds with a high turnover rate tend to have high transaction costs, which are paid out of the fund's income, and therefore reduce its return. Frequent selling can also produce short-term capital gains, which may mean you realize taxable investment income that you hadn't planned upon.

Past performance shows the fund's returns in previous years. While this measure doesn't guarantee future returns, it does tell you where the fund has stood in relation to comparable funds and appropriate benchmarks and whether its returns have been consistent or erratic. Performance is affected by the general direction of the markets and what's in the fund's portfolio, which reflects the thinking and the skill of the fund management. Before you invest in a strong-performing fund, it pays to check if the managers responsible for that performance are still at the helm. If they are, you have a better sense of what may happen in the future than if they've left.

One measure of **risk** is a fund's **volatility**, or its deviation—above and below—its average return. The amount of risk you're comfortable with will depend in large part on your time frame for holding the fund.

A DETAILED ROADMAP

You can find much of the information you need to evaluate a fund all in one place. The Securities and Exchange Commission (SEC) requires all mutual funds to publish a **prospectus** and provide a copy to potential investors before they purchase shares or along with the confirmation of an initial investment in a fund.

In addition to stating the fund's objective and explaining the way it invests, the prospectus explains the fund's fees, past performance, after-tax returns, and risk profile. It lists the portfolio holdings, identifies the fund manager, and, if there is a sales charge, explains the cost of choosing different classes of shares.

Funds also provide supplementary materials, such as the annual Statement of Additional Information (SAI), which details the fund's policies on borrowing, brokerage commissions, and other financial data. Most fund companies also have extensive websites that provide a great deal of information about their funds.

RATINGS & RANKINGS

The work of independent professional analysts is another important resource in evaluating funds. In addition to detailed analyses of the funds they cover, independent research firms, such as Standard & Poor's, Morningstar, and Lipper, also rate or rank mutual funds. A **rating** is based on how well a fund meets a specific set of criteria. A **ranking** is the relative standing of a fund when compared to funds in the same category.

For example, Standard & Poor's ranks funds on their three-year **Sharpe Ratio**, which is the fund's return minus the return on 3-month Treasury bills, divided by the fund's standard deviation. **Standard deviation** is a measure of volatility, or the extent to which the fund's return varies above and below its average return.

The top 10% of funds in each style peer group receive a 5 STARS rank, the next 20% receive 4 STARS, the next 40% receive 3 STARS, the next 20% receive

2 STARS, and the bottom 10% receive 1 STARS. In addition, each fund is assigned a numerical position in the hierarchy of all funds.

In contrast, Morningstar, which also uses a star system, rates funds based on risk-adjusted total return, combining performance and risk in one evaluation.

Lipper evaluates funds on the strength and consistency of their success in meeting their investment objectives and identifies the strongest as Lipper Leaders.

Of course, rankings and ratings don't tell the whole story. But if you understand the basis for the evaluations, they can provide a useful starting point.

These and other research firms provide some analyses on their websites, and you can also subscribe to receive more detailed reports. If you work with a broker or financial adviser, he or she may provide this research. You can also check to see if your public library carries any of these research reports.

TRANSPARENCY ISSUES

Most mutual funds trade frequently but publish a list of holdings quarterly. That raises the possibility of **portfolio overlap**, which means you might be more heavily invested in a single company than you're aware if several funds have added it to their portfolios. That, in turn, may affect the extent to which your overall portfolio is diversified and potentially increase your investment risk.

Fund Objective and Style

If you know what you want to achieve, you can probably find a fund that shares that goal.

Every mutual fund has an investment objective, which it describes in its prospectus. The fund's name often reflects the objective—for example, a fund that seeks a balance of growth and income might call itself the ABC Growth and Income Fund.

Most fund objectives are designed to provide a particular type of return, sometimes within a specific time frame. As a result, the fund objective has a major impact on the types of securities that dominate the fund's portfolio.

Explicit fund names are also good indicators of how the fund invests. That's largely because SEC rules require that any fund whose name suggests a certain type of investment must commit at least 80% of its assets to those securities.

SIZE MATTERS

One way that an equity fund may define its objective, and then invest to achieve it, is to concentrate on stocks issued by companies of a specific size, based on **market capitalization**, or **market cap**. Market cap is figured by multiplying the company's current price per share by the number of outstanding shares.

Companies are generally divided into three sizes—large-cap, mid-cap, and small-cap—and so are the funds that invest primarily in one of these groups.

Large-cap funds buy stock in established companies with capitalizations greater than $10 billion.

Mid-cap funds purchase equity in companies valued between $2 billion and $10 billion.

Small-cap funds buy stocks of companies with less than $2 billion. A fourth category, called micro-cap, focuses on even smaller companies.

Multi-cap funds invest in companies of all sizes.

Size typically affects the way an investment behaves as market conditions change. In general, though not in every case, the smaller the market cap, the greater the risk to your **principal**, or amount invested, and the greater the potential for a substantial return.

ALL IN THE TIMING

Bond funds, in contrast, tend to differentiate their investments based on issuer, rating, or term. Here, too, the name of the fund is generally a good indicator of the way it invests.

For example, a bond fund whose objective is the highest possible current income may concentrate on the lowest rated bonds that meet its criteria. Similarly, a fund seeking tax-free income will concentrate on municipal bonds, perhaps from a single state. And a fund whose objective is long-term income will buy high-rated corporate or Treasury issues, or both.

STYLE IN A BOX

A stylebox is visual shorthand for categorizing individual mutual funds by market cap and investment style. It's designed to help investors pinpoint a fund's basic characteristics and understand the fund's risk and return profile. The nine-category styleboxes illustrated here were originally developed by Morningstar as an asset allocation tool.

INVESTING WITH STYLE

Each fund manager adopts an **investing style**, or methodology, to help the fund meet its objective.

One approach is to buy securities that are selling for less than the manager believes they're worth. That's called **value investing**, and the assumption is that because the securities are undervalued, the price will rebound.

A contrasting style, which applies more directly to equities than to debt, is **growth investing**. Growth managers focus on stocks they think will increase substantially in price and have the potential to provide greater returns than the market as a whole. But these stocks also carry greater risk because their prices tend to be volatile.

Blend investing, sometimes called **core investing**, is a combination of these approaches, where the fund manager tries to find the right balance of undervalued investments and those with strong growth potential. **Contrarian** investing, on the other hand, means buying securities that other managers are shunning.

Differences in style help explain why funds with the same investment objective may produce different results, both in the short term and over longer periods. Under some market conditions, for example, value stocks may provide much stronger returns than growth stocks do, while the reverse may be true under different conditions. As a result, managers following a particular style may have some strong years and some lean ones.

ELEMENTS OF STYLE

A **conservative style** focuses on preserving principal by avoiding risk to principal. A moderate style tries to balance capital preservation with taking risks that may result in a greater return. An **aggressive style** takes bigger risks in pursuit of potentially even greater returns.

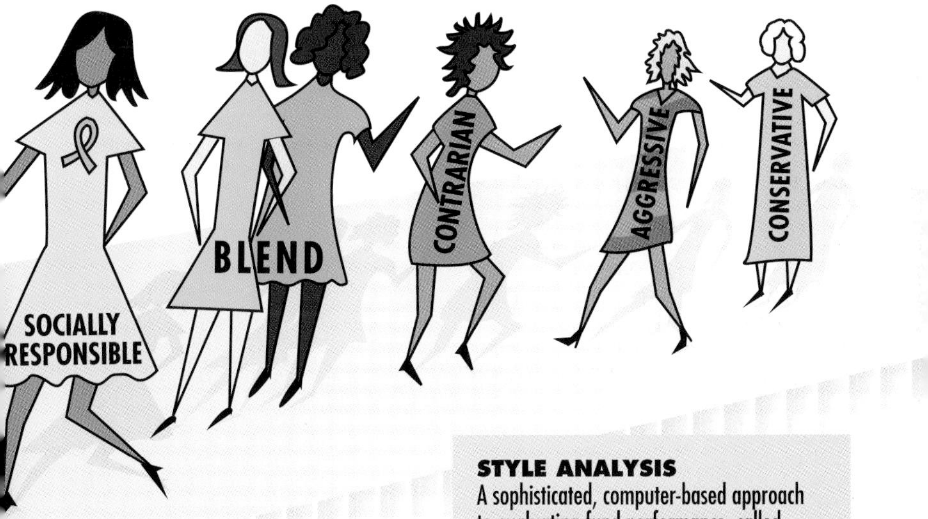
SOCIALLY RESPONSIBLE
BLEND
CONTRARIAN
AGGRESSIVE
CONSERVATIVE

STYLE ANALYSIS

A sophisticated, computer-based approach to evaluating fund performance, called **style analysis**, seeks to identify a fund's underlying investment style based on the way in which its returns correlate with a variety of style indexes.

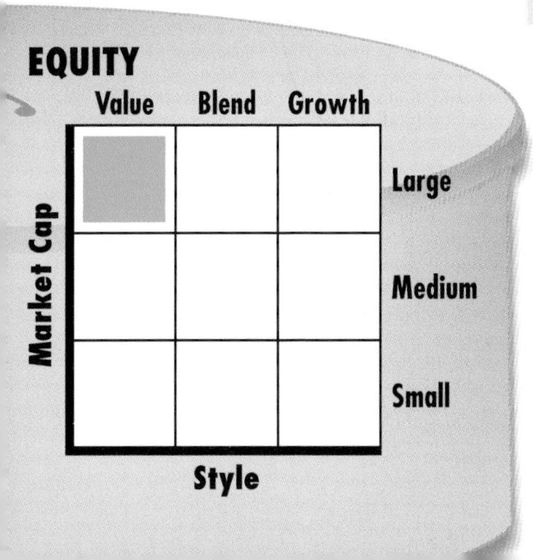
EQUITY
Value
Blend
Growth
Large
Medium
Small
Market Cap
Style

CATCH THE DRIFT?

You expect a fund to invest in a certain way based on its objective and style. But sometimes, to compensate for weak performance in its core investment category, a fund's managers may decide to alter the investment mix. That **style drift** could create an imbalance in your portfolio, exposing you unwittingly to greater risk.

Targeted Investments

Mutual funds aim at particular targets and try to hit them by making certain types of investments.

INVESTMENT OBJECTIVE

Every actively managed mutual fund—stock, bond, or money market—is established with a specific investment objective that fits into one of three basic goals:

- **Current income**
- **Some income and growth**
- **Future growth**

But within those categories, there's enormous variety that results from the way an individual fund invests. For example, funds that fit into the growth category can be subdivided by geographic area, or the home countries of the companies they invest in, by their timetable for the growth they seek, and by the level of risk they take to achieve their objective. Any fund that describes itself as seeking aggressive growth generally is taking more than average risk.

ANTICIPATING RISK

One risk you face as a mutual fund investor that's not included in the risk assessment that funds must provide about themselves—including risk to principal, interest rate risk, and currency risk—is the probability that a number of different funds with different objectives may invest in the same companies, creating what's sometimes known as **portfolio overlap**.

It may happen because all actively managed mutual funds try to provide the best possible results and sometimes deliberately buy investments outside their normal focus to improve their bottom line. If several of the funds you own all bulk up on the same star performer, you may have a much less diversified mutual fund portfolio than you intend—or even realize.

FUNDS TAKE AIM

These charts group funds into three categories by investment objective. They also illustrate the correlation between a fund's objective and the risks it may face.

INCOME FUNDS

Kind of fund	Investment objective	Potential risks	What the fund buys
Agency bond	Regular income plus return of principal	Value and return dependent on interest rates	Securities issued by US government agencies and related institutions
Corporate bond	Steady income, capital gains	Interest-rate changes and inflation, default	Highly rated corporate bonds, with various maturities
High-yield bond	Highest current income	High-risk bonds in danger of default	Low-rated and unrated corporate and government bonds
International money market	Income and currency gains	Changes in currency values and interest rates	CDs and short-term securities
Municipal bond	Tax-free income	Interest-rate changes and inflation, default	Municipal bonds in various maturities
Short-/inter-mediate-term debt	Income	Less influenced by changes in interest rate	Different types of debt issues with varying maturities, depending on type of fund
US Treasury bond	Steady income, capital gains	Interest-rate changes and inflation	Long-term government bonds

GROWTH AND INCOME

Kind of fund	Investment objective	Potential risks	What the fund buys
Balanced	Income and growth	Less growth during strong equity markets than all-equity funds. Dividend cuts	Part stocks and preferred stocks (usually 60%) and part bonds (40%)
Equity income	Income and growth	Less growth during strong equity markets than all-equity funds. Dividend cuts	Blue chip stocks and utilities that pay high dividends
Growth and income	Growth plus some current income	Less growth during strong equity markets than all-equity funds. Dividend cuts	Stocks that pay high dividends and provide some growth
Income	Primarily income	Interest-rate changes and reduced dividend payments	Primarily bonds, but some dividend-paying stocks

GROWTH FUNDS

Kind of fund	Investment objective	Potential risks	What the fund buys
Aggressive growth, also called capital appreciation	Long-term growth	Very volatile and speculative. Risk of above-average losses to get above-average gains	Stocks of new or under-valued companies expected to increase in value
Emerging markets	Growth	Can be volatile, putting principal at risk. Currency fluctuation, management, and political risks	Stocks in companies in developing countries
Global equity	Global growth	Gains and losses depend on currency fluctuation. Can be volatile, putting principal at risk	Stocks in various markets including the United States
Growth	Above-average growth	Can be volatile. Some risk to principal to get higher gains	Stocks in mid-sized or large companies whose earnings are expected to rise quickly
International equity	International growth	Potentially volatile, based on currency fluctuation and political instability	Stocks in non-US companies
Sector	Growth	Volatile funds, dependent on right market timing to produce results	Stocks in one particular industry, such as energy or transportation
Small-company growth	Long-term growth	Volatile and speculative. Risk of above-average losses to get higher gains	Stocks in small companies traded on the exchanges or over-the-counter (OTC)
Value funds	Growth, some income	Often out of step with overall market. May fail to rebound	Stocks in companies whose prices are lower than they seem to be worth

HEDGING

International fund managers may use a practice called hedging to protect the return on their funds. Hedging, in this context, means anticipating and offsetting possible future changes in the relative values of different currencies, specifically the dollar in relation to the currencies of countries where the fund invests. The most common tactic is to buy futures contracts that guarantee fixed exchange rates at specific points in the future. Funds that hedge may put up to 50% of their total assets in currency contracts rather than stocks or bonds. But other funds don't hedge at all, figuring that exposure to other currencies is part of the reason for investing overseas.

Fund Sales Charges

Mutual fund sales charges aren't necessarily a burden, but they are a load.

When you buy shares of a mutual fund from a fund company that pays intermediaries, such as brokers, to sell its funds, you pay a **sales charge**, or commission to cover that cost. That charge is known as a **load**, and the funds with sales charges are called load funds.

In most cases, a fund company offers either load funds or no-load funds, for which there are no sales charges. But some companies offer both types because they want to reach investors who buy directly from the fund as well as those who buy through an intermediary.

FRONT AND CENTER

Sales charges can be assessed at different times. When you buy a mutual fund with a **front-end load**, the fee is figured as a percentage of the amount you're investing, typically in the 4% to 5% range. Since the fee is subtracted up front, you actually purchase fewer shares than if no sales charge were levied. For example, if you're investing $5,000 in a fund that has a 4% front-end load, you'll actually be purchasing $4,800 worth of shares and paying a $200 sales charge.

BACK IT UP

You pay a **back-end load** on the other end of the transaction—when you sell shares. Unlike front-end loads, which are figured as a percentage of your purchase amount, back-end fees may be calculated in different ways, including as a percentage of the fund's NAV.

Also called a **contingent deferred sales charge (CDSC)**, the back-end load diminishes, usually by about one percentage point each year you own the shares. That means the longer you wait to sell, the lower the rate at which the sales charge is calculated. And if you hold your investment long enough, usually five to seven years, the back-end load will often disappear altogether.

KNOW WHEN TO HOLD THEM

Mutual fund companies try to encourage you to invest for the long term, using a variety of fees and charges as carrots—or sticks. One reason is to keep as much money as possible in the fund. Another is to limit transaction costs and the possibility of having to sell underlying investments at a loss if lots of investors want to redeem their shares at the same time. Major sell-offs affect the fund's NAV and reduce returns for long-term investors.

One fee designed to make short-term trading and market timing less profitable is the **early redemption**, or exit, fee, which you're charged if you sell your shares within a certain time frame set by the fund company. That period may range from five days to a year or more, depending on the fund. The fee you pay is subtracted from the proceeds of your sale.

Some funds also levy **exchange fees**, which they charge investors to move money from one fund to another. This fee is also designed to encourage investors to invest for the long term and discourage them from redeeming shares, thereby limiting the fund's potential need to sell off underlying investments.

EXIT FEE FOR EARLY REDEMPTION

EXCHANGE FEE

FUNDS WITH CLASS

Fund companies divide their shares into different classes, based on the way sales charges are levied. Each fund class has the same holdings and investment objectives. But because each class has different sales costs, fees, and expenses, there is variation in the fund's NAV and in the total return.

Although some fund companies offer several different classes, the most common are A, B, and C shares. **Class A** shares charge a load when you buy, and **Class B** shares charge back-end loads. **Class C** shares, otherwise known as **level loads**, charge an annual sales fee. The class of the shares you own also affects what you pay in annual operating and other expenses.

Generally, C shares charge a higher percentage of your account value to cover operating expenses than B shares, which in turn charge more than A shares. When the load on B shares disappears, they are sometimes converted by the fund company into A shares, which reduces 12b-1 and operating expense fees.

The SEC requires that a fund offering multiple share classes provide an analysis of comparative costs in its prospectus. It's worth investigating that comparison, because a particular share class may make better sense, based on how much you're investing and how long you plan to hold the shares.

BREAKPOINTS

A **breakpoint** is the amount of money you need to invest in a mutual fund in order to qualify for a reduced front-end sales charge. Though that amount varies from fund to fund, a typical example is a half a percent (0.5%) reduction once you reach $25,000, another half percent at $50,000, and so on.

You may reach a breakpoint and qualify for a reduced fee with a one-time purchase. Or, if you, and in some cases you and members of your household, hold investments in the same fund or the same fund family, those cumulative assets may count toward the required breakpoint total.

Rights of accumulation allow you to qualify for a breakpoint discount by combining past and new investments in a fund. And a **letter of intent** allows you to reach a breakpoint by stating that you plan to reach the threshold with investments that you'll make in the future.

Funds aren't required to offer breakpoints, but if they do, they're obligated to make sure you get the reduction you qualify for.

THE FIVE QUESTIONS

Investors who are researching mutual funds to add to their portfolios may want to find answers to these questions as part of the selection process:

1. What's the fund sponsor's reputation for leadership, clarity of communication, transparency, and business continuity?

2. What is the tenure and experience of the fund managers?

3. What's the fund's style?

4. What's the fund's expense ratio?

5. Has the fund provided consistently strong returns?

Mutual Fund Fees

When you're investing in mutual funds, fees are a fact of life.

Mutual fund fees fall into two categories: **shareholder fees** and **operating expenses**. You pay shareholder fees if you buy load funds, redeem shares within a restricted period, or allow your account balance to fall below the required minimum. But you pay operating expenses whenever you own fund shares. They're asset-based fees that are typically calculated daily and subtracted from the fund's net assets before investment gains or losses are credited to your account. Anything you pay in fees isn't reinvested. So the higher the fees, the more potential earnings you give up, or lose.

THE MATTER WITH FEES

The fact is that fees do affect your bottom line as a mutual fund investor. You can use the SEC Mutual Fund Cost Calculator at www.sec.gov to determine the impact of fees on your investment return using a number of different scenarios. For example, suppose you invested $55,000 and left it untouched for 10 years.

	Load	Return
SCENARIO 1		
	4.5% front load	10%
SCENARIO 2		
	4.5% front load	10%
SCENARIO 3		
	No load	10%
SCENARIO 4		
	No load	10%

OPERATING EXPENSES

Operating expenses cover the cost of running the fund and generally include:

- Investment management fees, which often account for the lion's share of the total
- Administrative fees
- 12b-1, or marketing and distribution, fees

These fees are usually quoted as an **expense ratio**, or a percentage of the fund's net assets, and range from less than 0.1% to 2.75% or higher in some cases. The fees vary from one fund company to the next, and from one fund to another within the same fund family.

Not surprisingly, actively managed funds tend to have higher management fees than passively managed index funds. And the more time and resources that are required to make investment decisions and execute transactions, the higher the fee is likely to be. This helps to explain why actively managed international or global funds tend to be the most costly.

Competitive pressure has brought some fund fees down, especially at some of the largest no-load companies. And other funds have been required to reduce their fees as part of legal settlements and new SEC disclosure rules.

WHAT THEY'RE PAID FOR

A fund uses management fees to compensate its manager, who's responsible for choosing securities for the fund's portfolio—and whose expertise often attracts investors to the fund.

When the fee is calculated as a percentage of the fund's assets under management, the manager is rewarded for increasing the value of the fund. In some funds, there may be a bonus for beating the fund's benchmark index. Additional performance payments may be made as well, depending on how the fund fares.

In other cases, fees paid to investment managers may be reduced, on a percentage basis, as the assets under management increase. That wouldn't necessarily reduce the dollar amount of the manager's com-

LEGAL LIMITS
NASD dictates maximum fees for mutual funds:

- Front-end loads: 8.5%
- 12b-1 fees: 1% (0.75% for marketing and 0.25% for shareholder services)
- For no-load funds, 12b-1 fees must be less than 0.25% for shareholder services

Lifetime cap on 12b-1 fees are based on the fund's overall sales. The only limit the SEC sets is a 2% maximum redemption fee charge.

Expense ratio	Worth after 10 years	COST OF INVESTING		
		Fees	+ Lost potential earnings	= Total cost
0.85%	$125,089	$9,960	$7,067	$17,567
1.25%	$120,033	$13,253	$9,269	$22,522
0.85%	$130,984	$7,837	$3,834	$11,672
1.25%	$125,794	$11,268	$5,576	$16,862

pensation, because the base would be larger. But it could save individual investors money.

12B-1 FEES
Named for a provision of the Investment Company Act of 1940 that authorizes them, 12b-1 fees pay for a fund's marketing and distribution expenses and certain shareholder services.

These fees, according to NASD rules, may be up to 1% of a load fund's total assets, with no more than 0.75% going toward marketing and distribution. Some funds use these fees to pay broker fees rather than charging a front-end load. Both load and no-load funds can use 12b-1 fees for shareholder services, capped at 0.25% of assets.

These tend to be the most controversial fees. Advocates argue that marketing adds value to the fund by attracting new investors. Opponents believe that these fees, which may have been relevant when the mutual fund industry was new, are no longer justified.

PUTTING THINGS IN PROSPECTUS
The best place to start when you're investigating fund fees is with the fund prospectus. Each fund must disclose and describe both its shareholder fees and operating expenses.

The fee table that's usually in the first few pages of the prospectus must list all the charges that you'll pay, either directly or indirectly. The one cost that's not reported is brokerage fees for transaction expenses, or the amount the fund pays to buy and sell shares, though those costs also affect the fund's—and your—total return.

Comparing the expense ratios of funds with similar investment objectives is an essential step in selecting a fund. But remember, while fees have a definite impact on your return over time, choosing funds solely on the basis of fees is no smarter than choosing investments exclusively on the basis of their tax consequences.

Fund Performance

There are several formulas for measuring mutual fund performance. The bottom line is measured by return and yield over several time periods.

Whether a mutual fund aims for current income, long-term growth, or a combination of the two, there are three ways to track its performance and judge whether or not it is profitable. Investors can evaluate a fund by:

- Following changes in share price, or **net asset value (NAV)**
- Figuring **yield**
- Calculating **total return**

You can compare a fund's performance to similar funds offered by different companies, or you can evaluate the fund in relation to other ways the money could have been invested—individual stocks or bonds, for example.

Because return is figured differently for each type of investment, there isn't a simple formula for comparing funds to individual securities.

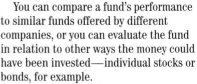

NAV CHANGE

$$\frac{\text{Value of fund}}{\text{Number of shares}} = \text{NAV}$$

for example

$$\frac{\$52,500,000}{3,500,000} = \$15$$

A fund's **NAV** is the dollar value of one share of the fund's stock. It's figured by dividing the current value of the fund minus fees and expenses by the number of its outstanding shares. A fund's NAV increases when the value of its holdings increases. For example, if a share of a stock fund costs $15 today and $9 a year ago, it means the value of its holdings increased, its expenses decreased, or a combination of the two caused the change.

YIELD

$$\frac{\text{Distribution per share}}{\text{Price per share}} = \text{Yield (\%)}$$

for example

$$\frac{\$.58}{\$10.00} = 5.8\%$$

Yield measures the amount of income a fund provides as a percentage of its NAV. A long-term bond fund with a NAV of $10 paying a 58 cent income distribution per share provides a 5.8% yield. You can compare the yield on a mutual fund with the current yield on comparable investments to decide which is providing a stronger return. Bond fund performance, for example, is often tracked in relation to individual bonds or bond indexes.

TOTAL RETURN

$$\frac{\text{Change in value + dividends}}{\text{Cost of initial investment}} = \frac{\text{Total}}{\text{Return (\%)}}$$

for example

$$\frac{\$832}{\$8,000} = 10.4\%$$

A fund's **total return** is the annual amount your mutual fund investment changes in value plus the distributions the fund pays on that investment. It's typically reported as **percentage return**, figured by dividing the dollar value of the total return by the amount of the initial investment. For example, an $8,000 investment with a one-year total return of $832 ($700 increase in value plus $132 in reinvested distributions) has an annual percentage return of 10.4%.

WATCHING RETURN

The most accurate measure of a mutual fund's performance is its **total return**, or change in value plus reinvested distributions. Total return is reported for several time periods, typically for as long as the fund has operated. When the figure is for periods longer than a year, the number is annualized, or converted to an annual figure. It's calculated as a **geometric mean**, which is more accurate for numbers multiplied in a sequence than a simple average return is.

Annualized figures reflect the impact of gains and losses over the period that's being tracked. But they don't report whether the return represents a fairly consistent performance from year to year or a seesaw of ups and downs.

Among the key factors that influence total return are the direction of the overall market in which the fund invests, the performance of the fund's portfolio, and the fund's fees and expenses.

Performance Patterns

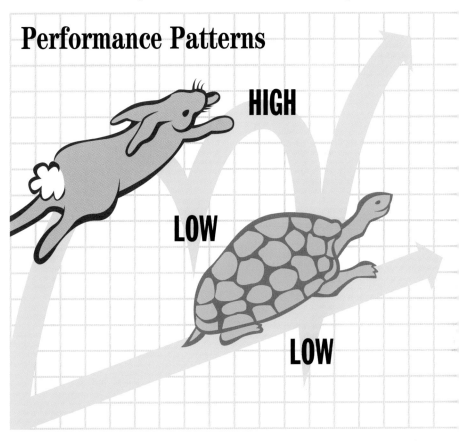

HIGH

LOW

LOW

THE IMPACT OF TIME

Most financial experts stress that mutual funds are best suited for long-term investing. They believe you should ignore the short-term peaks and valleys and be unconcerned about finding the top-performing funds of the year. For one thing, the individual fund or fund category that provides the strongest return in one year is unlikely to be in that position the following year.

The experts also point out that you can identify a number of funds in various categories that have provided returns consistent with the appropriate benchmark year after year, though these funds may never make it to the top—or the bottom—of the performance charts.

Holding a fund for an extended period also allows you to amortize the cost of the front-end load if you've purchased Class A shares. In the short term, paying this load reduces your return since the amount of the sales charge is subtracted before your principal is invested. If you stay in the fund, the effect of the sales charge disappears over time. But if you trade funds frequently, paying repeated sales charges can consume a big share of your potential earnings.

Another argument for maintaining a long-term perspective with a diversified portfolio of funds is that you decrease the risk of missing the periods of growth that often follow depressed or falling markets. It's also true that selling a fund when its NAV has dropped means locking in any losses to that point, though you might decide that is a better choice than taking the chance of having an even greater loss.

International Funds

Mutual funds are the easiest way to add international flavors to your investment menu.

By investing in more than one market, you're in a better position to benefit from economies that are growing while others are stalled or losing value. One way to diversify your portfolio more broadly is to buy shares in mutual funds that either focus on multinational companies that do business worldwide or invest in companies based in other countries. While they're often referred to generically as international funds, there are actually four specific categories of funds: **international, global, regional**, and **country**.

INTERNATIONAL FUNDS

Also known as **overseas funds**, international funds invest exclusively in stock or bond markets outside the United States. By spreading investments throughout the world, these funds balance risk by owning securities not only in mature, slower-growing economies but also in the more volatile economies of emerging nations.

GLOBAL FUNDS

Also called **world funds**, these funds include US stocks or bonds in their portfolios as well as those from other countries. The manager moves the assets around, depending on which markets are doing best at the time. That means that the percentage invested in US stocks can vary widely, depending on their performance in comparison with others around the world.

Despite what the name suggests, global funds often invest up to 75% of their assets in US companies.

REGIONAL FUNDS

These funds focus on a particular geographic area, like the Pacific Rim, Latin America, or Europe. Many mutual fund companies that began by offering international or global funds have added regional funds to capitalize on the growing interest in overseas investing and on the strength of particular parts of the world economy.

Like the more broad-based funds, regional funds invest in several different countries so that even if one market is in the doldrums, the others may be booming.

Regional funds tend to focus on groups of smaller countries or emerging markets, where one country may not issue enough securities to make a single country fund viable.

EUROPE

THE RISK OVERSEAS

When you invest in international markets, your return is affected not only by how well the investments perform but also by the changing values of your domestic currency and the currencies of the countries where you are invested.

For example, if the US dollar gains in value against the currencies of the countries where you're invested, any earnings will be worth less than they would be had you invested using the currency in which the investment was **denominated**, or priced. That's true because as the dollar increases in value, you need more of the other currency to equal a fixed number of dollars when your earnings are converted to, or exchanged for, dollars.

The good news, from an investor's perspective, is that the opposite is true as well. If the dollar loses value against other currencies, investment earnings in those currencies convert to greater gains if you've invested in dollars. Of course, when you invest internationally with mutual funds, the funds handle the currency fluctuations, as well as paying any non-US taxes that are due.

Many of the other risks of investing abroad are similar to the systematic and nonsystematic risks of investing at home. One difference, especially in emerging markets, is the risk of political instability.

COUNTRY FUNDS

These funds allow you to concentrate your investments in a single overseas country—even countries whose markets are closed to individual investors who aren't citizens. When a fund does well, other funds are set up for the same country, so that there may be many funds all investing in the same country. Many single-country funds are closed-end funds that are traded on a stock market once they have been established.

By buying stocks and bonds in a single country, you can reap the benefits of a healthy, well-established economy, or profit from the rapid economic growth as emerging markets start to industrialize or expand their export markets. The risk of investing in a single country, however, is that a downturn in the economy can create a drag on fund performance.

Closed-end funds that buy big blocks of shares in a country's industries can influence share prices and sometimes corporate policy—just as institutional investors may when they buy US stocks.

GERMANY

OLD OR NEW?

While markets around the world are increasingly linked electronically, the performance of an individual market is still determined primarily by the economic and political situation at home. Among the factors that influence an investor's experience in a particular market is whether it's mature or emerging.

A **mature market** is an industrialized country with established securities markets, substantial market volume, an efficient clearing and settlement system, and an official and effective oversight agency. An **emerging market** has a relatively new securities market, an evolving emphasis on stability and oversight, and a limited but growing list of traded securities.

Variable Annuities

A variable annuity is hard to classify. It's an investment, a retirement plan, and an insurance policy rolled into one.

Annuities are tax-deferred retirement savings plans offered by insurance companies. You purchase an annuity from an insurer and sign a contract agreeing to pay a **premium**, or certain amount of money, either as a lump sum or over time.

The insurer credits the premium and earnings to your account. When you're ready to begin withdrawing the money, the insurer will, if you choose, **annuitize** your account value, which means converting it to a stream of lifetime income. You'll have other withdrawal options, too, including taking the money as a lump sum or receiving systematic payments over a period of time.

Purchase a variable annuity with a lump sum or over time

PREMIUM

VARIABLE ANNUITY BASICS

With a **variable annuity**—which does not have a predetermined rate of return the way a **fixed annuity** does—you decide how your premium is invested by choosing from among a number of **subaccounts**, or investment options, which the annuity contract offers.

Subaccounts resemble mutual funds in that each subaccount owns a portfolio of underlying investments—stocks, bonds, cash equivalents, or a combination of stocks and bonds—purchased with money pooled from different investors. Your return depends on how well the subaccounts you've selected perform, which in turn is based on the performance of the specific investments in the account, what's happening in the market as a whole, and the fees and expenses.

COMPARING FEES

Variable annuities have annual, asset-based fees, just as mutual funds do, but on average they're higher. This means you must earn more on your annuity than on a comparable mutual fund to have the same total return. The details of these fees—how they are calculated and when they are taken out of your account—are described in the annuity's prospectus.

In addition, many annuities have **surrender fees**—typically 7% or more of the amount you invest—if you end the contract during the surrender-charge period, typically seven to ten years from the time you purchase the annuity. While most mutual funds similarly impose a redemption fee to discourage rapid turnover in the fund, that fee is usually smaller and in effect for a matter of days or months, not years.

INSURANCE PROTECTION TO BOOT

Most variable annuity contracts include a **death benefit** for which you pay a mortality and expense (M&E) fee. The death benefit guarantees that your beneficiaries will receive at least as much as you paid in premiums if you should die before you begin to receive annuity income. Some contracts may also lock in gains on a regular schedule. That means your beneficiaries would receive more than the premiums you paid into the annuity, even if the account balance drops below the principal amount.

Annuity advocates argue that having this protection encourages people who might otherwise avoid investing to benefit from its potential rewards while being insured against total loss.

Critics of annuities, and of the death benefit provision in particular, point out that M&E fees typically cost more than they're worth—unless the market takes a dramatic turn for the worse right after you purchase the annuity and then you die immediately. Otherwise, the likelihood of an account's value being less than your total premiums is usually quite small.

FREE-LOOK PERIOD

Every state has a law requiring a **free-look** period on annuities and life insurance. The period varies from state to state, but you generally get at least ten days from the day you buy an annuity to cancel it and get your money back without paying surrender charges.

Allocate money to subaccounts for performance and diversification

Adjust allocation if necessary

When you're ready, account value is annuitized to provide an income stream

Stock

Money market

Government bond

Corporate bond

Guaranteed account

TAX ISSUES

Earnings in a variable annuity grow tax deferred, and are taxed at your regular income tax rate when you begin withdrawals, usually after you're at least 59½. However, withdrawals before you reach 59½ may be subject to a 10% federal tax penalty.

Unlike money invested in a deductible IRA or employer sponsored plan, such as a 401(k), you invest post-tax income in a variable annuity that you purchase on your own. When you receive income from the annuity, the portion of the payment that is attributable to your premiums is a tax-free return of your premiums.

Also unlike traditional IRAs and employer plans, nonqualified annuities don't require you to begin withdrawals when you turn 70½. In fact, you can usually postpone taking income until you're 80, or even 90 in some states.

You may also find that an annuity is one of the options available in your employer sponsored plan—especially if it's a 403(b). In that case, your contributions as well as your earnings are tax deferred and, in most cases, you're required to begin taking withdrawals when you retire or reach 70½, whichever comes first.

RATING ANNUITY PROVIDERS

One of the primary concerns in choosing an annuity is whether or not the provider is going to be able to meet its long-term commitments. One way to make this assessment is to check out the company's financial situation using evaluations provided by several professional rating services. For example, both Standard & Poor's and Moody's Investors Service measure financial strength and ability to pay.

With a variable annuity, the principal you allocate to subaccounts—other than those that provide a fixed return— cannot be seized by the insurance company's creditors. But you're still dependent on the insurer to pay you lifetime income once you annuitize. Since that's money you'll be counting on, finding an insurer that is likely to meet its obligations to pay is of paramount importance.

STANDARD & POOR'S

Variable Annuity Policy Report
Universal Annuity

General Information

Policy Type	Variable Annuity	
Open to New Investors		Mir
S&P Rating	Y	Mir
	AA	Min

Insurance Company:
Travelers Insurance Company

A World of Options

Options are opportunities to make buy and sell decisions—if the market takes the right turns.

Buying an options contract gives you the right to buy or sell a particular financial product, called the **underlying instrument**, at a specific price within a preset time period before the contract expires.

If you **hold**, or own, an option, you are not obligated to **exercise** it, which means asserting your right to buy or sell. You may choose to exercise if doing so would produce a profit or limit a loss. But you could also sell the option in the marketplace or simply let it expire.

In contrast, when you **write**, or sell, an options contract, you are obligated to buy or sell the underlying instrument if the option holder exercises and you're designated to respond through a process known as **assignment**.

As a writer, you have no control over whether or not an option will be exercised. But you do have the right, at any time before the contract expires or is assigned, to get out of your obligation by buying an offsetting contract in the marketplace.

Types of

Calls

BUY
The right to buy

SELL
The obligation to sell

PUTS AND CALLS

Options contracts are either **calls** or **puts**, and you can buy or sell either type. You choose your approach based on what you think will happen to the underlying instrument in the marketplace.

When you **buy a call**, you have the right to buy the underlying instrument from the option seller at the exercise price. When you **buy a put**, you have the right to sell the underlying instrument to the seller at that price. If you **sell a call**, however, you must be prepared to sell the underlying instrument at the exercise price. And if you **sell a put** you must be prepared to buy the underlying instrument at the exercise price.

OPTIONS PRICES

Options have two types of prices: the strike price and the premium.

The **strike price**, or **exercise price**, is what you pay if you exercise an option to buy the underlying instrument. It's also the price you'll receive if you exercise your option to sell. The strike price—which is related to, though not the same as, the market price of the underlying instrument—is set by the options exchange that lists the contract, and it remains the same until the option expires or is adjusted.

The market price of the options contract, which is what you pay to buy it, is called the **premium**. It's also the amount you receive if you sell an option. Like stock prices, options premiums are constantly moving higher or lower as investor demand for the contract increases or decreases.

If you buy an option, you have a limited and predetermined risk since the most you can lose is the premium you pay.

When you **write**, or sell, an option, on the other hand, the premium you collect is your maximum potential return on the investment. If the option expires worthless, as you hope it will, you keep the entire premium. But if the option has value before it expires, and the holder exercises, your losses could be substantial if you had to buy the underlying instrument at above the market price or sell it below the market price.

An options contract gives the buyer rights and commits the seller to an obligation.

Options Contracts

Puts

BUY
The right to sell

HOLDER

SELL
The obligation to buy

WRITER

USING OPTIONS

You can buy and sell options contracts on individual stocks—known as **equity options**—on stock indexes, on interest rates, and on a number of other products.

When you buy an equity option, you're paying for the opportunity to benefit from changes in the stock's price without having to buy the stock. To use a hypothetical example, if you think that Alpha stock, which is currently trading at $50 a share, is going to increase in value in the next few months, you might buy 100 shares. That would cost you $5,000 plus sales charges.

An alternative would be to buy one call option on Alpha stock at a strike price of $60. If the premium were $2 a share, the contract would cost you $200 since each contract is typically for 100 shares. If the price of the stock goes up to $62, the value of your option might increase to $5 a share or higher. You could sell the contract for $500, or a $300 profit, before sales charges.

Of course, if you'd purchased the stock, you could sell it at a profit as well, collecting $6,200 before sales charges. The difference is that the options transaction would have produced a 150% gain while the stock transaction would have produced a 24% gain.

You can't guarantee the results of an options trade any more than you can a stock trade. If the stock rose to $59 and stayed there until the option expired, you would have lost the $200 you paid to purchase the call. But if you'd owned the stock, you could have realized a gain of $900, before sales charges, by selling your shares.

On the other hand, if the stock price dropped to $40 a share, all you would have lost had you purchased the call is the $200 premium. If you sold the stock to guard against further price decline, you would have lost $1,000.

THE OCC

The Options Clearing Corporation (OCC) becomes the actual buyer and seller of all listed options contracts, which means that every matched trade is guaranteed by the OCC, eliminating any counterparty risk. The OCC ensures that all matched transactions are settled on the day following the trade, that all premiums will be collected and paid, and that exercise notices are assigned according to established procedures.

The Value of Options

What an option is worth depends on tangible and intangible factors.

There is typically an active secondary market in options before their expiration date as options holders seek to sell to make a profit or limit a loss, and options writers want to buy to offset their positions. For example, someone who had sold a call on a particular stock at a particular exercise price might want to buy a call on the same stock with the same expiration date and at the same exercise price. That offsetting purchase takes the investor out of the marketplace, eliminating the obligation to make good on an exercise.

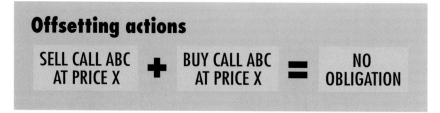

Offsetting actions

| SELL CALL ABC AT PRICE X | **+** | BUY CALL ABC AT PRICE X | **=** | NO OBLIGATION |

How Options Trade

The **premium**, or market price, of an option is closely tied to the current market price of the underlying instrument. In fact, the relationship between the two is so central to the way options trade that it's described in a special vocabulary.

An **at-the-money** option means that the market price and the strike price are the same.

An **in-the-money** option means the market price is higher than the strike price of a call option and lower than the strike price of a put option.

With an **out-of-the-money** option, the opposite is true: the market price is lower than the strike price of a call and higher than the strike price of a put. That makes it unlikely that the option will be exercised, especially if it's due to expire shortly.

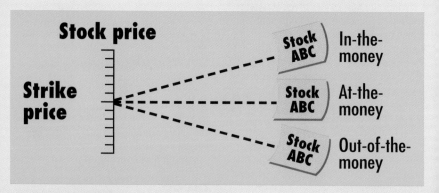

WASTING ASSETS

Options are **wasting assets**, which means that after a certain point in time they hold no value. Stocks, which you can hold indefinitely, always offer the potential for growth in value. Options, in contrast, have no value after their expiration date has passed. That means a conservative buy and hold strategy that might apply to stock investing doesn't work the same way with options investing.

As expiration nears, you have to monitor your positions closely to determine whether an option has moved in-the-money or out-of-the-money and should be acted on. Otherwise you risk missing an opportunity to realize a profit or limit a loss.

Intrinsic Value

An option's **intrinsic value** is what it would be worth at any given moment if you exercised it. For example, if you held a call on stock XYZ with a strike of $5, and XYZ is currently trading at $10, your call is in-the-money by $5, and therefore its intrinsic value is $5 per share, or $500 for the 100-share contract. If the stock were trading at $4, on the other hand, the option has an intrinsic value of $0, since it is out-of-the-money.

Even if a call has a $5 intrinsic value because it's in-the-money by $5, the premium isn't necessarily $500, since the cost of an option also takes into account its **time value**, or the potential that the option will continue to make gains before expiration. If the premium for your XYZ call is $700, or $7 per share, that means the time value that traders give your option is $2 per share. By the same token, an option with an intrinsic value of $0 might also be trading for $2, its time value. There's no fixed value for a given amount of time before expiration—it depends on how the market perceives the particular option.

As expiration nears, the time value of most options decreases, since the potential for price changes decreases. Near expiration, most options trade at or around their intrinsic value.

Finding values	For example
Share market price	$10
− Exercise price	− $ 5
Intrinsic value	**$ 5**
Premium	$ 7
− Intrinsic value	− $ 5
Time value	**$ 2**

TERM LIMITS

Every standard options contract is defined by its terms, which are standardized and set by the options exchange where the option is listed. Options with the same terms are **fungible**, or interchangeable.

An **options class** is the entire group of calls or puts available on a given underlying instrument. An **options series** is only those options in that class that have all the same terms. So any call for stock XYZ would be in the same class, but the XYZ calls that expire in April—called April XYZ calls—with a strike price of $50 would be considered a series.

Contract size: The size of the contract is how much of the underlying product will change hands if the option is exercised. For most equity options, the contract size is 100 shares.

Expiration month: Every option expires in a given month, set in the contract terms. The available expiration dates range from one month to two years away.

Strike price or exercise price: The strike price is the amount per share that the seller will receive and the buyer will pay for the shares that change hands, regardless of the market price for those shares at the time of exercise.

Delivery: There are two kinds of delivery. Physical delivery options mean the actual underlying instrument changes hands.

Cash-settled options call for cash to be paid in fulfillment of the contract. The amount of cash depends on the difference between the strike price and the value of the underlying instrument, and is determined using a formula that's defined in the contract.

Expiration style: American-style options may be exercised at any point before expiration. European-style options can only be exercised at expiration, not before.

Expiration month and strike price are usually the only terms that might vary within an options class. The other terms, such as the type of delivery and expiration style, are usually consistent for the entire class.

While standard options all expire within a year, it's possible to trade equity options that expire up to three years in the future. Those options are called Long-Term Equity Anticipation Securities®, or LEAPS. They trade just as regular options do.

Options Trading

You need to know exactly what you want to achieve before you begin a trade.

Trading options can be more complicated than trading stock. That's because while you initiate a stock trade with either an order to buy or an order to sell, an options order might be "buy to open," "buy to close," "sell to open," or "sell to close."

Basically, when you make an initial investment in an options contract, you are opening a position by either buying or selling the contract. At any point before the option expires, you can close your position. If you're holding a call option, and you can sell it for more than you paid to buy, you might close to realize a profit. You might also close to limit a potential loss if the option seems destined to remain out-of-the-money.

If you open a position by selling a contract, you might decide to close that position if you think that the option will be exercised, since you could then be required to make good on your obligation to buy or sell. In this case, since you sold to open, you'd buy to close.

EXECUTING A TRADE

When you make an options trade, you go through a brokerage firm, just as you do when you trade stocks. Whether you give the order over the phone or online, you'll have to provide detailed information about the option you're trading, including:

- The name or symbol of the option
- Whether you're opening or closing a position
- Whether you're buying or selling
- Whether you want a put or call
- The strike price
- The expiration month
- Whether you're paying cash or using a margin account
- Whether you want a limit order or market price

You'll have a chance to review your order and it's crucial that you double-check all the details. Once you've agreed to the trade, you'll receive confirmation that your order has been placed, which means it has been added to the line of orders waiting to be filled.

Every time you make a trade, you'll also pay a commission. The amount varies depending on the brokerage firm, but it's important to consider the costs of trading when planning your options strategies.

MAKING THE LIST

Each exchange decides on the options it's going to list, or make available for trading. The most widely traded options may be listed on all the exchanges, while others might be listed on only a few, or just one.

There are some basic standards that all the exchanges adhere to in selecting the companies on which they'll list equity options. Usually, eligibility for listing requires a minimum number of outstanding shares and a minimum market price for the stock. If a company is listed and fails to maintain the minimum require-

THREE WAYS TO BUY OPTIONS

Investor buys ten call options (1,000 shares) on stock X

Price: $55/share

Strike price: 60

Premium: $750

1. **HOLD TO MATURITY**

2. **TRADE BEFORE OPTION EXPIRES**

3. **LET THE OPTION EXPIRE**

TWO WAYS TO SELL OPTIONS

Investor owns 1,000 shares of stock X

Price: $55/share

Investor owns no shares of stock X

1. **WRITE TEN COVERED CALLS**
Strike price: 60
Collect premium: $750

2. **WRITE TEN UNCOVERED CALLS**
Strike price: 60
Collect premium: $750

ments, an exchange may decide to drop the listing.

All listed options are **fungible**, which means the contract terms are identical from exchange to exchange. That allows you to buy an option from one exchange and sell it on another to take advantage of the best available price. In most cases, though, you don't actually determine where the transaction takes place. Your brokerage firm and the exchange computers handle that for you.

FOLLOWING THE RULES

Listed options are traded on self-regulating exchanges (SROs) that are in turn regulated by the Securities and Exchange Commission (SEC)—the federal agency that governs the securities industry. For example, the SEC approves the standards that exchanges must use to list options,

though each exchange can make its own selections.

NOT ALWAYS YOUR OPTION

Even if you have an account with a brokerage firm and you're actively trading stocks, you'll need to be approved before you can trade options. The rules are meant to prevent you from making options trades that might be beyond your ability to cover or that might expose you to an inappropriate level of risk.

The brokerage firm will ask you for information about your investing experience and assets, and will require you to read a document about the risks of options trading. You may also be asked about your knowledge of options strategies. Based on your answers, the firm will approve you for a specific level of trading, which determines the strategies you may use.

IF STOCK PRICE RISES TO 65
Exercise options at strike price of 60 and then sell stock in marketplace

$5,000 from sale
− $750 premium
$4,250 PROFIT

IF STOCK PRICE RISES TO 58
Let options expire

less your
− $750 premium only
$750 LOSS

IF STOCK PRICE RISES TO 62
Sell contract before expiration

$2,000 from sale
− $750 premium
$1,250 PROFIT

IF STOCK PRICE RISES TO 60
Sell contract before expiration

$500 from sale
− $750 premium
$250 LOSS

IF STOCK PRICE DROPS TO 45
There are no takers for an option with a 60 strike price

less your
premium only
$750 LOSS

IF STOCK PRICE RISES TO 57
No takers—options expire

keep the
premium
$750 PROFIT

IF STOCK PRICE RISES TO 60
Buy 10 calls to cancel obligation and prevent losing stock

$750 premium collected
− $750 premium on offsetting calls
BREAK EVEN

IF STOCK PRICE RISES TO 57
No takers—options expire

keep the
premium
$750 PROFIT

IF STOCK PRICE RISES TO 65
Options are exercised. You must buy 1,000 shares of stock at $65 to sell at $60

$750 premium
− $5,000 loss on transaction
$4,250 LOSS

Options Strategies

Putting options to work for you is all about finding the right strategy for your needs.

Some of the most straightforward options strategies rely on buying, or **going long**. In contrast, writing, or selling, options is known as **going short**. If you hold an option, you're also known as the long. If you sell an option, you're the short.

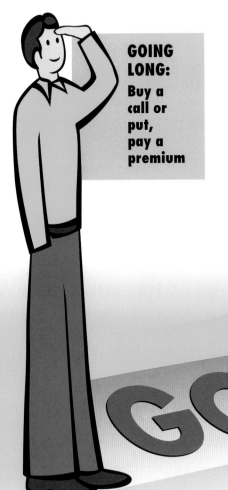

GOING LONG:

Buy a call or put, pay a premium

LONG CALLS

If you buy a call, you pay the premium for an option to buy shares of the underlying stock at a certain price before the expiration date. Generally, a long call means that you anticipate the underlying stock price will rise above the strike price of the call. If it does, you can either sell your option for more than you paid to buy it, or you can exercise the option to buy those shares for less than their current market value.

LONG PUTS

If you buy a put, you pay the premium for the right to sell shares of the underlying stock at a certain price before the expiration date. A long put usually means that you anticipate the underlying stock price will fall below the strike price of the option. If it does, you can either sell your option for more than you paid for it, or, if you hold shares of the underlying stock, sell them at the strike price for more than they're currently worth.

THE LONG AND SHORT OF IT

Buying a put is often compared to shorting stock, since both are strategies that take advantage of falling market prices. One benefit of buying a put rather than selling short is that you face a much smaller risk with a long put, since the most you can lose is the premium you pay. When selling short, your potential losses are unlimited if the price of the stock goes up instead of down.

PREMIUM

SHORT CALLS

Short options strategies are sometimes more risky than long calls and puts. If you write a call, it means you're selling someone else the right to buy—and you're agreeing to sell—shares of the underlying stock at the strike price before the expiration date. Choosing this strategy usually means that you anticipate the price of the stock to remain neutral or fall. As long as the stock price stays below the strike price of your short call, the option is out-of-the-money and you keep the premium.

If the stock price rises, however, you might choose to buy an offsetting call at a loss to prevent greater losses when the holder exercises the option. Alternatively, if you wrote a **covered call**, which means you already own the shares of underlying stock, you could surrender those shares to fulfill your obligation to sell. But you'd

GOING SHORT:
Sell a call or put, receive a premium

be receiving less for them than their market value.

If you wrote an **uncovered call**, which means you didn't own the shares, then you'd have to buy them at market price first and then sell them for less—at the exercise price—to meet your obligation.

SHORT PUTS

If you write a put, you're granting someone the right to sell—and you're agreeing to buy—shares of the underlying stock at the strike price at any time before expiration. A short put generally means you expect the market price of the stock to rise so that the put will expire worthless and you'll get to keep the premium.

If the reverse happens, and the market price falls below the strike price of the put, you might close out your position by buying an offsetting put. Otherwise, the option will almost certainly be exercised and you'll have to buy the option holder's shares for more than their market value.

You might also write a **cash-secured put**. That means when you write the option, you either purchase shares in a money market account or buy US Treasury bills so you know you'll have the cash available should you need to complete the purchase. Otherwise, you might be taking on more risk than you can afford.

SPREADING THE RISK

Spread strategies allow you to hedge against the kinds of losses you might face by simply going long or going short. The flip side is that using a spread limits your potential return.

Spread strategies require opening two options positions at the same time on the same underlying stock, usually by purchasing one and writing the other. Each option in the spread is referred to as a **leg**. In the most common version, known as a **vertical spread**, the two **legs** have different strike prices.

For example, you might use a spread to earn income on stock you own in LMN company. Rather than writing only a covered call,

which would mean running the risk that you'd have to sell your shares of LMN if the option were exercised, you could also buy a call at a slightly higher strike price than the one you wrote.

If the price of LMN stays below both strike prices, your profit is the premium you received for the short call, minus the premium you had to pay for the long call.

But if the price of LMN rises above both strike prices, you can close out both positions, and use the profit from selling your in-the-money long position to offset the cost of your in-the-money short position.

NAME THAT SPREAD
There are a variety of spread strategies that may be appropriate at different times. In addition to calendar spreads, which involve different expiration dates, you might try collars, straddles, and strangles.

Underlying Choices

Choosing an equity option also means choosing the underlying stock.

Once you've decided on an options strategy, the next step is to select the underlying product on which you'll purchase or write an option. In the case of equity options, that means choosing a stock.

EXTRA COMPLEXITY

There are some major differences between picking a stock to add to your portfolio and picking one on which to open an options position. When you're buying stock, you look for a company that seems poised for success, either because you expect its stock price to rise, it pays regular dividends, or both.

But when you're considering an options investment, you need to consider not only whether the stock's price will rise or fall, but also the amount of that increase or decrease. The amount of change, up or down, will help you determine the strike price at which you think you can make a profit.

You'll also need to choose a time frame for the price change to occur. When you buy a stock, for example, you can usually afford to wait to see if the price goes up. But when you choose an option, you must choose an expiration month. That's all the time you have for the underlying stock to perform as you anticipate.

WHEN YOU WRITE

If your strategy is to produce income by writing covered calls, you might choose a stock whose growth seems stalled—and one you wouldn't mind parting with if the price went up enough to put the option in-the-money. In that case, the options holder would no doubt exercise, and you would need to deliver the stock to fulfill your obligation.

If you're selling a put, you might select a stock that you'd like to add to your portfolio if the price were right. In that case, the premium you collect by selling will reduce the price you pay if the option holder exercises and you must fulfill your obligation to buy.

CONSIDERING WHAT'S PROBABLE

Even when you thoroughly research an equity, there's no guarantee that it will perform as you expect before the option expires. That's where **probability** comes in. Probability is a statistical measure of how likely a particular result will be, based on the historical volatility of the equity in question.

For example, an out-of-the-money option on a stock whose price is particularly **volatile**, which means it regularly moves significantly higher and lower than its average price, has a greater probability of moving in-the-money before expiration than an out-of-the-money option on a stock with low historical volatility. Of course, it's also more likely to move even more out-of-the-money.

RESEARCH METHODS

You can use the same types of research methodology to investigate the stocks on which you're considering options that you use when you're buying stocks.

You might look at some **fundamental analysis**, which evaluates the management of the company, its sales and earnings record, its product mix, its debt ratio, its competitors, and a raft of other data. Your broker may provide the firm's in-house assessment of the company and, in some cases, reports from independent analysts such as those at Standard & Poor's. Or, you can access independent analyst reports yourself. You might also investigate a **technical analysis** of recent price and volume movements in the general market and the sector to which the stock belongs, as well as price and volume data for the stock itself.

Many investors rely on both fundamental and technical data for options research as they do for stock research. You'll be exposed to a new vocabulary of Greek letters, known collectively as the Greeks, that options analysts use to discuss the movement of an option's theoretical price or volatility as the underlying stock's price or volatility changes or as expiration nears. Delta, for example, is a measure of how much an option price changes when the underlying stock's price changes.

PRICE RISE OR FALL?

WHEN YOU WANT TO BUY

If you identify a stock you want to buy but either don't have the cash on hand or want to hedge your bet, one alternative is to buy on margin. But you could also buy a call. Calls let you use leverage, as margin purchases do, but they may pose less potential risk.

When you buy a stock on margin you must invest 50% of the market price of the stock and maintain a cash reserve in your margin account in case the stock price drops far enough to require a margin call. If that happens, you may have to sell other assets you hold to cover the margin call.

In contrast, if you buy calls on the same stock, the premium you pay will typically cost significantly less than the 50% minimum you must put up to buy on margin. And if you've guessed wrong, and the value of the stock drops instead of rises, the option will expire out-of-the-money, so all you stand to lose is the premium you paid.

GIVING ORDERS

When you give an order to open or close an options position, you use the same language you do when you buy or sell

stocks. A **market order** means you want the trade to be executed at the current price.

If you're willing to trade only if the price is acceptable to you, you use a **limit order**. That puts a ceiling on the price you're

willing to pay to buy, and sets a floor for the lowest price you will accept. Limit orders may not be filled in a fast moving market. You may also be able to give a **stop-loss order**, which means you want your broker to sell

if the price goes above or below a certain level to limit further losses.

Hedging and Speculating

Options are flexible enough to fit a variety of investment strategies.

The more you know about options, the more you may use them in your investment portfolio. For example, you can use options to profit from either rising or falling stock prices. You can use options aggressively, by adopting some potentially riskier strategies, or conservatively, to hedge against risk.

HEDGING

BUILDING A HEDGE

Conservative investors use options to **hedge**, or limit risk. For instance, suppose you bought 100 shares of LMN stock, expecting it to increase in value. But since nothing in the stock market is guaranteed, perhaps you're concerned that if LMN's price drops sharply, you'll have a big loss.

To limit your risk, you might decide to buy a put, allowing you to sell your shares at a strike price lower than your purchase price. That way, if the market price of the stock dropped, your loss could be limited to the difference between what you paid for the shares and the strike price of the option, plus what you paid for the put.

Alternatively, if the market price increased, you might buy a put with a strike price that's higher than what you paid for each share. Using this strategy, you could lock in a profit if the stock price dropped during the contract term, since you could exercise your option and sell at the strike price.

Hedging has costs, however. You'll have to pay the premium to buy the put, which means reducing your potential profit from the trade. And if LMN stock continues to rise, you won't exercise your option but will still have paid the premium. For many investors, though, the hedge is worth the cost.

BEING BULLISH

You can use options in both rising and falling markets. In contrast, a straight-forward stock purchase is generally only profitable if the stock price rises—though you may choose to sell a stock short if you expect its price to fall.

When markets are rising, you might buy a call to lock in a purchase price for a particular stock. If the stock rises above the strike price of the call, you can buy shares at the strike price and either sell them at the higher market price for a profit or hold them in your portfolio. If the shares continue to rise in value, the transaction will continue to be profitable.

As an options writer, you may also profit from a rising stock price. For example, if you think the price of LMN stock will go up, you could write a put on LMN and collect income from the premium. If your assumption is right and the stock price rises above the strike price of the put, the option will be out-of-the-money, and you'll keep the premium as profit.

If, however, the stock price doesn't rise above the strike price, you'll either have to close out the position by buying the offsetting put at a loss or purchase the shares from the contract holder for less than their market value.

MANAGING RISK
For many investors, options are primarily risk management tools, or a way to protect against falling stock prices. But options are investments, not insurance policies. They always carry some risk, and returns are never guaranteed.

TAKING A FLIER

For aggressive investors, options can offer potentially large returns. Aggressive strategies are usually speculative.

For example, writing **uncovered calls** and **naked puts** on underlying stock that you don't own requires no investment on your part. And, if the option expires out-of-the-money, you keep the entire premium as profit.

The risk, of course, is that the option will move in-the-money and be exercised. Then you might have to purchase the underlying stock and sell it for much less than the market price, or, in the case of a put, buy the stock from the exerciser at much higher than the market price. The losses you face in these cases are potentially unlimited.

When bullish and bearish describe the stock market, bullish means that prices are going up and bearish means that prices are going down. But it's a little more complicated in options markets because call and put prices move in opposition. A call option usually rises in value when the underlying stock price goes up. But put prices usually rise in value as market prices go down.

FEELING BEARISH

Unlike most stock trading strategies, some options strategies can also be used to profit in a falling stock market. For example, if you think LMN stock is going to drop in price, you could buy puts on LMN. If the price of the stock drops below the strike price of your put, your option will move in-the-money and you can sell it for more than you paid for it.

You could also decide to write a call on LMN and receive income from the premium. If the price of the stock drops below the strike price of your call, your option is out-of-the-money and won't be exercised. That means you keep the premium as profit.

If, however, LMN rises in value above the strike price of your call, you'll either have to close out the option by buying an offsetting call and taking a loss, or by selling shares of LMN at the strike price—which might mean first buying them at their higher market price and taking a loss on the transaction.

Finding an Exit

Leaving an options position requires as much planning as entering one.

BUY OR SELL SHARES to meet your obligation

Exiting an equity options contract isn't always as simple as selling a stock or bond. Sometimes, you may not have to do a thing. Other times, you may have to buy or sell another option to close the position, or perhaps buy or sell shares of stock to meet your obligation if the option you sold has been exercised. It all depends on the position you've taken.

EXERCISING YOUR OPTIONS

If you've bought an option, which is also called **holding a long position**, and you don't exercise your options contract before it expires out-of-the-money, nothing will happen. You won't get any return on your investment, and the contract will no longer exist.

If you sold an option, which is also called **holding a short position**, and you don't close it out before expiration, you may have to buy or sell shares of stock to meet your obligation. If the option is out-of-the-money at expiration, though, the holder won't exercise, and you won't have to do anything.

An equity option doesn't have to be exercised or closed out exactly at expiration. That's because an option holder can act on an American-style option at any point before expiration, and in fact most do. As the underlying stock price changes, an option may move in-the-money and then back out-of-the-money. That means timing is an important part of planning— for exercising an option that you hold, or anticipating the exercise of an option that you wrote.

GIVING AN ASSIGNMENT

If you're ready to exercise an options position that you hold:

1 You notify your brokerage firm, which sends the exercise request on to The Options Clearing Corporation (OCC).

2 This clearinghouse randomly assigns exercise responsibility to a brokerage firm that represents someone who sold the same series of the option and so is holding the corresponding short position.

3 The brokerage firm will match the assignment to an investor that holds the short position, either making a random selection or following a particular system, such as the order in which positions were opened.

While you decide when to exercise a long position in an options contract, you might be assigned at any time if you hold a short position that's in-the-money. That means, for example, if you wrote a call, you'll have to sell the underlying shares to the exerciser at the strike price. And if you wrote a put, you'll have to buy those shares from the exerciser at the strike price.

AUTOMATIC EXERCISE

In some cases, expiring options may be automatically exercised on behalf of the holder. Automatic exercise usually occurs if the option is in-the-money by a predetermined amount. Some brokerage firms also practice automatic exercise for their clients when an option is in-the-money by a certain amount. If you hold an in-the-money option, you should check with your firm to see if and when your option might automatically be exercised and what the consequences might be.

DO NOTHING
or roll your
option

CLOSE OUT
POSITION
by offsetting
your trade

ROLLING ALONG

In some cases, you may have an open position that's about to expire, but you're reluctant to end the position altogether. One option, as expiration approaches, is to roll your option. Essentially, you close out your existing position and open a new one that's the same except for expiration date or strike price.

 If you **roll out**, you choose the same option but with a later expiration date. You might roll out if you think your transaction still has the potential to become profitable at a later date.

 If you **roll up**, you choose the same option but with a higher strike price. You might roll up if you purchased a call and you think the underlying stock price will continue to rise.

 If you **roll down**, you choose the same option but with a lower strike price. You might roll down if you think the underlying stock price won't change much, or it will go down.

A WORD TO THE WISE

While you can use rolling to increase your profits, you'll want to base any decision to roll on careful research. If you've chosen a reasonable strategy and the market has moved against you, it's possible that rolling out, up, or down could make that strategy profitable. But if you roll because you're frustrated with an unsatisfactory result, it may be a misguided trade. If you're not confident about what is likely to occur in the market, it may be better to cut your losses.

CLOSING OUT

If you hold an options position—whether long or short—you can always end the transaction by **closing out**, or offsetting your original trade.

Original position		To close out
Buy call	➤	Sell call
Buy put	➤	Sell put
Write call	➤	Buy call
Write put	➤	Buy put

Depending on whether your option has gone up or down in value since you opened the position, you may realize a profit by closing out, or you may take a loss. That loss may be less, however, than the size of the loss you might face if the option expired or were exercised.

If you hold a short position that's moved in-the-money, you'll have to close out if you don't want to be assigned if the option is exercised. Underlying stock prices often change quickly, which means options may move in-the-money and out-of-the-money rapidly as well.

That's one reason it's important to have a strategy for when you'll close out a position or exercise—perhaps when your option moves in-the-money by a certain amount. That means deciding ahead of time the amount of profit you'd like to take, or the maximum loss you're willing to accept.

ABOUT TO EXPIRE

All standardized equity and index options expire on the Saturday following the third Friday of their expiration month. Many brokerage firms impose a deadline for exercising or closing out well before Friday trading ends. That means you might not be able to wait until the last minute to decide on your exit strategy. Be sure to check with your brokerage firm about the actual cutoff date.

Index Options

You can get broad exposure to the stock market with index options.

Just as the underlying instrument of an equity option is a particular stock, so the underlying instrument of an **index option** is a specific index, such as the Standard & Poor's 500 Index. Fluctuations in the value of the index and time until expiration affect the premium for an index option just as those factors affect the premium of an equity option.

TRACKING MARKET MOVEMENT

Index options are attractive to individual investors because they offer the same ability to hedge or speculate as equity options. Rather than anticipating the movement of an individual stock, though, index options let you adopt strategies based on the movement of the market as a whole or of a particular sector.

For example, if you anticipate that the stock market in general will rise, you can buy calls on the S&P 500. If, instead, you bought calls on the individual stocks in the index, you would need to execute a far greater number of transactions, commit a lot more money, and spend time monitoring your positions.

Index options also reduce the risk that one particular company's stock won't perform as you expected. Instead, the value of your option will be determined by the collective performance of a large number of companies. For example, if you anticipate that the telecommunications sector is poised for a move, buying a telecom index option will allow you to profit from that move—assuming your assumption is correct—without having to select one particular telecommunications company.

And because indexes are so diversified, index options can be a simple way to hedge a diverse portfolio. If you buy a put on a broad stock index, your put will rise in value as the stocks in your portfolio lose value. If the stock market makes gains, your put will be out-of-the-money, but what you paid in premium should be offset by increases in the value of your portfolio. You might decide to roll out, and repurchase the put with a later expiration date, to continue the hedge.

NO PERFECT HEDGE

One risk of hedging with index options is that the movement of the index may not exactly match the movement of your portfolio. The more carefully you choose an index—by comparing its make-up and volatility to your own portfolio—the greater the potential it will work as a hedge. But there's no way to guarantee a perfect match.

CASH-SETTLED OPTIONS

Most equity options are **physical delivery** contracts, which require shares of the underlying instrument to change hands. Index options, in contrast, are **cash settled**, which means the exerciser receives a certain amount of money. With index options, the cash settlement value is the difference between the value of the index at closing and the strike price of the option, times the multiplier.

For example, if Index ABC closes at 1,050, you hold a call with a strike price of 1,000, and the multiplier is 100, your cash settlement is $5,000.

Index closes at	1,050
Strike price	−$1,000
	50
Multiplier	x 100
Your cash settlement	**$5,000**

MULTIPLE MULTIPLIERS

A standard equity options contract covers 100 shares of stock, and you multiply the premium by 100 to find the contract cost. If the contract is adjusted, as it would be in a stock split, the multiplier is also adjusted. For example, if the underlying stock splits 3-for-2, the adjusted option covers 150 shares, and you multiply the premium by 150. In cash-settled options, the market listing the option sets the multiplier that determines the settlement.

MANCE MARKET MOVEMENT

HEDGE
SPECULATE
DIVERSIFY
REDUCE RISK

USING LEVERAGE

Index options demonstrate the potential for **leverage** that options trading provides. Leverage is the ability to use a small investment to control a much larger one. For example, to buy just one share of each of the 500 stocks tracked in the S&P 500 would require an immense amount of capital. But you can participate in the movement of those stocks at a fraction of that price by purchasing S&P 500 options.

While leverage has a certain appeal, there are risks as well. Whenever you buy an option, your risk is limited to the premium you pay. But if you write an option, the losses you risk are potentially unlimited. For example, if you write an index put, you open the transaction with a net credit because you collect the premium. But if the underlying index plummets in value, you'll face a steep cash settlement.

OTHER INSTRUMENTS

Options are available on a wide variety of underlying instruments, including exchange-traded funds (ETFs), futures contracts, limited partnership interests, and American depositary receipts (ADRs).

OTHER OPTIONS

Just as stockholders can hedge with index options, bondholders can hedge using interest rate options, which are essentially options on US or other government bonds. You can use these options to offset a drop in rates between the date you purchase the option and the date the bond matures. If the money from the maturing bond has to be reinvested at a lower rate, the profit from trading the option may make up for some of the loss.

Related, though unlisted, derivative products, called **interest rate caps**, allow institutional investors to protect their portfolios against interest rate increases. In a rising rate environment, an insurance company might expect its policyholders to borrow against their policies at below-market rates and invest the money to earn a higher rate. So it might buy the rate cap to offset its lending losses.

Institutional investors with large overseas holdings sometimes hedge their portfolios by purchasing options on the currencies in which their money is invested. Since the investment's value depends on the relationship between the currencies, using options can equalize sudden shifts in value.

STYLE MATTERS

Most index options are European-style, which means they can be exercised only at expiration, not before.

Researching Options

Investigating before investing is essential when you're trading options.

Before you begin any options trade, you'll want to evaluate whether the underlying stock or stock index of the option you're considering is likely to rise or fall in value, and the time frame within which it may do so. That generally also requires assessing the market as a whole.

IDENTIFYING RESOURCES

You can do much of your options research online. In addition to general financial websites, you can check industry sites such as www.888options.com, the website of the Options Industry Council (OIC), which offers options education as well as trading data. The websites of the options exchanges also offer premium quotes and other information for the options they list.

You might also use subscription-based options newsletters. These publications offer options information and often provide specific trade ideas. Newsletters are usually the work of options experts, but there's no guarantee that their insights will prove correct. If you're considering a newsletter, you should carefully review the long-term track record of the author as well as the appropriateness of the information and analysis for your investing style.

USING BENCHMARKS

Another way to analyze the options marketplace is by using the appropriate **benchmarks**. A benchmark is a yardstick against which you compare a security or an option. In stock trading, for example, the Standard & Poor's 500 Index is often used as a benchmark for large-company stocks. You compare the return on a particular stock to the return of the index to see how the stock has performed in relation to the market in general.

One benchmark that's popular with options investors is the Chicago Board Options Exchange (CBOE) Volatility Index, or VIX. Rather than tracking average return, VIX tracks the overall implied vola-

- **Benchmarks**
- **Put/call ratio**
- **VIX (implied volatility)**
- **Pricing formulas**

tility of S&P 500 index options. **Implied volatility** is a measure of how actively investors think that the S&P 500 and, by extension, the stock market in general and a single stock in particular, will fluctuate.

The higher the VIX, the greater the expectation that prices will change quickly—though there are no guarantees that investor sentiment is an accurate predictor of what will happen. That's why you may also want to track the market price of the stocks underlying your options contracts closely. This is particularly important as their expiration dates get closer since you may need to close a position to realize a gain or protect against a greater loss.

RELEVANT RATIOS
You can get a sense of current market trends and what they seem to suggest for the near term by looking at certain indicators. One example is the **put/call ratio**, which compares the number of put and call contracts

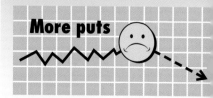

More puts

Implied volatility is a measure of the market's prediction of how volatile a stock will be. **Historic volatility**, on the other hand, is an actual measure of how much a stock's price fluctuated in the past.

IS THE PRICE RIGHT?

Options analysts use complex formulas, or models, to calculate the **theoretical price** of an option—meaning what the price logically ought to be—based on a number of factors. By comparing the actual trading price of an option to its theoretical value, you can determine whether the option is trading for more or less than it's worth.

The Black-Scholes formula is one of the best-known pricing models. Because the formula itself is very complicated, you'll probably use a web-based calculator. But it can be helpful to know the variables in the formula, since changes in those factors will influence the premium of an option you hold or one you're considering.

These variables include:
- Price of the underlying stock
- Strike price
- Time until expiration
- Volatility
- Whether the underlying stock distributes dividends
- Interest rates

For example, it's usually a good idea to follow changes in national interest rates, since they affect the premiums on options. And you might use the Black-Scholes formula to estimate how the premium of a particular option might change if interest rates move up or down 100 basis points, which is one percentage point. It's important to remember, though, that an options formula calculates only theoretical price. Market demand determines the actual price, no matter what its theoretical value.

The Black-Scholes Formula

$$C = S_0 \Phi \left[\frac{\ln\{\frac{S_0}{K}\} + (r + \frac{1}{2}\sigma^2)\, n}{\sigma\sqrt{n}} \right] - Ke^{-rn} \Phi \left[\frac{\ln\{\frac{S_0}{K}\} + (r - \frac{1}{2}\sigma^2)\, n}{\sigma\sqrt{n}} \right]$$

NOBEL EFFORTS

The Black-Scholes formula was devised by three mathematicians: Fischer Black, Myron Scholes, and Robert Merton. They published their formula in 1973, and won the Nobel Prize in 1997 for their achievement. Other options pricing formulas include the Cox-Ross-Rubenstein model and the Whaley model.

STICK TO IT

Once you open an options position, it's important to stick with the strategy you adopted when you made the decision to invest. That might mean closing out your option if the premium or the market price of the underlying stock exceeds the level you set as your exit point when you opened the position.

For the same reason, it's important to continue to use the same benchmarks that helped frame your decision when you opened your position. If you chose an option because of its theoretical value, for example, you should determine your exit strategy using the same criteria, rather than making a decision based on its relative volatility.

that have been opened for a particular options class. As a rule, when there are more puts than calls it means that investor sentiment anticipates falling prices for the market in general or for the stock in particular. The opposite is true when calls predominate.

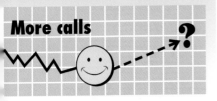

More calls

Reading an Options Chart

Options information is widely available, if you know how to read it.

If you're looking for options trading information, you can find tables reporting the previous day's trades in the financial press. And you can find options chains of all the options currently available on a particular stock or other underlying instrument online. One place to begin is at www.888options.com, the website of the Options Industry Council (OIC).

UNDERSTANDING THE CODE

An options **ticker symbol** is made of three, four, or five letters and has three distinct elements. The first part, called the options root symbol, stands for the underlying interest, and, in the case of an equity option, is generally derived from the company's stock symbol—though it may be different. The second part of the symbol contains letters that identify whether the option is a call or a put and the month of its expiration. Each expiration month is identified with two letters, one for calls and one for puts. For example, A indicates a January call and X indicates a December put.

The third part of the symbol reports the last two digits of the strike price, ranging from a low of $5 to a high of $100. In fact, though, each letter does quadruple duty, so that **A** indicates a $5 strike, and also strikes of $105, $205, and $305. You decipher which strike price is being indicated based on the current market price of the underlying stock.

The standard symbol format is:

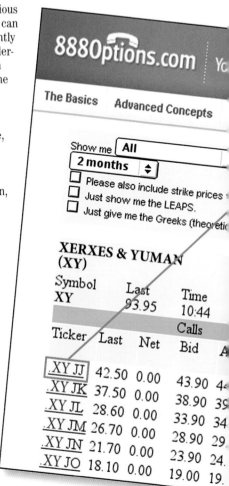

8880ptions.com | Yo

The Basics   Advanced Concepts

Show me [**All**]

[2 months ◆]

☐ Please also include strike prices
☐ Just show me the LEAPS.
☐ Just give me the Greeks (theoretic

XERXES & YUMAN (XY)

Symbol XY	Last 93.95	Time 10:44

| | | | Calls | |
Ticker	Last	Net	Bid	A
.XY JJ	42.50	0.00	43.90	44
.XY JK	37.50	0.00	38.90	39
.XY JL	28.60	0.00	33.90	34
.XY JM	26.70	0.00	28.90	29.
.XY JN	21.70	0.00	23.90	24.
.XY JO	18.10	0.00	19.00	19.

Options root symbol

XYZ D M—Strike price

Expiration month and type (call or put)

Call options—options to buy—are reported separately from **put options**—options to sell.

GETTING WIRED

Options, like futures contracts, have historically been bought and sold on exchange trading floors, using a sometimes rough and tumble auction-style system known as **open outcry**. But the winds of electronic change, which have revolutionized stock trading, are stirring up options trading as well.

Order routing and execution on the US options exchanges—the American Stock Exchange, the Boston Options Exchange, the Chicago Board Options Exchange, the International Securities Exchange, the Pacific Exchange, and the Philadelphia Stock Exchange—are increasingly handled electronically. Traders on exchange floors are using hand-held computers to record transactions, replacing yesterday's paper order cards. The Boston and the ISE are entirely electronic.

What's more, options that once traded on only one exchange may now trade on several simultaneously, a move that supporters say provides a more efficient and liquid market.

Listed under **ticker** are the stock symbol, in this case Xerxes & Yuman (XY), and two letters that indicate the type of option, the expiration and strike price. **J** indicates a call expiring in October. The second **J** indicates a 50 strike price.

Last is the most recent price for the option. Online, it's typically updated regularly during the day if trading is active. The last price for the October 50 call was 42.50, or $4,250 per contract on 100 shares. The ask price for the October put was 0.05, or 5 cents.

Bid reports what buyers are willing to pay for options and **ask** what sellers are willing to accept.

Net indicates how much the options price has changed, if it has. A positive number means an increase and a negative one, in red, a decrease.

---

ation for Options Education

Contact Us | Press | Help

search »

quote »

xplorer   Online Classes   Seminars & Events   Resources & Data

and Puts ⬍ on [XY]   starting [0 ⬍] months from today, for

al exchanges.

ased on the Black-Scholes formula).

[Get Option]

93.95

-0.03 ▼

Bid	Ask	Open	High	Low	Close	Vol
0.00	0.00	93.55	93.99	93.52	93.98	493200

Oct

Puts

Open Interest	Strike	Ticker	Last	Net	Bid	Ask	Vol Open Interest
537	50	XY VJ	0.00	0.00	0.00	0.05	251
79	55	XY VK	0.05	0.00	0.00	0.05	37
141	60	XY VL	0.05	0.00	0.00	0.05	1770
00	65	XY VM	0.05	0.00	0.00	0.05	2669
09	70	XY VN	0.05	0.00	0.00	0.05	2271
	75	XY VO	0.05	0.00	0.00	0.05	1213

Open interest on an option is the number of open, outstanding positions that have not been closed out. Open interest includes both long and short puts or calls.

You can set the limits of the searches you want to conduct, choosing to display all strike prices for both **calls** and **puts** on a particular underlying investment, or only those options that are in-the-money or close to being in-the-money.

In this example, all puts and calls with an October **expiration date** and a 50 **strike price** are being displayed. The calls are to the left and the puts to the right of the screen's center column.

The bold numbers to the right of the stock name show the most recent **market price** for the underlying stock—$93.95—and the **net gain or loss** from the day's opening price—down 0.03 cents.

Volume reports the number of trades during the previous trading day. The number is unofficial but gives a sense of the activity in each option. Generally, trading increases as the expiration date gets closer if the strike price is in-the-money. But many factors contribute to trading volume and can be hard to isolate.

Futures: Derivative Products

Futures are complex and volatile, but also useful investments.

FUTURES ARE OBLIGATIONS TO BUY OR SELL a specific commodity—such as corn, gold, or Treasury bonds—on a specific day for a preset price.

DERIVATIVE INVESTMENTS

Futures belong to the group of financial products known as **derivatives** because their prices reflect, or are derived from, the value of the commodity underlying the futures contract. Commodities can be consumable, such as soybeans and silver, or financial, such as the Euro or a particular stock.

Futures developed from **forward contracts** that were originally used by commodity producers—corn farmers for example—to lock in the price they were to be paid for corn when it was harvested some months later. With the contract in hand, the farmer could be protected if corn prices dropped.

Futures contracts formalized the forward contract process, imposing standard contract terms for **grade**, or quality, quantity, and delivery month. With the imposition of standard terms, it became possible to trade futures contracts on an organized exchange, creating a futures marketplace.

Buying or selling a futures contract does not transfer ownership, as buying or selling a stock does. Rather, the contract spells out the terms of the deal, including the rights and obligations of the buyer and seller, the underlying product—also called the underlying instrument—to be purchased or sold, the quantity, and the price.

LEVERAGE AND RISK

Leverage, in financial terms, means using a small amount of money to control an investment of much greater value.

Futures contracts are highly leveraged instruments because, under most circumstances, you can buy or sell a futures contract with a **good faith deposit** called an **initial margin** of less than 10% of the underlying item's value. For example, if you buy a gold contract worth $35,000 when the futures contract represents 100 ounces of gold and the gold futures price is $350 an ounce, the

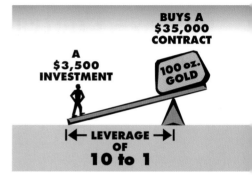

BUYS A $35,000 CONTRACT

A $3,500 INVESTMENT

100 oz. GOLD

|← **LEVERAGE** →| OF **10 to 1**

required good faith deposit might be $3,500. That gives you 10-to-1 leverage since you control the $35,000 investment with your $3,500 deposit.

During periods when the price of gold is volatile, it could change by $30, $40, or even $50 within a short period of time. If the price went up $50, to $400 an ounce, the value of your futures contract on 100 ounces of gold would jump $5,000 ($50 an ounce x 100 ounces = $5,000). But, of course, the opposite could also happen. If the price of an ounce of gold dropped $50, the value of your futures contract would drop $5,000.

So while leverage means that the initial amount required to buy a futures contract, known as opening a futures position, is relatively small, changes in the price of the contract are magnified in relation to your initial deposit.

MAKING A PROFIT

If you buy a futures contract, you make a profit if the price of the underlying item rises above the contract price. That's because you are able to buy the item at the lower contract price rather than at the current, higher price.

If you sell a futures contract, you make a profit if the price of the underlying item falls below the contract price. That's because you are able to sell at a higher price than the current market price. But because the returns are unpredictable and the stakes are high, most individual investors tend not to trade futures.

How Leverage Works

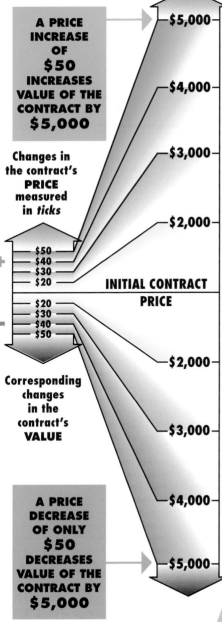

A PRICE INCREASE OF $50 INCREASES VALUE OF THE CONTRACT BY $5,000

Changes in the contract's **PRICE** measured in *ticks*

$5,000

$4,000

$3,000

$2,000

+
$50
$40
$30
$20

INITIAL CONTRACT PRICE

–
$20
$30
$40
$50

$2,000

Corresponding changes in the contract's **VALUE**

$3,000

$4,000

A PRICE DECREASE OF ONLY $50 DECREASES VALUE OF THE CONTRACT BY $5,000

$5,000

Futures contracts expire on a specific day each month and are dropped from trading. US contracts expire on the third Saturday of the expiration month and can be exercised or offset on or before the third Friday.

Futures Contracts

You don't need to invest much to enter a futures contract, but you need nerve—and luck—to ride this financial roller coaster.

To trade futures, you give an order to buy or sell a commodity on a particular date in the future—such as October wheat, December pork bellies, or June Eurodollars. The price is determined in trading on the exchange where there's a market in that commodity.

But you pay just the **good faith deposit**, or initial margin. Briefly, a futures margin is a performance bond that's available to the futures broker to meet a customer's obligations for potential losses on a futures position. That's different from buying stock on margin, where you must provide at least 50% of the purchase price, and the balance is a loan arranged through the firm.

CHANGING PRICES

Both over the term of a futures contract and throughout a regular trading day, the price of liquidating a futures position changes constantly. The changes in contract value are caused by fluctuations in the price of an offsetting contract, which in turn is caused by changes in the cash price of the underlying commodity, among other factors. The difference between the price of a contract and the price of an offsetting contract represents the profit or loss of the position.

At the end of each trading day, the exchange's **clearinghouse**, an agency that's responsible for clearing and settling its trades, moves money either in to or out of its members' accounts, based on the

Winning and Losing with a Futures Contract

	JULY 1	JULY 14	AUGUST 24
	You buy one September wheat contract of 5,000 bushels at $3.50 a bushel, worth $17,500	Wheat prices rise to $3.90. Contract is now worth $19,500	Wheat prices drop to $3.25. Contract is now worth $16,250
		$2,000 PROFIT	
$17,500			$1,250 LOSS
		Exchange credits your account— this is profit if you sell an offsetting contract now	You must add money now to your account to meet the required maintenance margin
	You put the required 10% into your margin account		
$1,750			
	$1,750 INITIAL MARGIN		
$0			

THE LANGUAGE OF FUTURES

Futures trading involves contracts that cancel, or offset, each other: For every buy there's a sell and vice versa. The language of futures trading reflects this phenomenon.

To Enter the Market	Which Means	To Offset Your Position	Which Means
GO LONG	ENTER A FUTURES CONTRACT TO **BUY**	**GO SHORT**	ENTER A FUTURES CONTRACT TO **SELL**
GO SHORT	ENTER A FUTURES CONTRACT TO **SELL**	**GO LONG**	ENTER A FUTURES CONTRACT TO **BUY**

shifting value of their contracts. The process is called **marking to market**.

After you've opened a position, you must maintain the required margin level, called the **maintenance margin**, of your account at all times, adding money if required to cover the loss if the value of your contract drops. Maintenance margin requirements may differ from initial margin requirements.

CONTROLLING RISK

Initial and maintenance margin levels are generally set by the futures exchange where the contract is listed, though an individual clearinghouse or firm may require higher levels. Margin helps control the risk to which traders are exposed. If market prices start to move rapidly and the market **volatility** increases, margin rates can be increased. This helps to ensure that traders don't expose themselves to risks that exceed the capital in their account. Higher margin requirements can also slow trading, as traders are able to take fewer positions with the same amount of money.

A TWO-PARTY SYSTEM

There are two parties to every futures transaction—the **buyer**, who is called the long, and the **seller**, who is called the short. If you want to enter the futures market, you can **go long** or **go short**. When an order is filled, the contract typically goes into a pool at the exchange's clearinghouse with all the other filled orders. And if you want to leave the futures market, cancelling your obligation under the contract, you offset your position with an equal number of the same futures contract on the opposite side of the market.

> When you go short, it's because you expect a contract's price to drop, or you're hedging a bet that it will rise. It's similar to selling a stock short—which you do for similar reasons.

For example, if you have purchased, or have a long position in, three September US Treasury note futures and want to leave the market, you would sell, or take a short position in, three September US Treasury note futures.

To offset a futures contract, you don't have to find the investor who was on the other side of your original futures contract and hope that person also wants to offset his or her position. That's because once a futures position has been cleared by a futures clearing firm, the clearing firm becomes the buyer for every seller and the seller for every buyer. This means that when you give the order to offset your existing futures position, the clearing firm will see to it that your old futures position is cancelled by your new, offsetting trade.

OPEN INTEREST

When you buy or sell a futures contract, you open a position in the futures market. To close the position you buy an offsetting contract. The number of contracts that have been opened in the market but not yet closed by offset or delivery is called the open interest. When a futures contract expires, its **open interest** becomes zero.

DELIVERY ISSUES

If you don't offset your futures position, you must make or take delivery of the item underlying the contract at expiration. The person with the short position is required to make delivery, and the person with the long position is required to take delivery. The contract specifies where, when, and how delivery may take place.

Physical delivery is the exception rather than the rule. The overwhelming majority—some experts estimate more than 98%—of futures contracts are terminated before expiration.

Some futures contracts, called cash-settled contracts, don't permit physical delivery. Rather, they are settled—if they're not offset—with a cash payment determined by the price change in the last two trading days before expiration.

Hedgers and Speculators

Futures have a reputation for attracting high-risk speculators. But they perform the important function of stabilizing prices.

There are two distinct classes of players in the futures markets.

Hedgers are interested in the commodities. They can be producers, like farmers, mining companies, foresters, and oil drillers. Or they can be users, like bakers, paper mills, jewelers, and oil distributors. In general, producers sell futures contracts while users buy them.

Speculators, on the other hand, trade futures strictly to make money. If you buy and sell futures contracts but never use the commodity itself, you are a speculator. Speculators identify the contracts in which they're interested, based on which way they think the market is going in a particular commodity.

HEDGER'S FARMSTAND

CORN ALWAYS 58¢ PER LB.

HOW HEDGERS USE THE MARKET

Hedgers are interested in protecting themselves against price changes that will undercut their profit. For example, a textile company may want to hedge against rising cotton prices as a result of boll weevil infestation. In August, the company buys 100 December cotton futures, representing five million pounds of cotton at 58 cents a pound.

During the fall, the cotton crop is infested and the prices shoot up. The December contract now trades at 68 cents. But the textile maker has hedged against exactly this situation. In December it can take delivery of cotton at 58 cents a pound, 10 cents less than the market price, and save $500,000 (10 cents x 5 million pounds).

Or the company can sell the futures contracts for more than it paid for them and use the profit to offset the higher price it will have to pay for cotton in the cash market. If the hedge works perfectly, hedgers make up in one market what they lose in the other. But, of course, the perfect hedge seldom exists.

HOW SPECULATORS USE THE MARKET

Speculators hope to make money in the futures market by betting on price moves. A speculator may load up on orange juice futures in November, for instance, betting that if a freeze sets in and damages the Florida orange crop, prices of orange juice and the futures contracts based on them will soar.

If the speculators are right, and the winter is tough, the contracts on orange juice will be worth more than they paid. The speculators can then sell their contracts at a profit. If they're wrong, and there's a bumper crop, the bottom will fall out of the market, and the speculators will be squeezed dry by falling prices.

costs in the event of a freeze, and orange farmers couldn't earn enough money in a good year to pay their production costs.

Speculators also keep the market active. If only those who produced or used the commodities were trading, there would not be enough activity to keep the market going. Buy and sell orders would be paired slowly, erasing the protection that hedgers get when the market responds quickly to changes in the cash market.

INFLUENCES ON FUTURES CONTRACT PRICES

The price of a futures contract is influenced by natural and political events, but it's also affected by the economic news that the government releases, the length of time the contract has to run, and by what speculators are doing and saying.

Virtually every day of every month, the government releases economic data, sells Treasury bills, or creates new policies that influence the price of futures contracts for both natural and financial commodities. News on new home sales, for example, directly influences the price of lumber futures, as hedgers and speculators try to link the probable rise or fall in the demand for lumber to what will happen in the construction industry.

If a producer agrees to hold a commodity for future delivery, the contract will reflect storage, insurance, and other carrying costs to cover daily expenses until delivery. Generally, the further away the delivery date, the greater the carrying costs. Even so, prices rarely go up regularly in consecutive months. When the prices do increase this way, the relationship is called a **contango**.

Speculation also influences a commodity's price. Sudden demand for a contract—sparked by rumor, inside information, or other factors—can drive its price sky-high. Or the reverse can happen when rumors or events make investors scramble to sell.

SPECULATORS ARE INDISPENSABLE

Speculators are crucial to the success of the futures market because they complete a symbiotic relationship between those wishing to avoid risk and those willing to take it.

Since hedgers, in planning ahead, want to avoid risk in what are often undeniably risky businesses, others have to be willing to accept it. Unless some speculators are willing to bet that orange juice prices will rise while others bet that prices will fall, an orange juice producer could not protect against dramatically increased

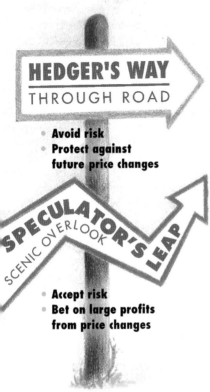

HEDGER'S WAY
THROUGH ROAD

- Avoid risk
- Protect against future price changes

SPECULATOR'S LEAP
SCENIC OVERLOOK

- Accept risk
- Bet on large profits from price changes

> Investing in futures is different from investing in stocks, bonds, and mutual funds because futures markets are **zero sum markets**. That means for every dollar somebody makes (before commissions), somebody else loses a dollar. Put bluntly, that means that any gain is at somebody else's expense.

How Futures Trading Works

Though they have different goals, hedgers and speculators are in the market together. What happens to the price of a contract affects them all.

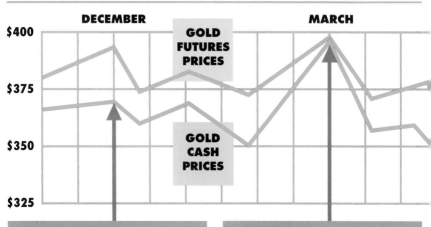

DECEMBER

GOLD IS $370 AN OUNCE IN THE CASH MARKET AND $385 FOR THE JUNE CONTRACT

In December, the price of gold in the cash market—what a buyer would pay for immediate delivery—is $15 less than the price of the June contract.

PRODUCERS (HEDGERS)

Gold producers hedge by selling futures contracts. The gold producers sell June futures contracts because they won't have gold ready for delivery until then.

Earned in December sale   **$385**

USERS (HEDGERS)

Gold users hedge by buying futures contracts. The gold users buy June futures contracts because that's when they need the gold.

Cost of December buy   **– $385**

SPECULATORS

Speculators buy gold futures contracts if they think the price is going up.

Cost of December buy   **– $385**

> This hypothetical illustration does not include commissions or other trading costs that would affect the cost of trading futures contracts. It also assumes that all participants purchased contracts at the same price.

MARCH

GOLD IS $395 AN OUNCE IN THE CASH MARKET. THE JUNE CONTRACT IS SELLING FOR $398

In March, the price of gold has gone up to $395 in the cash market. The June futures contract is selling for $398.

PRODUCERS (HEDGERS)

The producers can't sell their gold because it isn't ready yet. They do nothing.

USERS (HEDGERS)

This upswing in the cash price is exactly what the users were trying to protect themselves against. They wait for the expiration date.

SPECULATORS

The speculators sell, thinking gold has reached its peak. One clue is that the contract price is so close to the cash price. If speculators thought higher prices in the cash market were likely in the near future, they would be willing to pay higher prices for futures contracts.

    This time the speculators made money in the market if they sold in March when the contract price reached its peak.

Price from March sell	**$398**
Cost of December buy	**– 385**
Result of trade [profit]	**$ 13**

OPTIONS ON FUTURES

Buying a **put** or **call** option on a futures contract enables an options buyer to speculate on a price change with limited risk. The most the buyer can lose is the **option premium**, or the cost of the option.

Buying a call option on a futures contract gives the buyer the right to buy, or go **long**, a particular futures contract at a specific price during the life of the option. Buying a put option on a futures contract similarly gives the buyer the right to sell, or go **short**. An options buyer isn't obligated to exercise the option, but may do so at any point before the option expires.

A buyer might buy a call option on gold futures, anticipating a rise in gold prices. If the price does go up, then the buyer will exercise the option, buy the gold futures at the preset price and close out the position by selling an offsetting contract at the higher current market price. The buyer's profit is the price difference between the offsetting contracts, minus the price of the option premium.

If the price of gold falls, then the buyer lets the option expire unexercised and loses only the price of the option premium. By using the options alternative, the buyer is protected against the unlimited losses that are possible with futures contracts.

JUNE

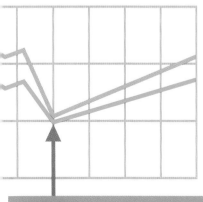

JUNE

CONTRACTS EXPIRE WHEN GOLD IS $350 AN OUNCE IN THE CASH MARKET AND $352 IN THE FUTURES MARKET

In June, when the contract expires, both the producers and the users equalize their profit or loss in the futures market through offsetting trades in the cash market.

PRODUCERS (HEDGERS)

Because the price of the gold futures contract had dropped, the producers made money on the offsetting trade.

Earned in December sale	$385
Cost of June buy	– 352
Result of trade [profit]	$ 33

Even though producers had to sell their gold in the cash market for less than the anticipated price, the profit from their futures trades gave them the expected level of profit.

Earned in cash market	$350
Futures profit	+ 33
Gross profit	$383

USERS (HEDGERS)

The users lost money on the futures contracts because it cost more to sell the offsetting contracts than they had paid to buy.

Earned in June sell	$352
Cost of December buy	– $385
Result of trade (loss)	– $ 33

Since it cost the users less to buy gold in the cash market than they had expected, the total cost was what they anticipated.

Cost in cash market	$350
Cost of futures trade	+ 33
Actual cost of gold	$383

In any given futures contract, the profit or loss of the hedgers could be reversed, depending on the rise or fall of the futures price. In the end, however, their profit or loss in the futures trade would be offset by profit or loss in the cash market. The speculators could lose as frequently—maybe more frequently—than they gained, depending on changing prices and the timing with which they entered and left the market.

The oldest futures contracts date back to 17th-century Japan, when **rice tickets** provided landlords who collected rents in rice with a steady secondary income source. They sold warehouse receipts for their stored rice, giving the holder the right to a specific quantity of rice, of a specific quality, on a specific date in the future.

The buyers who paid for the tickets could cash them in at the appointed time or sell them at a profit to someone else. Like futures contracts today, the tickets themselves had no real worth, but they represented a way to make money on the changing value of the underlying commodity—the rice.

Buying and Selling Futures

Futures are traded on exchanges that offer markets in everything from pork bellies to stock indexes.

Typically, exchange-traded contracts are traded only on the exchange that issues them. Exchanges provide speedy clearing of trades, an accurate record of prices, and a system to ensure that an investor's obligations to buy or sell are met.

MAKING A TRADE

To trade futures, you open an account with a futures brokerage firm known as a **futures commission merchant (FCM)**, who will execute and record your trades. You may deal directly with the FCM or go through an introducing broker (IB) or commodity trading advisor (CTA). Your money and assets are held in a separate account, segregated from the firm's own money. You pay a commission and fees to trade futures as you do when you buy or sell stocks and bonds.

When you're ready to trade, you give your broker an order to buy or sell one or more futures contracts, either to open a position or to cancel a position you hold with an offsetting trade. The broker sends your order to an exchange floor or enters it in an electronic trading system.

When an order is filled, the details of the purchase and corresponding sale are matched, recorded, and confirmed.

MARKET REGULATION

Futures markets in the United States are regulated at three levels, just as securities markets are. Each exchange is a self-regulating organization (SRO), responsible for the operation of the exchange and the conduct of its member firms.

The **National Futures Association** (NFA) is an SRO authorized by Congress. Like the NASD in the securities industry, it is responsible for oversight of the firms and individuals who deal with the investing public, including FCMs, IBs, CTAs, commodity pool operators (CPOs), and sales people. It has the authority to discipline or bar those who violate its rules of professional conduct.

The **Commodity Futures Trading Commission** (CFTC) is the futures market equivalent of the Securities and Exchange Commission (SEC). It's the federal agency that's responsible for ensuring that investors have the information they need to make informed decisions and that the derivatives markets are open, competitive, and financially sound. Like other federal regulatory agencies, it has the power to prosecute those who violate its rules.

EXCHANGE RULES

Each exchange develops the terms and conditions of the futures contracts it lists for trading. The same or similar futures contracts may be traded on more than one exchange, but normally one exchange's contract on a particular commodity dominates its competitors in terms of trading volume and liquidity.

Where the Exchanges Are

Futures are traded on regulated exchanges, also called designated contract markets (DCMs). In the United States, the list includes:

The Chicago Board of Trade (www.cbot.com)

The Chicago Climate Futures Exchange (www.chicagoclimatefuturesexchange.com/ccfe.html)

The Chicago Futures Exchange (www.cboe.com/cfe), a subsidiary of the Chicago Board Options Exchange

The Chicago Mercantile Exchange (www.cme.com)

HedgeStreet, Inc. (www.hedgestreet.com)

The Kansas City Board of Trade (www.kcbt.com)

The Minneapolis Grain Exchange (www.mgex.com)

The New York Board of Trade (www.nybot.com)

The New York Mercantile Exchange (www.nymex.com), which has a division called the Commodity Exchange

OneChicago (www.onechicago.com)

The Philadelphia Board of Trade (www.phlx.com/pbot)

The US Futures Exchange, also known as Eurex US (www.eurexus.com)

How Trading Works

Historically, futures traders arrived at **price discovery**, or what the buyer would pay and the seller accept, through an often frenetic open outcry auction system on exchange floors. Each commodity traded in a specific area. But while floor trading still exists, transactions are increasingly handled electronically, making the system even faster and more efficient.

A **trading pit** is shaped like a ring and tiered into three or four levels. During **open outcry**, traders jockey for position to see over the heads of the traders in front of them. Some pits are divided into sections so several different commodities can be traded at the same time.

Electronic trading systems, operating alongside live trading, fill orders using an electronic matching system. Completed trades are reported back to the brokerage firm that originated them. The firm confirms the trade with the customer who placed the order. Depending on the exchange, **e-trading** hours may overlap with floor trading hours, but also extend later into the evening, or even overnight.

Only member brokerage firm traders and some individual members, called **locals**, can actually trade on the floor.

Large **electronic display boards** circle the trading floor. They're constantly updated with new trade data, which is simultaneously sent out to the rest of the world by quote machine.

Consumable Commodities

Modern life depends on raw materials—the products that keep people and businesses going. Anticipating what they'll cost is what fuels the futures market.

Commodities are the raw materials that are consumed in the process of creating food, fuel, clothes, cars, houses, and the thousands of other products that people buy—the wheat in bread, the silver in earrings, the oil in gasoline. Most producers and users buy and sell commodities in the **cash market**, commonly known as the **spot market**, because the full cash price is paid on the spot.

DETERMINING CASH PRICES

Commodity prices are based on **supply and demand**. If a commodity is plentiful, its price will be low. If it's hard to come by, the price will be high.

Supply and demand for many commodities move in fairly predictable seasonal cycles. Tomatoes are cheapest in the summer when they're plentiful and most flavorful, and most expensive in the winter when they're out of season. Soup manufacturers plan their production season to take advantage of the highest-quality tomatoes at the lowest prices.

But it doesn't always work that way. If a drought wipes out the Midwest's wheat crop, cash prices for wheat surge because bakers buy up what's available to avoid a short-term crunch. Or if political and economic turmoil threatens the oil supply, prices at the gas pumps jump in anticipation of supply problems.

MINIMIZING FUTURE RISK

Since people don't know when such disasters will occur, they can't plan for them. That's why **futures contracts** were invented—to help businesses minimize risk. A baker with a futures contract to buy wheat for $3.20 a bushel is protected if the spot price jumps to $3.70—at least for the purchase covered by the contract.

Farmers, loggers, and other commodity producers can only estimate the demand for their products and try to plan accordingly. But they can get stung by too much supply and too little demand—or the reverse. Similarly, manufacturers have to take orders for future delivery without knowing the cost of the raw materials they will need to make their products. That's why they buy futures contracts on the products they make or use: to smooth out the unexpected price bumps.

What's in a Contract and What Can Affect Its Price

PRICES RISE WHEN
Bad weather ruins US wheat crop

WHAT THE CONTRACT IS FOR AND WHAT IT COSTS

ONE WHEAT CONTRACT IS 5,000 BUSHELS

If wheat is $3.72 a bushel, one contract is worth **$18,600**

PRICES FALL WHEN
Russia has bumper crop of wheat

CASH PRICES AS CLUES

The fluctuation in cash prices provides clues to what consumers can expect to pay in the marketplace for products made from the raw materials.

Unlike the stock market, though, where a particular economic situation is likely to have a similar impact—up or down—on many of the equities being traded, in the cash market each product operates independently of the others.

Futures prices tend to track cash prices closely, but not identically. The difference between the futures contract

CONTRACTS ON COMMODITIES

Currently, the futures contracts that are available on organized exchanges for consumable commodities cover a variety of grains, fibers, and textiles, several types of food products, fats and oils, precious and nonprecious metals, lumber, and energy products.

Every contract on a particular product has standard terms that include the specific **grade**, or quality, the quantity, the delivery month, how the price is calculated, and the minimum **tick**, or the allowable incremental price change. You find the current value of the contract by multiplying the current price times the official quantity.

While the same forces of supply and demand affect the shopper in the supermarket or the driver at the gas pumps, the futures market doesn't deal in five pounds of sugar or ten gallons of gas. Efficiency demands that commodities be sold in large quantities.

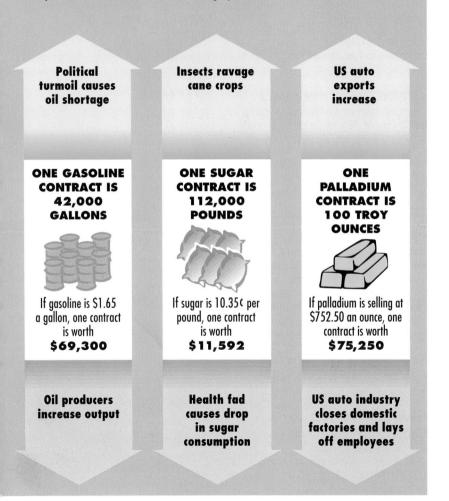

Political turmoil causes oil shortage

ONE GASOLINE CONTRACT IS 42,000 GALLONS

If gasoline is $1.65 a gallon, one contract is worth **$69,300**

Oil producers increase output

Insects ravage cane crops

ONE SUGAR CONTRACT IS 112,000 POUNDS

If sugar is 10.35¢ per pound, one contract is worth **$11,592**

Health fad causes drop in sugar consumption

US auto exports increase

ONE PALLADIUM CONTRACT IS 100 TROY OUNCES

If palladium is selling at $752.50 an ounce, one contract is worth **$75,250**

US auto industry closes domestic factories and lays off employees

price and the cash price of the underlying commodity is called the **basis**.

The prices tend to change constantly, though rarely dramatically, from day to day. But during a period of several months or a year, you may find significant increases or decreases in some products and surprisingly little change in others.

CORNERING THE MARKET

Some commodities traders aren't satisfied with the money they can make by betting on price fluctuations. They'd rather control prices by engineering a financial **corner**, or monopoly, on the commodity itself. Frederick Phillipse has the dubious distinction of introducing the technique in North America. In 1666, he successfully cornered the market on wampum—Native American money—by burying several barrels of it. Fur traders had to pay his prices to carry on their business.

Financial Commodities

Stocks, bonds and currencies are the commodities of the investment business.

You may not think of currencies, stock indexes, and interest rates as commodities, but they are. Money is as much the raw material of domestic and international trade as wheat is the raw material of bread.

Just as farmers, mining companies, and jewelry manufacturers can be dramatically affected by changes in the price of corn, copper, and gold, so changes in currency values, the direction of the stock market, and interest rates can have enormous impact on the financial community.

Like other commodities, financial futures contracts trade on specific exchanges, where they are often among the most actively traded products.

Financial Futures in Action

THE HEDGERS

Mutual fund with a portfolio of stocks similar to S&P 500 Index stocks when near-term price declines expected	**Hedges by taking a short position** to protect stock portfolio against falling stock prices	**If index rises**, gains on portfolio are matched by losses on short futures hedge **If index drops**, losses on portfolio are offset by profits on short futures hedge
Pension fund that plans to buy portfolio of stocks similar to S&P 500 Index stocks next month	**Hedges by taking a long position** to protect against rising prices until money is available to purchase stocks	**If index rises**, increased cost of buying stocks is offset by gains on long futures hedge **If index drops**, buying costs are less but fund has losses on the long futures hedge

THE SPECULATORS

Speculators who anticipate where S&P 500 Index will be in the future	**Buy S&P futures** when they think the index will rise **Sell S&P futures** when they think the index will fall	**If the index rises**, there's a gain on futures position, and **if it falls**, there's a loss **If the index falls**, there's a gain on futures position, and **if it rises**, there's a loss

EXPECTING THE UNEXPECTED

There are **hedgers** in the financial futures market as there are in other futures markets. Pension and mutual fund managers, securities firms, and international companies, to name a few, rely on financial commodities to run their businesses or meet their obligations to clients. So they use financial futures to protect themselves against unexpected losses or to reduce the cost of purchases.

For example, a US company that sells its product in England and is paid in British pounds must convert the pounds to dollars before recording the payment on its books. If the price of the product was fixed and value of the pound falls against the dollar, the US company is, in effect, paid less for its product, since the pounds will convert into fewer dollars.

To hedge against this possibility, the company may sell pound futures. If the value drops, the company can use the profit from the futures transaction to offset the losses on the invoice payment.

KEEPING MARKETS LIQUID

As in other futures markets, **speculators** keep the markets active by constant trading. Speculators buy or sell futures contracts depending on which way they think the market is going. World politics, trading patterns, and the economy are the unpredictable factors in these markets. Rumor, too, plays a major role.

Financial speculators are no more interested in taking delivery of $100,000 in Treasury bonds than grain speculators are in 5,000 bushels of wheat. What they're interested in is making money. So at what seems to be a good time, they sell a contract they own and take their profits. Or they may sell to cut their losses.

WHAT'S THERE TO DELIVER?

The key difference between financial futures and other futures contracts is that most of the financial products are intangible, with no physical or account-able existence. This means there is nothing to deliver if the contract is not offset. In the rare circumstance when that occurs, the contracts are settled in cash.

Instead of dollars per gallon of heating oil or cents per bushel of corn, the value of an index contract is calculated by multiplying a fixed dollar amount by the current value of the index. A contract on the Standard & Poor's MidCap 400 is determined by multiplying $500 times the index, the Dow Jones Industrial Average (DJIA) by multiplying $10 times the index, and the Nasdaq 100 by multiplying $100 times the index.

For example, if the S&P MidCap 400 was 692 at expiration, a futures contract on the index would be worth $346,000. Similarly, if the DJIA was at 10,550, a contract on it would be worth $105,500.

An interest rate futures contract is also cash settled. Its value is figured as a dollar amount times points of 100%, or, in the case of US and UK government bonds, in 32nds of 100 to correspond to the way that those bonds are priced. For example, to find the value of a five-year Treasury note, you multiply $100,000 times the closing price.

ARBITRAGE

Some professional traders use **arbitrage** to capitalize on price discrepancies between similar products in different markets. For example, stock indexes and futures contracts on those indexes don't move in lockstep. When they are out of sync, arbitragers, using sophisticated computer programs that follow the shifts

THE PRICE FEEDBACK LOOP

Investor confidence is one of the factors affecting the price of financial instruments. So traders who buy and sell these products track futures prices—widely considered an expression of investor sentiment—for clues about where actual prices will move. In turn, futures traders track actual prices for clues about futures prices.

in price, can make money by simultane-ously buying the one that's less expensive and selling the one that's more expensive. Because arbitragers trade huge numbers of contracts at the same time, tiny price differences can result in large profits if their timing is right.

Since many arbitragers make the same decisions at the same time, their activity can affect the markets in which they trade, narrowing or eliminating the price discrepancies between the markets.

OVER-THE-COUNTER

Highly sophisticated investors, such as corporations, financial institutions, and public agencies use over-the-counter (OTC) futures contracts as tools to manage financial risk by hedging their long-term commitments to buy, sell, or lend—especially when the deal involves multiple currencies. They work directly with dealer banks to handle the transactions, which are typically negotiated by specialized traders.

Because of their complexity and the extent to which they may be leveraged, OTC derivatives can pose potentially large risks. For example, while the deals usually don't require collateral, there is no exchange or clearinghouse to guarantee that the parties will make good on their commitments. And because they're tailored to specific requirements, they're often highly illiquid.

QUADRUPLE WITCHING

Once every quarter—on the third Saturday of March, June, September, and December—stock options, stock index options, stock index futures, and single stock futures all expire at the same time. The phenomenon, which can trigger intense Friday trading to resolve all open positions before the deadline, is known as quadruple witching day. That's one more witch than there used to be, before single stock futures began trading in 2002.

Futures Risks

If you see risks for what they are, you may be able to contain them.

The futures market was founded on the principle of **risk transfer**. Investors seeking to minimize their exposure to certain risks transferred those risks to others who were either trying to protect against an opposite risk, or were willing to take the risk in the hope of making a profit.

That's still the case with futures. But because of the way these products work, there's also the risk that a transaction may result in a loss that exceeds the amount of your initial margin and could potentially cost an almost unlimited amount.

THE ROLE OF THE EXCHANGES

Futures exchanges monitor and act to control price **volatility**. In most cases, the exchange where a futures contract is traded establishes a daily **price limit** that prevents the price of that particular contract from rising or falling beyond a preset limit. In this **lock limit system**, when the high or low price limit is reached, trading is stopped, or locked.

The price limit is set in relation to the **closing price** on the previous trading day and specifies, in dollars or cents, how far the price can move. For example, if gold traded at $350 per troy ounce the previous day, the current day's price limit might be $35. That means no trades could be executed at prices above $385 or below $315. (A troy ounce, the traditional unit of weight for precious metals, is 31.1035 grams.)

Daily price limits are not permanent and exchanges may adjust them. During the **delivery month** of a futures contract, when the contract expires, price limits are often lifted, allowing extreme volatility.

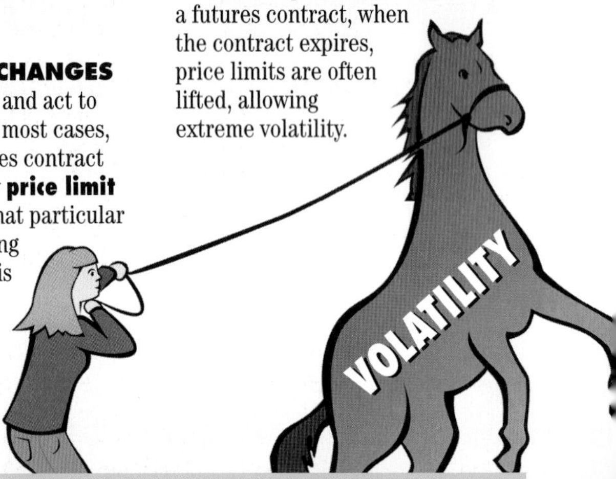

VOLATILITY

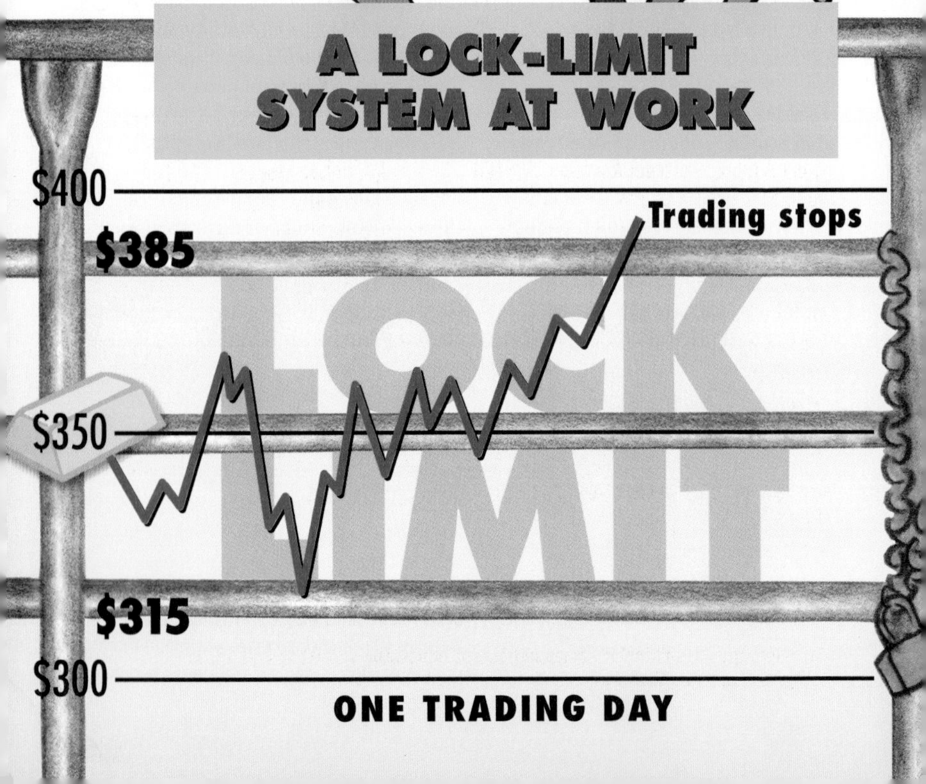

A LOCK-LIMIT SYSTEM AT WORK

$400

$385

Trading stops

LOCK LIMIT

$350

$315

$300

ONE TRADING DAY

From an investor's perspective, the risk of daily price limits is that you can't always liquidate your position before lock down. When the market re-opens, the stabilized price may be well above or below what you need to make a profit—or avoid a loss—with an offsetting contract.

CONTINGENT ORDERS

Just as the exchanges try to control volatility through the daily price limit, you may use **contingent orders**, also called restricted orders, to exert control on the prices you pay to buy or receive when you sell.

A **limit order**, the most common variety, names the price at which you will buy or sell a contract. In a volatile market, the transaction may never be completed, however, because the market price may move through the limit price too quickly to be acted upon.

Stop orders specify a price at which a broker should buy or sell a particular contract. When the stop price is reached, the order converts to a market order and the broker must execute the trade at the best current price. The downside is that

you could end up paying more or selling for less than you want.

A contingent order may be a **day order**, which means it expires if it has not been filled by the end of the trading day. Good-till-canceled (GTC), or **open orders**, on the other hand, do not expire until they are filled or cancelled.

SPREAD TRADING

One risk management technique that futures traders use to try to limit their potential losses is to simultaneously buy and sell futures contracts on the same or related underlying commodities at the same time. That's known as a **spread** and each side of the spread is known as a **leg**.

Since realizing a profit depends on making more money on one leg than you lose on the other, what you want is a spread where the price difference widens after you open the postions. In this example, you buy single stock futures contracts on A and sell them on B. When the price difference between them increases from $15 to $18, you make money when you offset your opening positions. But when the difference narrows from $15 to $10, you lose money.*

	PRICE DIFFERENCE WIDENS			PRICE DIFFERENCE NARROWS	
Opening positions ($15 spread)	Offsetting contract prices ($18 spread)	Profit or loss	Offsetting contract prices ($10 spread)	Profit or loss
Buy 100 Stock A futures at $25	Sell 100 Stock A futures at $30	100 x $5 = $500	Sell 100 Stock A futures at $30	100 x $5 = $500
Sell 100 Stock B futures at $10	Buy 100 Stock B futures at $12	100 x –$2 = –$200	Buy 100 Stock B futures at $20	100 x –$10 = –$1000
Net gain or loss		$300		–$500

Of course, it's always possible that you'll sustain losses on both legs of a single stock futures spread. When this happens you could lose more than you would have lost on an outright futures position in one of the stocks.

*This example doesn't include commissions and other transaction costs, which apply whether you have gains or losses.

Futures Investment Decisions

You can take different paths to futures investing.

To invest successfully in futures contracts, you need to assess where the market is headed as accurately as possible. One resource is professional analysis, which may be either fundamental or technical. In fact, most futures traders rely on both perspectives in making their decisions.

They use fundamental research to examine market conditions, and then technical research to support or question their price predictions.

FINDING INFORMATION
You can access analysts' research information through your brokerage firm, the exchanges, and other investment professionals. You can also find futures trading information, including real-time or slightly delayed contract prices, on the website of the exchange that lists the contract you're considering, on the websites of brokerage firms that execute futures transactions, and in a variety of print and online material. And you can check the financial press for reports on daily trading activity.

FUNDAMENTAL ANALYSIS

FUNDAMENTAL DIFFERENCES
Fundamental analysts try to determine the supply of a particular commodity and the corresponding demand. Changes in contract prices, which drive profit or loss, are largely based on whether there is a surplus, which drives prices down, or a shortage, which drives prices up.

With agricultural commodities, the analyst looks at weather forecasts, projected crop yields, likelihood of crop failures due to disease, financial factors affecting farmers' activities, and the prices of alternative, competing commodities. The lumber market is driven by housing starts. Copper mining futures are affected by labor and political unrest in countries with significant mining output.

The concerns are different with financial commodities. For example, demand for a particular currency is affected in part by US consumers buying products priced in that currency. So analysts may look at the volume of Japanese electronics that US consumers are buying. The more those products are in demand, the higher the value of the Japanese yen tends to be against the dollar.

TECHNICAL ANALYSIS

BEING TRENDY
Technical analysis ignores supply and demand, looking instead at the futures market itself—including price behavior, trading volume, and open interest, which is the number of outstanding contracts on the commodity that have not been offset.

For example, technical analysts chart prices to detect the pattern in which they've been moving, to determine a trendline, and to assess when the direction is going to change. Using sophisticated computer programs, they digest and analyze reams of data on the complex relationship linking trading volume and price trends.

A HANDLE ON PRICES
The usual price pattern for agricultural commodities is higher contract prices for later delivery months. For example, in August, prices for December corn futures will be higher than for September corn futures, and March prices will be higher than for December for the same commodity.

The difference in price represents the **carrying charge**, or cost, of storing the product during the months after harvest. An inverted market, or **backwardation**, occurs when a there's a supply shortage in a particular commodity. In the short term, hoarding increases the price of the nearest delivery months' contracts, while prices for contracts farther out tend to fall.

MANAGED FUTURES

As opposed to trading futures through an individual trading account, you may choose to participate in the futures market through a **managed account** or a **commodity pool**.

A managed account is your own individual futures trading account, except that you have given a registered professional account manager, sometimes called a commodity trading advisor (CTA), a written power of attorney to make all the trading decisions. You may need to commit more money to open a managed account than to trade yourself. And you'll pay management fees in addition to the usual transaction fees.

Commodity pools combine your money with money from other pool participants to create an account that is similar in operation to a stock mutual fund, but is not a mutual fund. Because a commodity pool is usually structured as a limited partnership, you share in the gains and losses in proportion to your investment, but your risk is limited to the amount of your investment. That means you are also protected from the margin calls which can occur in this highly volatile market.

Another potential advantage of a commodity pool is the greater diversification you can usually achieve. That's because the pool has so much more money to invest in a broad

START ON THE RIGHT FOOT

Before you trade futures—individually, through a managed account, or as part of a commodity pool—you can learn more about the risks and potential returns by reviewing a booklet called "A Guide to Understanding Opportunities and Risks in Futures Trading." It's published by the National Futures Association (NFA). You can download the text at www.NFA.futures.org or request a copy by calling 800-621-3570.

www.NFA.futures.org

range of futures contracts than you would investing on your own.

You should review the disclosure documents that the commodity pool operator gives you to determine the fees involved and the trading philosophy and practice. For newly formed pools, you need to find out whether active trading has begun, or is contingent upon raising a minimum amount of pool money. In the latter case, you'll want to know what is being done with your money in the interim until the pool begins trading.

Both CTAs and commodity pool operators must be registered with the CFTC and be members of the NFA. You can check the credentials of firms and individuals in the futures industry by using NFA's Background Affiliation Status Information Center (BASIC) on the NFA website (www.NFA.futures.org).

Alternative Investments

Variety can spice up the investment stew.

The group of investments described as *alternative* comprises a number of different products, including but not limited to hedge funds, private equity, nontraded real estate investment trusts (REITs), and certain partnerships or limited liability corporations (LLCs). They differ from stocks, bonds, and other traditional investments in several ways, ranging from how they're structured and sold to the role they may play in a diversified portfolio.

MOVING INTO THE MAINSTREAM

What's considered an alternative investment at one time—usually when it's available only to very high net worth investors—may become a more traditional investment later on. For example, the increasing use of certain derivatives, such as equity options and commodities products, has helped move them into the mainstream.

MEETING THE TEST

One way that most alternative investments differ from more traditional investments is that they are offered privately rather than being publicly traded. Some of them are registered with the Securities and Exchange Commission (SEC) though most are not. In either case, the SEC imposes restrictions on who is eligible to invest—which is not the case with publicly traded securities or other investment products.

Specifically, SEC rules require that to be considered an **accredited investor**—and therefore eligible to invest in hedge funds or private equity partnerships—an individual must have a net worth of at least $1 million or an annual income of at least $200,000 if single, or $300,000 if married, in the two most recent years. There must also be a reasonable expectation for that level of income to continue. Institutional investors are also accredited, as are charitable organizations or trusts with assets of at least $5 million.

PRIVATE

Accred Inves

DIVERSIFIED PORTFOLIO

UPPING THE ANTE

Should individuals be required to have a net worth of $5 million to be accredited investors? The argument in favor is that while increasing numbers of people have accumulated a net worth of $1 million, they may not necessarily have enough investment experience to put money into alternative products.

EXPANDING HORIZONS

Most individual investors make their first alternative investments through private banks, brokerage firms, asset managers, or insurance companies. These firms offer funds that invest in a portfolio of funds—or even a fund that owns funds of funds. More rarely, they offer SEC-registered hedge funds or private equity funds.

Registered investments are often more liquid, and investment minimums are substantially lower, making it possible for more people to participate. For example, the minimum required for a registered investment is likely to be closer to $25,000 than the $250,000 to $1 million required for a typical hedge fund or private equity partnership.

COUNTING THE COST

The price tag on alternative investing includes not only the required minimum commitment but also substantial fees. The investment minimums vary widely, from as little as $2,500 for some private nontraded REITs to $1 million or more for some hedge funds.

The fees, which can be substantial, are computed differently for various investments. In the case of hedge funds and private equity partnerships, the issue is the percentage of profits.

INVESTMENT FEES

Hedge funds	1% to 2% annual asset-based fees plus 18% to 20% of fund profits
Private equity funds	1.5% to 2% annual asset-based fees plus 18% to 20% of fund profits
Private, nontraded REITs and other direct investments	Up to 16% up front, amortized over the investment term

FROZEN FAIRLY SOLID

Alternative investments are often highly illiquid. That means there's no secondary market where they can be traded easily, and the buy-back programs that some of these investments offer are often limited and may impose stiff fees. From the sponsor's perspective, illiquidity is an advantage since it means that the partnership or corporation does not ordinarily have to buy back shares that investors want to sell. That's different from a mutual fund, which may have to liquidate some its holdings to meet demands for cash.

One reason that alternative investments require a longer-term commitment is that their managers may employ strategies that take an extended period to produce results. The term of the investment, also described as a **lock-up period**, isn't the same for all the products but does apply to most of them. In hedge funds, for example, it's often one year but could be less. In private equity it may be unlimited.

As a potential investor, you should always take into account the specific provisions that apply to a particular investment that you may be considering.

FUNDS OF FUNDS

Funds of hedge funds (FOHF) are investment funds that build a diversified portfolio of existing hedge funds. The FOHF manager is responsible for researching, choosing, and monitoring the funds in the fund, tasks that may exceed the expertise of an individual investor or investment adviser. The appeal of a fund of funds is that it offers exposure to a range of hedging strategies that, overall, may have the effect of reducing portfolio risk.

Fees are one potential drawback to a fund of funds. In addition to the management fees you pay to own the fund of funds, there are management fees associated with each of the funds within the FOHF. And in addition to the performance fees the underlying funds charge, your fund of funds manager may also be eligible for a performance bonus, which you, as a shareholder, will pay as well.

Investors who buy a fund of funds may know which hedge funds their FOHF owns, or they may not. Levels of transparency vary. In fact, in some cases, certain investors may have information about the portfolio while others don't.

Hedge Funds

If you're not exactly sure what a hedge fund does, you have lots of company.

Hedge funds, like mutual funds, raise a pool of money to invest and pay out profits, after fees, to their investors. But the similarity ends there.

To begin with, hedge funds are only lightly regulated and are only occasionally required to report their holdings. They also employ a number of leveraged trading techniques that mutual funds can't use. And there's no easy way to price the assets of some of the more illiquid hedge funds or to verify that the returns are accurate, so they lack the transparency that mutual funds provide.

Hedge funds may be set up as limited partnerships (LPs) or limited liability corporations (LLCs). US investors can buy funds set up in different jurisdictions. When a fund is offered by a US company and available domestically, it's described as an onshore fund. If the fund is offered by a US company based in another jurisdiction—sometimes identified generically as a tax haven—it's described as an offshore fund. Investing offshore is legal as long as you report any earnings and pay the taxes that are due.

BASIC ANATOMY

When a hedge fund is established, it's generally designed to pursue a particular strategy that governs the investments the manager makes and how the fund is structured.

For example, a fund that specializes in **merger arbitrage** will concentrate its investments in companies that are involved in a corporate merger, or seem likely to be.

The fund will typically buy shares in a target company and sell short shares in the acquiring company. If the deal is done, the fund ends up with equal and opposite positions in the acquiring company and may realize a profit on the **spread**, or difference in prices.

HEDGE FUNDS PROS AND CONS

Hedge funds are controversial, partly because they control such enormous amounts of money. While there is no official count of how many funds there are, or how much they're investing, research companies estimate that there are about 8,000 hedge funds with combined portfolios of $1 trillion. To put that in perspective, there are between 7,000 and 8,000 open-end mutual funds investing about $8 trillion.

Those concerned about hedge funds point to the risk the funds might pose to the capital markets. They maintain, for example, that if a number of large hedge funds made similar bets at the same time—and they were wrong—they could suffer major losses and roil the entire market.

Those who feel that hedge funds play a necessary role in the economy argue that the funds serve high net worth clients and pension funds, insurance companies, and other institutional investors that aren't fully served by more traditional strategies. Advocates point out that the large amounts of money that the funds invest provide liquidity that makes the markets somewhat less volatile than they might otherwise be.

They also point out that hedge funds are typically less volatile than equity mutual funds, and so may be a valuable risk management tool.

NEW RULES

A Securities and Exchange Commission (SEC) rule scheduled to take effect in 2006 requires certain hedge fund managers to register as **registered investment advisers (RIAs)** if they manage more than $25 million in assets and have more than 14 clients. All RIAs must act as fiduciaries, which requires them to make investment recommendations that are in the best interests of their clients.

But the new rule does not restrict the types of investment strategies that RIAs may use, limit the types of investments they may make, or change certain other characteristics of hedge funds. For example, the rule doesn't limit leverage or prohibit performance fees.

If the market as a whole became profitable, the fund would make more money on the stocks it held long than it would lose on the ones it had sold short. If the opposite occurred, and the market faltered, the fund would lose money on the stock that it owned but could profit from the short sales.

The goal of a long/short strategy is to realize a bit more on the profitable side of the trade than you lose on the other. While any two-sided trade means sacrificing some of the potential gain that comes with correctly anticipating the way the market will move, it also protects against steep losses if the market moves in the opposite direction. That's the concept of hedging, or playing both sides of the fence.

IN THE BEGINNING

Hedge funds began in the 1940s as a relatively conservative approach to limiting investment risk. By taking opposite positions on the same or similar investments, a fund positioned itself to take advantage of the fact that some investments will be losing value while others are gaining—and that you can't reliably predict which will be which.

Using this approach, a fund might identify firms that it expected to prosper and then purchase, or go long, their stock. At the same time, the fund would identify other firms that seemed to be at risk, and sell those stocks short.

AN EVOLUTIONARY TALE

In the 1990s, many newer hedge funds were investing aggressively. Fund managers sought large gains by exploiting a variety of pricing discrepancies in the marketplace—in currency values, for example, or the disparity between the values of a company's stocks and its bonds. These managers also employed greater leverage, controlling large positions with a small amount of capital, and used derivatives to hedge their positions.

While there were notable successes and sometimes huge profits, one of the more prominent hedge funds—Long Term Capital Management—suffered huge losses that roiled the markets. That development precipitated initial steps towards some, if limited, transparency, including the introduction of hedge fund indexes.

Hedge Fund Investing

What's essential to hedge fund investing is finding the information you need.

One sign that hedge funds are becoming part of mainstream investing is the development of hedge fund indexes by Standard & Poor's, Dow Jones, and other index providers. By making timely and reliable pricing information available to the market, an index enhances the transparency of the sample of funds it tracks and establishes a performance standard, or **benchmark**, against which the industry as a whole can be measured.

DEFINING FEATURES

In addition to the ordinary considerations of constructing a financial index, there are a number of special challenges to creating a hedge fund index. That's because, for an index to be useful, it must report performance of its sample funds in an accurate and timely way. But that information, by and large, isn't readily available since hedge funds aren't required to provide daily pricing information.

The index provider must set standards for inclusion, determine the number of funds that constitute a representative sample, and then monitor the funds it includes to verify that they continue to meet all its criteria.

To be included in an index, a hedge fund must agree to provide regular valuations that can be independently verified. It must also have the capacity to accept new investments as the index is likely to serve as the basis of a representative index fund. That's because the index fund must invest in the hedge funds as it seeks to replicate the index performance.

INDEX INVESTING

S&P and other hedge fund index providers license their indexes to investment companies, who use them as the basis for establishing and marketing hedge fund index funds.

The companies that offer these index funds set the minimums for the initial and subsequent investments. They typically offer limited liquidity and may repurchase shares once a quarter or on some other schedule if investors want to sell. That's in contrast to an open-end mutual fund, which buys back shares every day and a hedge fund, which might not allow redemptions for a year or more.

As is the case with most hedge funds,

VARIATIONS ON A THEME

All hedge funds are not alike. They vary both in investment style and the types of strategies they use. The most common types are grouped into three styles:

 Arbitrage, which focuses on discrepancies in the prices of closely related securities, such as stocks, bonds, or convertible bonds

 Event-driven, which seeks profits based on specific events in the marketplace, such as mergers, acquisitions, and bankruptcies

 Directional or tactical, which capitalizes on the characteristic ebb and flow of market movements in equities, commodities, and interest rates

HEDGE FUND ➡

a majority of index fund shareholders are high net worth individual investors and an increasing number of institutional investors. But, because of their substantially lower required minimum investment and increased transparency, hedge fund index funds may be attractive to affluent individual investors looking for ways to diversify their portfolios.

DUE DILIGENCE

Hedge funds provide potential investors with a document called an **investment memorandum**, which explains the fund's structure, identifies its strategy, and describes the qualifications of the management team. It can be a useful starting point in researching the fund, but it's only the beginning of what you need to know.

First and foremost, you need to understand what the fund does—ideally well enough to be able to explain it to someone else. You'll want to learn more about how complex or straightforward the manager's investment strategy is, including the plans for using leverage, short selling, and derivative products. It's also important to know how the fund is organized, how large it is, how many investors are participating, the amount that insiders have invested, and whether the fund has an independent accountant.

Due diligence also includes background and regulatory checks on the fund's managers and on any submanagers whom the fund may use to run parts of the portfolio. And last but not least, you should know about the fund's back-office operations, including whether or not the fund processes trades. Since the success of a hedge fund often hinges on timely execution, trading delays could affect a fund's performance.

In reality, researching a hedge fund—or any other privately offered investment—is a job for an objective, professional third-party analyst. A number of index providers also use professional analysts to research the hedge funds that are included in their indexes, as do brokerage firms offering a fund of hedge funds.

☑ Organization
☑ Investment strategy
  ● Short selling?
  ● Leverage?
☑ Size, number of investors
☑ Amount invested?
☑ Independent accountant

A CLASS DEBATE

One of the ongoing debates about hedge funds is whether or not they constitute an asset class. Depending on their investment strategy, hedge funds may invest in traditional asset classes, such as stocks or bonds, or in derivatives, such as commodities. From one perspective, those underlying investments determine the hedge fund's asset class—as is the case with mutual funds. The opposite perspective is that while hedge funds invest in traditional asset classes, they use nontraditional strategies, and produce returns that aren't correlated with the returns on their underlying investments. As such, they constitute a distinctive asset class that may help you manage portfolio risk.

HEDGE FUND
INDEX
FUND ➡
Straighter route
to potential
gains

WINDS OF CHANGE

Hedge funds continue to evolve as their numbers increase and they identify new opportunities for producing substantial returns. While there are always pricing anomalies that can yield a profit, arbitrage opportunities don't necessarily keep pace with demand. As a result, some hedge funds are diversifying their portfolios, using a percentage of their assets for private equity investments or small business loans.

Private Equity Investments

Nothing ventured, nothing gained is the principle driving private equity investing.

Private equity is an umbrella term for raising private money to invest in business ventures. The firms that raise and manage this pool of cash tend to specialize in either **venture capital** or corporate buyouts.

Venture capital is often described as the engine of a country's economic growth since it enables private companies to get started and grow while fostering invention and experimentation. Venture capital firms expect to make substantial profits on their investments, though some of the companies in which they invest may provide disappointing returns or fail entirely.

Buyout firms, on the other hand, typically purchase existing private or public companies, restructure them, and then either sell them to other private investors or take them public.

VENTURE CAPITA

POOLED INVESTMENT FUN

RAISING CAPITAL
Before venture capital firms make their investments they raise a pool of capital from accredited investors who meet standards set by the Securities and Exchange Commission (SEC).

This **pooled investment fund** is typically organized as a **limited partnership** in which the firm is the general partner and the investors are limited partners. Unlike most investors, who are passive, venture capital firms take an active role in the management of the companies they invest in. To cover those costs, the firm charges the fund's investors an annual management fee of 1% to 2% of assets in the fund plus a percentage—often as much as 20% to 30%—of any eventual profits the fund makes.

WHO'S AT THE REINS
The success of a private equity investment depends in large part on the sponsoring firm's management expertise. That helps to explain a popular piece of advice in private equity circles: "Bet the jockey, not the horse."

INVESTING STAGES
Not all companies looking for venture capital are at the same stage in their growth, so firms tend to specialize:

- Early stage companies are in the first or second phase of developing their products and probably already have some patents or established intellectual property

- Expansion stage companies need an injection of capital to grow to the next level

- Later stage companies vulnerable to takeover need a final boost of funds to reach the mass necessary to go public or be acquired

Venture capital firms—often called VCs—may make straight equity investments or offer a combination of equity and debt. They may invest in a range of industry sectors, geographic locations, and growth stages or specialize in a particular sector, place, or stage.

TAKING CONTROL

Buyout firms historically invest in later-stage, often large, companies that are vulnerable to takeover for a variety of reasons. In some cases, the buyers combine cash with substantial amounts of debt to purchase target companies in what are often described as **leveraged buyouts**, or LBOs.

By taking the newly purchased companies private, at least for a time, the buyout firms can make potentially radical changes in structure and management without having to explain their actions or their cost to shareholders.

The buyout firms attract investors for the same reasons that venture capital firms do: the long-term prospect of substantial returns despite the substantial fee that the buyout firm takes off the top.

THE INVESTORS

The great majority of investors in venture capital firms are high net worth individuals, pension funds, banks, endowments, foundations, insurance companies, and other institutional investors. Minimum investment thresholds make private equity funds prohibitively expensive for most individual investors and new funds offered by successful firms are often closed to new investors in any case.

However, affluent individuals can sometimes gain access to private equity partnerships by investing in a **fund of funds**, which holds interests in a selection of these partnerships. In most cases, though, investing through a fund of funds is likely to mean another layer of fees on top of those owed to the partnership, with a substantial percentage of the eventual profits going to the fund of funds managers.

WHEN WILL IT END?

During the term of a private equity investment, those who invest are not able to cash out, and in most cases do not receive any income. The good news is that there may be a substantial reward for accepting the high risk and illiquidity in the form of eventual returns that may be higher than if the money had been invested in the stock market over the same period of time.

There are generally three potential exit strategies for venture capital investments:

Initial public offering (IPO)

While an IPO may sound the most exciting, it is, on average, no more or less lucrative for investors than other strategies. In an IPO, the private company is transformed into a company with publicly traded shares. As an investor in the private company, you receive stock in the now-public company equivalent to your investment interest.

In most cases there are restrictions on how soon you can sell your new shares on the open market. This **lock-up period** is usually at least six months and often graduated, which allows you to sell an increasingly larger portion of your shares over a two-year period.

Merger or acquisition

The most common, and often most successful, exit event is a merger or acquisition. In this case, the private company is bought by or merged with another established company, which might or might not be public. As an original investor, you receive equity in the new company or a cash payment, or both.

Secondary buyout

A recapitalization, also called a **secondary buyout**, occurs when one venture capital firm sells its stake to another, at which point investors in the original fund are cashed out.

AT THE GATE

The most expensive LBO of the 1980s, and the most notorious, was the $31 billion takeover of RJR Nabisco. Future deals may well eclipse that amount, but perhaps not the drama.

Real Estate Investment Trusts

You can invest in real estate that you have no intention of living in.

A **real estate investment trust (REIT)** is a corporation that has been established to make money in real estate. A REIT uses funds, pooled from a group of investors, to buy buildings, or, less often, to buy mortgages on buildings. Most REITs specialize in a particular type of real estate—such as hotels, shopping centers, self-storage units, hospitals and nursing homes, or office buildings—and may concentrate their purchases in a specific geographic area.

As with most corporations, the REIT's management team is responsible for running a profitable business, which means, with REITs in particular, generating a steady stream of revenue for its investors.

Investors' pooled money is used to purchase properties or mortgages

WARNIN

REIT dividends may be taxed at regular rate

INCOME SOURCES

Equity REITs that invest directly in buildings generate income from rent, which is, in turn, paid to investors as a monthly or quarterly **dividend**. Dividends often increase as rents increase, which means the investment can act as a hedge against inflation. On the downside, rents, and therefore dividends, may drop if there is a market downturn and rental spaces go empty. That can happen, too, if the properties the REIT owns aren't attractive to potential renters or if the market for a particular type of property is saturated.

Because of the way REITs pay income, they provide a relatively stable cash flow, which makes them a suitable investment for people who are looking for a supplemental, steady stream of income. For example, REIT income may be used to bolster pension or other retirement income, pay college expenses, set up a charitable remainder trust, or make new investments.

PUBLIC OR PRIVATE

There are two ways you can invest in a REIT. Some REITs are **public corporations**, listed on a national exchange, like the New York Stock Exchange (NYSE) or the Nasdaq Stock Market, or on a quotation service, like the OTC Bulletin Board. You can buy and sell shares in these REITs the same way you do shares in any publicly traded company.

Private, nontraded REITs, on the other hand, are available only through **direct participation programs (DPPs)** offered by the REIT's sponsor and distributed through brokerage firms or other financial institutions. A nontraded REIT usually pools money from 1,000 or more investors to purchase the properties it will manage. As an investor, you are part owner of the actual physical buildings the REIT owns rather than a shareholder in the REIT corporation.

To invest in a nontraded REIT, you need to meet financial suitability standards—often a minimum of $150,000 net worth (excluding your home or car) or a gross annual income of $45,000 plus net worth of $45,000 and sometimes more—as well as make a minimum initial investment established by the REIT.

Nontraded REITs, as their name implies—have no formal **secondary market**—no NYSE or Nasdaq where you can liquidate your shares or resell your interest. Since a REIT's investment term is typically between 8 and 12 years, and may be longer, you'll need to be able to do without that capital you've invested in the REIT for that period of time.

REIT RISK SCALE

Lower		Higher
Low-income housing	Industrial and commercial properties	Single-family housing

90%

90% of the REIT's taxable income is distributed to the investors

REIT management team

Investors can claim depreciation of REIT assets against REIT income

Corporate income tax

DIFFERENT RETURNS

While both public and private REITs invest in income-producing real estate, there are differences in the way they are structured that may affect your return.

Managers of public REITs are subject to the usual market pressure to meet short-term expectations. As a result, share prices tend to fluctuate in response to market conditions, rather than what's happening to real estate values. That can mean paying a premium for the REIT shares or selling at a discount to the actual value of the properties.

Nontraded REITs, on the other hand, can provide a hedge against marketplace **volatility** because they aren't traded. But you have to be sure you can afford their illiquidity since there's no secondary market in which to trade them.

BEFORE YOU INVEST

As with any other investment, you should research the REIT before you commit your money. With both types of REITs, you should review the expertise and track record of the management team, and the REIT's business plan and sources of outside capital. For a traded REIT, you'll want to evaluate debt levels and performance history. With a nontraded REIT, you may want the opinion of a third-party profes-

sional evaluator, which your brokerage firm is likely to have secured.

TAX ADVANTAGES TO BOOT

Under special IRS rules, REITs must distribute 90% of their taxable income as dividends to investors. In return, REITs don't have to pay corporate income taxes. On the plus side, that means that REITs provide a higher return than most other corporations. The downside, however, is that you'll owe tax on REIT dividends at your regular federal income tax rate, which may be as high as 35%, instead of the maximum 15% rate that applies to qualifying equity dividends.

While this tax provision may seem to nullify the benefits of the generally higher returns, there is an offsetting tax benefit of private, nontraded REIT investing. That is, you can claim depreciation of the real estate assets against your dividend income.

This means that you may not owe income tax on those earnings until some date in the future, when your tax rate might be lower. Even better, in some cases you may be able to defer taxes until the REIT sells its properties, in which case you owe tax at the lower long-term capital gains tax rate.

DIVERSIFIED HOLDINGS

Dear REIT 123 Global Shareholders:

Since the end of the first quarter, we completed two acquisitions.

On April 29, REIT 123 purchased 78 retail self-storage and truck rental facilities operated under the Y-H brand name for $312 million. The facilities are located in 69 cities in 24 states. Under the terms of two separate lease agreements, the self-storage facilities will be leased for an initial term of 20 years. The lease can be renewed for two ten-year periods. The truck rental facilities will be leased for an initial term of 10 years.

On May 5, REIT 123 acquired an office manufacturing and warehouse facility in Manufacturing Town from North Star Group, the largest commercial printer in the region for approximately $27.7 million. North

INDEX

INDEX